The Boost Graph Library

The C++ In-Depth Series

Bjarne Stroustrup, Editor

"I have made this letter longer than usual, because I lack the time to make it short."
—BLAISE PASCAL

T he advent of the ISO/ANSI C++ standard marked the beginning of a new era for C++ programmers. The standard offers many new facilities and opportunities, but how can a real-world programmer find the time to discover the key nuggets of wisdom within this mass of information? The C++ In-Depth Series minimizes learning time and confusion by giving programmers concise, focused guides to specific topics.

Each book in this series presents a single topic, at a technical level appropriate to that topic. The Series' practical approach is designed to lift professionals to their next level of programming skills. Written by experts in the field, these short, in-depth monographs can be read and referenced without the distraction of unrelated material. The books are cross-referenced within the Series, and also reference *The C++ Programming Language* by Bjarne Stroustrup.

As you develop your skills in C++, it becomes increasingly important to separate essential information from hype and glitz, and to find the in-depth content you need in order to grow. The C++ In-Depth Series provides the tools, concepts, techniques, and new approaches to C++ that will give you a critical edge.

Titles in the Series

Accelerated C++: Practical Programming by Example, Andrew Koenig and Barbara E. Moo

The Boost Graph Library: User Guide and Reference Manual, Jeremy G. Siek, Lie-Quan Lee, and Andrew Lumsdaine

C++ In-Depth Box Set, Bjarne Stroustrup, Andrei Alexandrescu, Andrew Koenig, Barbara E. Moo, Stanley B. Lippman, and Herb Sutter

C++ Network Programming, Volume 1: Mastering Complexity Using ACE and Patterns, Douglas C. Schmidt and Stephen D. Huston

Essential C++, Stanley B. Lippman

Exceptional C++: 47 Engineering Puzzles, Programming Problems, and Solutions, Herb Sutter

Modern C++ Design: Generic Programming and Design Patterns Applied, Andrei Alexandrescu

More Exceptional C++: 40 New Engineering Puzzles, Programming Problems, and Solutions, Herb Sutter

The Boost Graph Library

User Guide and Reference Manual

Jeremy Siek
Lie-Quan Lee
Andrew Lumsdaine

✦ Addison-Wesley

Boston • San Francisco • New York • Toronto
Montreal • London • Munich • Paris • Madrid • Capetown
Sydney • Tokyo • Singapore • Mexico City

Many of the designations used by manufacturers and sellers to distinguish their products are claimed as trademarks. Where those designations appear in this book, and Addison-Wesley was aware of a trademark claim, the designations have been printed with initial capital letters or in all capitals.

The authors and publisher have taken care in the preparation of this book, but make no expressed or implied warranty of any kind and assume no responsibility for errors or omissions. No liability is assumed for incidental or consequential damages in connection with or arising out of the use of the information or programs contained herein.

The publisher offers discounts on this book when ordered in quantity for special sales. For more information, please contact:

Pearson Education Corporate Sales Division
One Lake Street
Upper Saddle River, NJ 07458
(800) 382-3419
corpsales@pearsontechgroup.com

Visit AW on the Web: www.aw.com/cseng/

Library of Congress Cataloging-in-Publication Data
Siek, Jeremy G.
     The Boost graph library : user guide and reference manual/ Jeremy G. Siek, Lie-Quan Lee, Andrew Lumsdaine
        p. cm.
     Includes bibliographical references and index.
     ISBN 0-201-72914-8 (alk. paper)
     1. C++ (Computer language).   2. Graph theory.   I. Lee, Lie-Quan. II. Lumsdaine, Andrew.   III. Title.

006.6—dc21

2001053553

ISBN 0-201-72914-8
Text printed on recycled paper
1 2 3 4 5 6 7 8 9 10—MA—0504030201
First printing, December 2001

To Richard and Elisabeth.
—J.G.S.

To Yun.
—L-Q.L.

To Wendy, Ben, Emily, and Bethany.
—A.L.

Contents

Foreword

When I first looked at this book, I felt envious. After all, what led me to the discovery of generic programming was the desire to build a library like the Boost Graph Library (BGL). In 1984 I joined the faculty of Polytechnic University in Brooklyn with some vague ideas about building libraries of software components. Well, to tell you the truth that was my secondary interest—my real interest at that time was to construct formal underpinnings of natural language, something like Aristotle's Organon, but more complete and formal. I was probably the only assistant professor in any Electrical Engineering or Computer Science department who meant to obtain tenure through careful study of Aristotle's Categories. Interestingly enough, the design of the Standard Template Library (STL)—in particular the underlying ontology of objects—is based on my realization that the whole-part relation is a fundamental relation that describes the real world and that it is not at all similar to the element-set relation familiar to us from set theory. Real objects do not share parts: my leg is nobody else's leg. STL containers are like that: two containers do not share parts. There are operations like *std::list::splice* that move parts from one container to another; they are similar to organ transplant: my kidney is mine until it is spliced into somebody else.

In any case, I was firmly convinced that software components should be functional in nature and based on John Backus's FP system. The only novel intuition was that functions should be associated with some axioms: for example, the "Russian peasant algorithm" that allows one to compute the nth power in $O(\log n)$ steps is defined for any object that has an associative binary operation defined on it. In other words, I believed that algorithms should be associated with what we now call concepts (see §2.3 of this book), but what I called structure types and what type-theorists call *multi-sorted algebras*.

It was my great luck that Polytechnic had a remarkable person on its faculty, Aaron Kershenbaum, who combined deep knowledge of graph algorithms with an unusual desire to implement them. Aaron saw potential in my attempts to decompose programs into simple primitives, and spent a lot of time teaching me graph algorithms and working with me on implementing them. He also showed me that there were some fundamental things that cannot be done functionally without prohibitive change in the complexity. Although it was often possible for me to implement linear time algorithms functionally without changing the asymptotic complexity, it was impossible in practice to implement logarithmic time algorithms without making them linear. In particular, Aaron explained to me why priority queues were so important for many graph algorithms (and he was well qualified to do so: Knuth in his Stanford GraphBase book [22] attributes the discovery of how to apply binary heaps to Prim's and Dijkstra's algorithms to Aaron).

It was a moment of great joy when we were able to produce Prim's and Dijkstra's algorithms as two instances of the same generic—we called it "high-order" then—algorithm. It is quite remarkable how close BGL code is to what we had (see, for example, a footnote to §13.4.2). The following code in Scheme shows how the two algorithms were implemented in terms of the same higher-order algorithm. The only difference is in how distance values are combined: using addition for Dijkstra's and by selecting the second operand for Prim's.

```
(define dijkstra
  (make−scan−based−algorithm−with−mark
    make−heap−with−membership−and−values + < ))

(define prim
  (make−scan−based−algorithm−with−mark
    make−heap−with−membership−and−values (lambda (x y) y) < ))
```

It took me a long time—almost 10 years—to find a language in which this style of programming could be *effectively* realized. I finally found C++, which enabled me to produce something that people could use. Moreover, C++ greatly influenced my design by providing a crisp C-based machine model. The features of C++ that enabled STL are templates and overloading.

I often hear people attacking C++ overloading, and, as is true with most good mechanisms, overloading can be misused. But it is an essential mechanism for the development of useful abstractions. If we look at mathematics, it has been greatly driven by overloading. Extensions of a notion of numbers from natural numbers to integers, to rational numbers, to Gaussian integers, to p-adic numbers, etc, are examples of overloading. One can easily guess things without knowing exact definitions. If I see an expression that uses both addition and multiplication, I assume distributivity. If I see less-than and addition, I assume that if $a < b$ then $a + c < b + c$ (I seldom add uncountable cardinals). Overloading allows us to carry knowledge from one type to another.

It is important to understand that one can write generic algorithms just with overloading, without templates: it does, however, require a lot of typing. That is, for every class that satisfies, say, random access iterator requirements, one has to define all the relevant algorithms by hand. It is tedious, but can be done (only signatures would need to be defined: the bodies will be the same). It should be noted that generics in Ada require hand-instantiation and, therefore, are not that helpful, since every algorithm needs to be instantiated by hand. Templates in C++ solve this problem by allowing one to define things once.

There are still things that are needed for generic programming that are not yet representable in C++. Generic algorithms are algorithms that work on objects with similar interfaces. Not identical interfaces as in object-oriented programming, but similar. It is not just the handling of binary methods (see §2.1.3) that causes the problem, it is the fact that interfaces are described in terms of a single type (single-sorted algebra). If we look carefully at things like iterators we observe that they are describable only in terms of multiple types: the iterator type itself, the value type, and the distance type. In other words, we need three types to define the interfaces on one type. And there is no machinery in C++ to do that. The result of this is that we cannot define what iterators are and, therefore, cannot really compile generic algorithms. For example, if we define the reduce algorithm as:

```
template <class InputIterator, class BinaryOperationWithIdentity>
typename iterator_traits<InputIterator>::value_type
reduce (InputIterator first, InputIterator last, BinaryOperationWithIdentity op)
{
    typedef typename iterator_traits<InputIterator>::value_type T;
    if (first == last) return identity_element (op) ;
    T result = *first;
    while (++first != last) result = op (result, *first) ;
    return result;
}
```

but instead of: *++first != last* we write: *++first<last*, no compiler can detect the bug at the point of definition. Though the standard clearly states that *operator<* does not need to be defined for Input Iterators, there is no way for the compiler to know it. Iterator requirements are just words. We are trying to program with concepts (multi-sorted algebras) in a language that has no support for them.

How hard would it be to extend C++ to really enable this style of programming? First, we need to introduce concepts as a new interface facility. For example, we can define:

```
concept SemiRegular : Assignable, DefaultConstructible {} ;
concept Regular : SemiRegular, EqualityComparable {} ;
concept InputIterator : Regular, Incrementable {
    SemiRegular value_type;
    Integral distance_type;
    const value_type& operator* () ;
} ;

value_type (InputIterator)
reduce (InputIterator first, InputIterator last, BinaryOperationWithIdentity op)
(value_type (InputIterator) == argument_type (BinaryOperationWithIdentity) )
{
    if (first == last) return identity_element (op) ;
    value_type (InputIterator) result = *first;
    while (++first != last) result = op (result, *first) ;
    return result;
}
```

Generic functions are functions that take concepts as arguments and in addition to an argument list have a list of type constraints. Now full type checking can be done at the point of definition without looking at the points of call, and full type-checking can be done at the points of call without looking at the body of the algorithm.

Sometimes we need multiple instances of the same concept. For example,

OutputIterator merge (InputIterator [1] *first1, InputIterator* [1] *last1,*
　　　　　　　InputIterator [2] *first2, InputIterator* [2] *last2,*
　　　　　　　OutputIterator result)
(bool operator< (value_type (InputIterator [1] *), value_type (InputIterator* [2] *)),*
value_type (InputIterator [1] *) == value_type (InputIterator* [2] *),*
output_type (OutputIterator) == value_type (InputIterator [2] *));*

Note that this merge is not as powerful as the STL merge. It cannot merge a list of *float*s and a vector of *double*s into a deque of *int*s. STL algorithms will often do unexpected and, in my opinion, undesirable type conversions. If someone needs to merge *double*s and *float*s into *int*s, he or she should use an explicit function object for asymmetric comparison and a special output iterator for conversion.

C++ provides two different abstraction mechanisms: object-orientedness and templates. Object-orientedness allows for exact interface definition and for run-time dispatch. But it cannot handle binary methods or multi-method dispatching, and its run-time binding is often inefficient. Templates handle richer interfaces and are resolved at compile-time. They can, however, cause a software engineering nightmare because of the lack of separation between interfaces and implementation. For example, I recently tried compiling a 10-line STL-based program using one of the most popular C++ compilers, and ran away in shock after getting several pages of incomprehensible error messages. And often one needs run-time dispatch that cannot be handled by templates. I do believe that introduction of concepts will unify both approaches and resolve both sets of limitations. And after all, it is possible to represent concepts as virtual tables that are extended by pointers to type descriptors: the virtual table for input iterator contains not just pointers to *operator** and *operator++*, but also pointers to the actual type of the iterator, its value type, and its distance type. And then one could introduce pointers to concepts and references to concepts!

Generic programming is a relatively young subdiscipline of computer science. I am happy to see that the small effort—started twenty years ago by Dave Musser, Deepak Kapur, Aaron Kershenbaum and me—led to a new generation of libraries such as BGL and MTL. And I have to congratulate Indiana University on acquiring one of the best generic programming teams in the world. I am sure they will do other amazing things!

Alexander Stepanov
Palo Alto, California
September, 2001[1]

---

[1] I would like to thank John Wilkinson, Mark Manasse, Marc Najork, and Jeremy Siek for many valuable suggestions.

Preface

The graph abstraction is a powerful problem-solving tool used to describe relationships between discrete objects. Many practical problems can be modeled in their essential form by graphs. Such problems appear in many domains: Internet packet routing, telephone network design, software build systems, Web search engines, molecular biology, automated road-trip planning, scientific computing, and so on. The power of the graph abstraction arises from the fact that the solution to a graph-theoretic problem can be used to solve problems in a wide variety of domains. For example, the problem of solving a maze and the problem of finding groups of Web pages that are mutually reachable can both be solved using depth-first search, an important concept from graph theory. By concentrating on the essence of these problems—the graph model describing discrete objects and the relationships between them—graph theoreticians have created solutions to not just a handful of particular problems, but to entire families of problems.

Now a question arises. If graph theory is generally and broadly applicable to arbitrary problem domains, should not the software that implements graph algorithms be just as broadly applicable? Graph theory would seem to be an ideal area for software reuse. However, up until now the potential for reuse has been far from realized. Graph problems do not typically occur in a pure graph-theoretic form, but rather are embedded in larger domain-specific problems. As a result, the data to be modeled as a graph are often not explicitly represented as a graph but are instead encoded in some application-specific data structure. Even in the case where the application data are explicitly represented as a graph, the particular graph representation chosen by the programmer might not match the representation expected by a library that the programmer wants to use. Moreover, different applications may place different time and space requirements on the graph data structure.

This implies a serious problem for the graph library writer who wants to provide reusable software, for it is impossible to anticipate every possible data structure that might be needed and to write a different version of the graph algorithm specifically for each one. The current state of affairs is that graph algorithms are written in terms of whatever data structure is most convenient for the algorithm and users must convert their data structures to that format in order to use the algorithm. This is an inefficient undertaking, consuming programmer time and computational resources. Often, the cost is perceived not to be worthwhile, and the programmer instead chooses to rewrite the algorithm in terms of his or her own data structure.

This approach is also time consuming and error prone, and will tend to lead to sub-optimal solutions since the application programmer may not be a graph algorithms expert.

Generic Programming

The Standard Template Library (STL) [40] was introduced in 1994 and was adopted shortly thereafter into the C++ Standard. The STL was a library of interchangeable components for solving many fundamental problems on sequences of elements. What set the STL apart from libraries that came before it was that each STL algorithm could work with a wide variety of sequential data structures: linked-lists, arrays, sets, and so on. The iterator abstraction provided an interface between containers and algorithms and the C++ template mechanism provided the needed flexibility to allow implementation without loss of efficiency. Each algorithm in the STL is a function template parameterized by the types of iterators upon which it operates. Any iterator that satisfies a minimal set of requirements can be used regardless of the data structure traversed by the iterator. The systematic approach used in the STL to construct abstractions and interchangeable components is called *generic programming*.

Generic programming lends itself well to solving the reusability problem for graph libraries. With generic programming, graph algorithms can be made much more flexible, allowing them to be easily used in a wide variety applications. Each graph algorithm is written not in terms of a specific data structure, but instead to a graph abstraction that can be easily implemented by many different data structures. Writing generic graph algorithms has the additional advantage of being more natural; the abstraction inherent in the pseudo-code description of an algorithm is retained in the generic function.

The Boost Graph Library (BGL) is the first C++ graph library to apply the notions of generic programming to the construction of graph algorithms.

Some BGL History

The Boost Graph Library began its life as the Generic Graph Component Library (GGCL), a software project at the Lab for Scientific Computing (LSC). The LSC, under the direction of Professor Andrew Lumsdaine, was an interdisciplinary laboratory dedicated to research in algorithms, software, tools, and run-time systems for high-performance computational science and engineering.[2] Special emphasis was put on developing industrial-strength, high-performance software using modern programming languages and techniques—most notably, generic programming.

Soon after the Standard Template Library was released, work began at the LSC to apply generic programming to scientific computing. The Matrix Template Library (MTL) was one of the first projects. Many of the lessons learned during construction of the MTL were applied to the design and implementation of the GGCL.

---

[2]The LSC has since evolved into the Open Systems Laboratory (OSL) *http://www.osl.iu.edu*. Although the name and location have changed, the research agenda remains the same.

An important class of linear algebra computations in scientific computing is that of sparse matrix computations, an area where graph algorithms play an important role. As the LSC was developing the sparse matrix capabilities of the MTL, the need for high-performance reusable (and generic) graph algorithms became apparent. However, none of the graph libraries available at the time (LEDA, GTL, Stanford GraphBase) were written using the generic programming style of the MTL and the STL, and hence did not fulfill the flexibility and high-performance requirements of the LSC. Other researchers were also expressing interest in a generic C++ graph library. During a meeting with Bjarne Stroustrup, we were introduced to several individuals at AT&T who needed such a library. Other early work in the area of generic graph algorithms included some codes written by Alexander Stepanov, as well as Dietmar Kühl's master's thesis.

With this in mind, and motivated by homework assignments in his algorithms class, Jeremy Siek began prototyping an interface and some graph classes in the spring of 1998. Lie-Quan Lee then developed the first version of the GGCL, which became his master's thesis project.

During the following year, the authors began collaborating with Alexander Stepanov and Matthew Austern. During this time, Stepanov's disjoint-sets-based connected components implementation was added to the GGCL, and work began on providing concept documentation for the GGCL, similar to Austern's STL documentation.

During this year the authors also became aware of Boost and were excited to find an organization interested in creating high-quality, open source C++ libraries. Boost included several people interested in generic graph algorithms, most notably Dietmar Kühl. Some discussions about generic interfaces for graph structures resulted in a revision of the GGCL that closely resembles the current Boost Graph Library interface.

On September 4, 2000, the GGCL passed the Boost formal review (managed by David Abrahams) and became the Boost Graph Library. The first release of the BGL was September 27, 2000. The BGL is not a "frozen" library. It continues to grow as new algorithms are contributed, and it continues to evolve to meet users' needs. We encourage readers to participate in the Boost group and help with extensions to the BGL.

What Is Boost?

Boost is an online community that encourages development and peer-review of free C++ libraries. The emphasis is on portable and high-quality libraries that work well with (and are in the same spirit as) the C++ Standard Library. Members of the community submit proposals (library designs and implementations) for review. The Boost community (led by a review manager) then reviews the library, provides feedback to the contributors, and finally renders a decision as to whether the library should be included in the Boost library collection. The libraries are available at the Boost Web site *http://www.boost.org*. In addition, the Boost mailing list provides an important forum for discussing library plans and for organizing collaboration.

Obtaining and Installing the BGL Software

The Boost Graph Library is available as part of the Boost library collection, which can be obtained in several different ways. The CD accompanying this book contains version 1.25.1 of the Boost library collection. In addition, releases of the Boost library collection can be obtained with your Web browser at *http://www.boost.org/boost_all.zip* for the Windows zip archive of the latest release and *http://www.boost.org/boost_all.tar.gz* for the UNIX archive of the latest release. The Boost libraries can also be downloaded via FTP at *ftp://boost.sourceforge.net/pub-/boost/release/*.

The zip archive of the Boost library collection can be unzipped by using WinZip or other similar tools. The UNIX "tar ball" can be expanded using the following command:

gunzip −cd boost_all.tar.gz | tar xvf −

Extracting the archive creates a directory whose name consists of the word *boost* and a version number. For example, extracting the Boost release 1.25.1 creates a directory *boost_1_25_1*. Under this top directory, are two principal subdirectories: *boost* and *libs*. The subdirectory *boost* contains the header files for all the libraries in the collection. The subdirectory *libs* contains a separate subdirectory for each library in the collection. These subdirectories contain library-specific source and documentation files. You can point your Web browser to *boost_1_25_1/index.htm* and navigate the whole Boost library collection.

All of the BGL header files are in the directory *boost/graph/*. However, other Boost header files are needed since BGL uses other Boost components. The HTML documentation is in *libs/graph/doc/* and the source code for the examples is in *libs/graph/example/*. Regression tests for BGL are in *libs/graph/test/*. The source files in *libs/graph/src/* implement the Graphviz file parsers and printers.

Except as described next, there are no compilation and build steps necessary to use BGL. All that is required is that the Boost header file directory be added to your compiler's include path. For example, using Windows 2000, if you have unzipped release 1.25.1 from *boost_all.zip* into the top level directory of your C drive, for Borland, GCC, and Metrowerks compilers add *-Ic:/boost_1_25_1* to the compiler command line, and for the Microsoft Visual C++ compiler add */I "c:/boost_1_25_1"*. For IDEs, add *c:/boost_1_25_1* (or whatever you have renamed it to) to the include search paths using the appropriate dialog. Before using the BGL interface to LEDA or Stanford GraphBase, LEDA or GraphBase must be installed according to their installation instructions. To use the *read_graphviz()* functions (for reading AT&T Graphviz files), you must build and link to an additional library under *boost_1_25_1/libs/graph/src*.

The Boost Graph Library is written in ISO/IEC Standard C++ and compiles with most C++ compilers. For an up-to-date summary of the compatibility with a particular compiler, see the "Compiler Status" page at the Boost Web site *http://www.boost.org/status/-compiler_status.html*.

How to Use This Book

This book is both a user guide and reference manual for the BGL. It is intended to allow the reader to begin using the BGL for real-life graph problems. This book should also be interesting for programmers who wish to learn more about generic programming. Although there are many books about how to use generic libraries (which in almost all cases means how to use the STL or Standard Library), there is very little available about how actually to build generic software. Yet generic programming is a vitally important new paradigm for software development. We hope that, by way of example, this book will show the reader how to do (and not simply use) generic programming and to apply and extend the generic programming paradigm beyond the basic container types and algorithms of the STL.

The third partner to the user guide and reference manual is the BGL code itself. The BGL code is not simply academic and instructional. It is intended to be used.

For students learning about graph algorithms and data structures, BGL provides a comprehensive graph algorithm framework. The student can concentrate on learning the important theory behind graph algorithms without becoming bogged down and distracted in too many implementation details.

For practicing programmers, BGL provides high-quality implementations of graph data structures and algorithms. Programmers will realize significant time saving from this reliability. Time that would have otherwise been spent developing (and debugging) complicated graph data structures and algorithms can now be spent in more productive pursuits. Moreover, the flexible interface to the BGL will allow programmers to apply graph algorithms in settings where a graph may only exist implicitly.

For the graph theoretician, this book makes a persuasive case for the use of generic programming for implementing graph-theoretic algorithms. Algorithms written using the BGL interface will have broad applicability and will be able to be reused in numerous settings.

We assume that the reader has a good grasp of C++. Since there are many sources where the reader can learn about C++, we do not try to teach it here (see the references at the end of the book—*The C++ Programming Language*, Special ed., by Bjarne Stroustrup [42] and *C++ Primer*, 3rd ed., by Josee Lajoie and Stanley B. Lippman [25] are our recommendations). We also assume some familiarity with the STL (see *STL Tutorial and Reference Guide* by David R. Musser, Gillmer J. Derge, and Atul Saini [34] and *Generic Programming and the STL* by Matthew Austern [3]). We do, however, present some of the more advanced C++ features used to implement generic libraries in general and the BGL in particular.

Some necessary graph theory concepts are introduced here, but not in great detail. For a detailed discussion of elementary graph theory see *Introduction to Algorithms* by T. H. Cormen, C. E. Leiserson, and R. L. Rivest [10].

Literate Programming

The program examples in this book are presented using the literate programming style developed by Donald Knuth. The literate programming style consists of writing source code and documentation together in the same file. A tool then automatically converts the file into both a pure source code file and into a documentation file with pretty-printed source code. The literate programming style makes it easier to ensure that the code examples in the book really compile and run and that they stay consistent with the text.

The source code for each example is broken up into *parts*. Parts can include references to other parts. For example, the following part labeled "Merge sort function definition" refers to the parts labeled "Divide the range in half and sort each half" and "Merge the two halves." An example often starts with a part that provides an outline for the entire computation, which is then followed by other parts that fill in the details. For example, the following function template is a generic implementation of the merge sort algorithm [10]. There are two steps in the algorithm, sorting each half of the range and then merging the two halves.

⟨ Merge sort function definition xxiia ⟩ ≡

```
template <typename RandomAccessIterator, typename Compare>
void merge_sort (RandomAccessIterator first, RandomAccessIterator last, Compare cmp)
{
   if (first + 1 < last) {
       ⟨Divide the range in half and sort each half xxiib⟩
       ⟨Merge the two halves xxiic⟩
   }
}
```

Typically, the size of each part is limited to a few lines of code that carry out a specific task. The names for the parts are chosen to convey the essence of the task.

⟨ Divide the range in half and sort each half xxiib ⟩ ≡

```
RandomAccessIterator mid = first + (last − first) / 2;
merge_sort (first, mid, cmp);
merge_sort (mid, last, cmp);
```

The *std::inplace_merge* ( ) function does the main work of this algorithm, creating a single sorted range out of two sorted subranges.

⟨ Merge the two halves xxiic ⟩ ≡

```
std::inplace_merge (first, mid, last, cmp);
```

Parts are labeled with a descriptive name, along with the page number on which the part is defined. If more than one part is defined on a page, the definitions are distinguished by a letter.

Sometimes a file name is used for the label of a part. This means that the part is written out to a file. Many of the examples in the book are written out to files, and can be found in the *libs/graph/example/* directory of the Boost distribution. The following example shows the *merge_sort* ( ) function being output to a header file.

⟨ *merge-sort.hpp* xxiii ⟩ ≡

   #ifndef *MERGE_SORT_HPP*
   #define *MERGE_SORT_HPP*

   ⟨*Merge sort function definition xxiia*⟩

   #endif // *MERGE_SORT_HPP*

The Electronic Reference

An electronic version of the book is included on the accompanying CD, in the file ***bgl-book.pdf***.
The electronic version is searchable and is fully hyperlinked, making it a useful companion
for the printed version. The hyperlinks include all internal references such as the literate
programming "part" references as well as links to external Web pages.

Acknowledgments

We owe many debts of thanks to a number of individuals who both inspired and encouraged
us in developing the BGL and in writing this book.

A most profound thanks goes to Alexander Stepanov and David Musser for their pio-
neering work in generic programming, for their continued encouragement of our work, and
for contributions to the BGL. We especially thank David Musser for his careful proofreading
of this book. Matthew Austern's work on documenting the concepts of the STL provided a
foundation for creating the concepts in the BGL. We thank Dietmar Kühl for his work on
generic graph algorithms and design patterns; especially for the property map abstraction.
This work would not have been possible without the expressive power of Bjarne Stroustrup's
C++ language.

Dave Abrahams, Jens Maurer, Dietmar Kühl, Beman Dawes, Gary Powell, Greg Colvin
and the rest of the group at Boost provided valuable input to the BGL interface, numerous
suggestions for improvement, and proofreads of this book. We also thank the following BGL
users whose questions helped to motivate and improve BGL (as well as this book): Gordon
Woodhull, Dave Longhorn, Joel Phillips, Edward Luke, and Stephen North.

Thanks to a number of individuals who reviewed the book during its development: Jan
Christiaan van Winkel, David Musser, Beman Dawes, and Jeffrey Squyres.

A great thanks to our editor Deborah Lafferty; Kim Arney Mulcahy, Cherly Ferguson,
and Marcy Barnes, the production coordinators; and the rest of the team at Addison–Wesley.
It was a pleasure to work with them.

Our original work on the BGL was supported in part by NSF grant ACI-9982205. Parts
of the BGL were completed while the third author was on sabbatical at Lawrence Berkeley
National Laboratory (where the first two authors were occasional guests). All of the graph
drawings in this book were produced using the dot program from the Graphviz package.

License

The BGL software is released under an open source "artistic" license. A copy of the BGL license is included with the source code in the LICENSE file.

The BGL may be used freely for both commercial and noncommercial use. The main restriction on BGL is that modified source code can only be redistributed if it is clearly marked as a nonstandard version of BGL. The preferred method for the distribution of BGL, and for submitting changes, is through the Boost Web site.

Part I

User Guide

Chapter 1

Introduction

In this chapter, we provide a broad overview of some of the interfaces and components available in the BGL. We begin with a quick review of graph terminology using a network of Internet routers as an example of a system that can be modeled as a graph. The generic interfaces that are defined by the BGL are introduced in §1.2 and we discuss the concrete graph classes that implement these interfaces in §1.3. Finally, §1.4 gives a preview of the BGL generic graph algorithms.

1.1 Some Graph Terminology

A graph model for a network of Internet routers is shown in Figure 1.1. The circles (representing routers) are labeled a through e, and the connections between them are labeled with the average transmission delay.

In the terminology of graph theory, each router in the example network is represented by a *vertex* and each connection is represented by an *edge*.[1] A *graph* G consists of a *vertex set* V and an *edge set* E. Thus, we write $G = (V, E)$. The size of the vertex set (the number of vertices in the graph) is expressed as $|V|$ and the size of the edge set as $|E|$. An edge is written as an ordered pair consisting of the vertices connected by the edge. The ordered pair (u, v) indicates the edge that connects vertex u to vertex v.

The router network of Figure 1.1 can be expressed using set notation as follows:

$$
\begin{aligned}
V &= \{a, b, c, d, e\} \\
E &= \{(a, b), (a, d), (b, d), (c, a), (c, e), (d, c), (d, e)\} \\
G &= (V, E)
\end{aligned}
$$

A graph can be directed or undirected, meaning the edge set in the graph consists respectively of directed or undirected edges. An edge of a *directed graph* is an ordered pair (u, v)

---

[1] Another popular name for vertex is *node*, and another name for edge is *arc*.

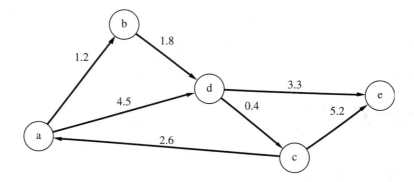

Figure 1.1 A network of Internet routers. The connections are labeled with the transmission delay (in milliseconds).

with u as the *source* vertex and v as the *target* vertex. The directed edge (u, v) is distinct from the edge (v, u). In an *undirected graph* an edge always connects the two vertices in both directions, so the vertex ordering in an edge does not matter; (u, v) and (v, u) are the same edge. An edge connecting a vertex to itself such as (u, u) is called a *self-loop* and is typically not allowed in an undirected graph. Two or more edges that connect the same two vertices, such as (u, v) and (u, v), are called *parallel edges*. A graph that allows parallel edges is called a *multigraph*.

If a graph contains an edge (u, v), then vertex v is said to be *adjacent* to vertex u. For a directed graph, edge (u, v) is an *out-edge* of vertex u and an *in-edge* of vertex v. For an undirected graph, edge (u, v) is said to be *incident on* the vertices u and v. The adjacency set for each vertex in the directed graph of Figure 1.1 follows.

$$
\begin{aligned}
Adjacent[a] &= \{b, d\} \\
Adjacent[b] &= \{d\} \\
Adjacent[c] &= \{a, e\} \\
Adjacent[d] &= \{c, e\} \\
Adjacent[e] &= \{\}
\end{aligned}
$$

The following are the out-edges for each vertex:

$$
\begin{aligned}
OutEdges[a] &= \{(a, b), (a, d)\} \\
OutEdges[b] &= \{(b, d)\} \\
OutEdges[c] &= \{(c, a), (c, e)\} \\
OutEdges[d] &= \{(d, c), (d, e)\} \\
OutEdges[e] &= \{\}
\end{aligned}
$$

Similarly, the following are the in-edges for each vertex:

$$
\begin{aligned}
InEdges[a] &= \{(c,a)\} \\
InEdges[b] &= \{(a,b)\} \\
InEdges[c] &= \{(d,c)\} \\
InEdges[d] &= \{(a,d),(b,d)\} \\
InEdges[e] &= \{(c,e),(d,e)\}
\end{aligned}
$$

1.2 Graph Concepts

One of the primary responsibilities of a generic library is to define the interfaces that allow algorithms to be written independently of any particular data structure. Note that by *interface* we do not merely mean a set of function prototypes. Instead, we mean a set of syntactic requirements—things like function names and numbers of arguments—as well as semantic requirements (executing the function must have certain effects) and time and space complexity guarantees.

Using the terminology from the book *Generic Programming and the STL* [3], we use the word *concept* to refer to this richer notion of an interface. The STL defines a collection of iterator concepts that provide a generic mechanism for traversing and accessing sequences of objects. Similarly, the BGL defines a collection of concepts that specify how graphs can be inspected and manipulated. In this section we give an overview of these concepts. The examples in this section do not refer to specific graph types; they are written as function templates with the graph as a template parameter. A generic function written using the BGL interface can be applied to any of the BGL graph types—or even to new user-defined graph types. In §1.3 we discuss the concrete graph classes that are provided in the BGL.

1.2.1 Vertex and Edge Descriptors

In the BGL, vertices and edges are manipulated through opaque handles called *vertex descriptors* and *edge descriptors*. Different graph types may use different types for their descriptors. For example, some graph types may use integers, whereas other graphs may use pointers. The descriptor types for a graph type are always accessible through the ***graph_traits*** class. The motivation and use of traits classes are described in §2.4 and the ***graph_traits*** class in particular is discussed in §14.2.1.

Vertex descriptors have very basic functionality. By themselves they can only be default constructed, copied, and compared for equality. Edge descriptors are similar, although they also provide access to the associated source and target vertex. The following function template[2] shows an implementation a generic function that determines if an edge is a self-loop.

---

[2]For aesthetic reasons, we prefer ***typename*** to the equivalent ***class*** for declaring template parameters.

```
template <typename Graph>
bool is_self_loop (typename graph_traits<Graph>::edge_descriptor e, const Graph& g)
{
  typename graph_traits<Graph>::vertex_descriptor u, v;
  u = source (e, g);
  v = target (e, g);
  return u == v;
}
```

1.2.2   Property Maps

Graphs become useful as models for particular problem domains by associating objects and quantities to vertices and edges. For example, in Figure 1.1 each vertex has a name consisting of a single character, and each edge has a transmission delay. In the BGL we refer to attached objects or attached quantities as *properties*. There are a wide variety of implementation techniques that can be used to associate a property with a vertex or edge. These include properties as data members of a struct, separate arrays indexed by vertex or edge number, hash tables, and so on. However, to write generic graph algorithms we need a uniform syntax for accessing properties, regardless of how they are stored. This uniform syntax is defined by the property map concepts.

A property map is an object that provides a mapping from a set of key objects to a set of value objects. The property map concepts specify only three functions: *get(p_map, key)* returns the value object for the *key*, *put(p_map, key, value)* assigns the *value* to the value object associated with the *key*, and *p_map[key]* returns a reference to the value object. The following example is a generic function that prints the name of a vertex given a name property map.

```
template <typename VertexDescriptor, typename VertexNameMap>
void print_vertex_name (VertexDescriptor v, VertexNameMap name_map)
{
  std::cout << get (name_map, v);
}
```

Similarly, the transmission delay of an edge can be printed using the following function:

```
template <typename Graph, typename TransDelayMap, typename VertexNameMap>
void print_trans_delay (typename graph_traits<Graph>::edge_descriptor e,
  const Graph& g, TransDelayMap delay_map, VertexNameMap name_map)
{
  std::cout << "trans-delay(" << get (name_map, source (e, g)) << ","
            << get (name_map, target (e, g)) << ") = " << get (delay_map, e);
}
```

The *print_vertex_name* () and *print_trans_delay* () functions are used in the next section.

Property maps are discussed in detail in Chapter 15, including techniques for creating user-defined property maps. How to add properties into a graph and obtain the corresponding property map is described in §3.6.

1.2.3 Graph Traversal

The graph abstraction consists of several different kinds of collections: the vertices and edges for the graph and the out-edges, in-edges, and adjacent vertices for each vertex. Similar to the STL, the BGL uses iterators to provide access to each of these collections. There are five kinds of graph iterators, one for each kind of collection:

1. A *vertex iterator* is used to traverse all the vertices of a graph. The value type of a vertex iterator is a vertex descriptor.

2. An *edge iterator* is used to traverse all the edges of a graph. The value type of this iterator is an edge descriptor.

3. An *out-edge iterator* is used to access all of the out-edges for a given vertex u. Its value type is an edge descriptor. Each edge descriptor in this iterator range has u as the source vertex and a vertex adjacent to u as the target vertex (regardless of whether the graph is directed or undirected).

4. An *in-edge iterator* is used to access the in-edges of a vertex v. Its value type is an edge descriptor. Each edge descriptor in this iterator range has v as the target vertex and a vertex that v is adjacent to as the source.

5. An *adjacency iterator* is used to provide access to the vertices adjacent to a given vertex. The value type of this iterator is a vertex descriptor.

Like descriptors, each graph type has its own iterator types that are accessible through the **graph_traits** class. For each of the iterators just described, the BGL interface defines a function that returns a **std::pair** of iterator objects: the first iterator points to the first object in the sequence and the second iterator points past the end of the sequence. For example, the following function prints the names of all of the vertices in a graph:

```
template <typename Graph, typename VertexNameMap>
void print_vertex_names(const Graph& g, VertexNameMap name_map)
{
  std::cout << "vertices(g) = { ";
  typedef typename graph_traits<Graph>::vertex_iterator iter_t;
  for (std::pair<iter_t, iter_t> p = vertices(g); p.first != p.second; ++p.first) {
    print_vertex_name(*p.first, name_map); std::cout << ' ';
  }
  std::cout << "}" << std::endl;
}
```

Applying this function to a graph object that models the router network of Figure 1.1 produces the following output:

> *vertices* (*g*) = { *a b c d e* }

The following code prints the transmission delay values that are attached to each of the edges in the graph. In this function we use the *tie* ( ) function (from *boost/tuple/tuple.hpp*) to allow direct assignment from a *std::pair* into two scalar variables—in this case, *first* and *last*.

```
template <typename Graph, typename TransDelayMap, typename VertexNameMap>
void print_trans_delays (const Graph& g, TransDelayMap trans_delay_map,
  VertexNameMap name_map)
{
  typename graph_traits<Graph>::edge_iterator first, last;
  for (tie (first, last)  =  edges (g) ; first != last; ++first) {
    print_trans_delay (*first, g, trans_delay_map, name_map) ;
    std::cout << std::endl;
  }
}
```

The output of this function for the graph of Figure 1.1 is

> *trans−delay* (*a* , *b*)   = **1.2**
> *trans−delay* (*a* , *d*)   = **4.5**
> *trans−delay* (*b* , *d*)   = **1.8**
> *trans−delay* (*c* , *a*)   = **2.6**
> *trans−delay* (*c* , *e*)   = **5.2**
> *trans−delay* (*d* , *c*)   = **0.4**
> *trans−delay* (*d* , *e*)   = **3.3**

In addition to the *vertices* ( ) and *edges* ( ) functions, there are *out_edges* ( ), *in_edges* ( ), and *adjacent_vertices* ( ) functions. These functions take a vertex descriptor and graph object as arguments and return a pair of iterators.

Most algorithms do not need to use all five types of traversal, and some graph types cannot provide efficient versions of all iterator types. Care should be taken not to use concrete graph types with algorithms that require operations not supported by that type. If you attempt to use a graph type that does not provide a required operation, then a compile error will occur. The compile error may even include some information to help you figure out which operation was missing. See §2.5 for more details.

The available operations for a particular graph type is given in the documentation for that type. The "Model Of" section summarizes the provided operations by listing the concepts satisfied by the graph type. The operations required by each algorithm are given in the documentation for the algorithm by listing the concepts required of each parameter.

1.2.4 Graph Construction and Modification

The BGL also defines interfaces for adding and removing vertices and edges from a graph. In this section, we give a brief example of one way to create a graph that models the router network of Figure 1.1. First we use *add_vertex()* to add the five nodes representing routers to the graph, then we use *add_edge()* to add edges representing connections between the routers.

```
template <typename Graph, typename VertexNameMap, typename TransDelayMap>
void build_router_network (Graph& g, VertexNameMap name_map,
   TransDelayMap delay_map)
{
  ⟨Add routers to the network 9a⟩
  ⟨Add connections to the network 9b⟩
}
```

The *add_vertex()* function returns a vertex descriptor for the new vertex. We use this vertex descriptor to assign a vertex name to the vertex in a name property map:

⟨ Add routers to the network 9a ⟩ ≡

```
typename graph_traits<Graph>::vertex_descriptor a, b, c, d, e;

a = add_vertex (g); name_map [a] = 'a';
b = add_vertex (g); name_map [b] = 'b';
c = add_vertex (g); name_map [c] = 'c';
d = add_vertex (g); name_map [d] = 'd';
e = add_vertex (g); name_map [e] = 'e';
```

The *add_edge()* function returns a *std::pair*, where the first member of the pair is an edge descriptor for the new edge and the second is a Boolean flag that indicates whether an edge was added (some graph types will not insert an edge if an edge with the same source and target is already in the graph).

⟨ Add connections to the network 9b ⟩ ≡

```
typename graph_traits<Graph>::edge_descriptor ed;
bool inserted;

tie (ed, inserted) = add_edge (a, b, g);
delay_map [ed] = 1.2;
tie (ed, inserted) = add_edge (a, d, g);
delay_map [ed] = 4.5;
tie (ed, inserted) = add_edge (b, d, g);
delay_map [ed] = 1.8;
tie (ed, inserted) = add_edge (c, a, g);
delay_map [ed] = 2.6;
tie (ed, inserted) = add_edge (c, e, g);
delay_map [ed] = 5.2;
```

```
tie(ed, inserted) = add_edge(d, c, g);
delay_map[ed] = 0.4;
tie(ed, inserted) = add_edge(d, e, g);
delay_map[ed] = 3.3;
```

In some cases it is more efficient to add or remove multiple vertices or edges simultaneously instead of one at a time. The BGL interface includes functions for accomplishing this.

1.2.5 Algorithm Visitors

Many of the algorithms of the STL have a function object parameter that provides a mechanism for customizing the behavior of the algorithm to a particular application. For example, the *std::sort()* function contains a comparison parameter *compare*.

```
template <typename RandomAccessIterator, typename BinaryPredicate>
void sort(RandomAccessIterator first, RandomAccessIterator last,
          BinaryPredicate compare)
```

The *compare* parameter is a function object (sometimes called a *functor*). Its use is illustrated by the following example.

Consider the case of a program for maintaining an address book. Sorting an array of addresses by the last name of the contact can be accomplished by calling *std::sort()* with an appropriate function object. An example of such a function object is the following:

```
struct compare_last_name {
  bool operator()(const address_info& x, const address_info& y) const {
    return x.last_name < y.last_name;
  }
};
```

Sorting the array of addresses is accomplished with a call to *std::sort()*, passing in the customized comparison function.

```
std::vector<address_info> addresses;
// ...
compare_last_name compare;
std::sort(addresses.begin(), addresses.end(), compare);
```

The BGL provides a mechanism similar to function objects for customizing the behavior of graph algorithms. These objects are called *algorithm visitors*. The BGL visitor is a multifunction object. Instead of just the single *operator()* of a function object, a BGL visitor defines multiple functions that are invoked at certain defined *event points* within an algorithm (the event points differ with each algorithm).

Despite the name, BGL visitors are somewhat different from the visitor pattern described in the "Gang of Four" (GoF) Patterns Book [14]. A GoF visitor provides a mechanism for performing new operations on an object structure without modifying the classes. Like the GoF visitor, the purpose of the BGL visitor is to provide a mechanism for extension. However the difference is that a BGL visitor extends algorithms, not object structures.

In the following example we print out the Internet routers from Figure 1.1 in breadth-first order by extending the *breadth_first_search* ( ) function with a visitor. The visitor prints the vertex name on the *discover vertex* event (see §4.1.1 for a description of breadth-first search).

The visitor class is defined according to the interface described by the BFSVisitor concept.

```
template <typename VertexNameMap>
class bfs_name_printer
  : public default_bfs_visitor { // inherit default (empty) event point actions
public:
  bfs_name_printer (VertexNameMap n_map) : m_name_map (n_map) { }
  template <typename Vertex, typename Graph>
  void discover_vertex (Vertex u, const Graph& ) const {
    std::cout << get (m_name_map, u) << ' ';
  }
private:
  VertexNameMap m_name_map;
};
```

We then create a visitor object of type *bfs_name_printer* and pass it to *breadth_first_search* ( ). The *visitor* ( ) function used here is part of the named-parameter technique that is described in §2.7.

```
bfs_name_printer<VertexNameMap> vis (name_map);
std::cout << "BFS vertex discover order: ";
breadth_first_search (g, a, visitor (vis));
std::cout << std::endl;
```

The output is as follows:

```
BFS vertex discover order: a b d c e
```

The edges of the breadth-first search tree are depicted by the black lines in Figure 1.2.

1.3　Graph Classes and Adaptors

The graph types provided by the BGL fall into two categories. The first is the graph classes that are used to store a graph in memory. The second is graph adaptors that create a modified view of a graph or that create a BGL graph interface based on some other type.

1.3.1　Graph Classes

The BGL contains two primary graph classes: *adjacency_list* and *adjacency_matrix*.

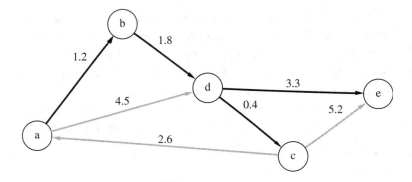

Figure 1.2 The path taken during a breadth-first search.

The main BGL component for representing graphs is the ***adjacency_list***. This class generalizes the traditional adjacency-list representation for a graph. The graph is represented by a collection of vertices where, with each vertex, there is stored a collection of out-edges. The actual implementation of the collection of vertices and edges can vary to meet particular needs. The ***adjacency_list*** class has several template parameters: ***EdgeList***, ***VertexList***, ***Directed***, ***VertexProperties***, ***EdgeProperties***, and ***GraphProperties***.

- ***EdgeList*** and ***VertexList*** specify the classes used to store the vertex list and edge lists for the graph. These parameters allow tradeoffs between traversal speed and insertion/removal speed and tradeoffs in memory consumption. In addition, the ***EdgeList*** parameter determines whether parallel edges may be inserted into the graph.

- ***Directed*** specifies whether the graph is directed, undirected, or bidirectional. By convention, a directed graph provides access to out-edges only, whereas a bidirectional graph provides access to in-edges as well as out-edges.

- ***VertexProperties***, ***EdgeProperties***, and ***GraphProperties*** specify the property types that are attached to the vertices, to the edges, and to the graph itself.

Complete documentation for the ***adjacency_list*** class can be found in §14.1.1.

The BGL class for representing dense graphs (graphs where $|E| \approx |V|^2$) is the ***adjacency_matrix***. In an ***adjacency_matrix***, access to an arbitrary edge (u, v) is efficient (constant time). The ***adjacency_matrix*** can represent both directed and undirected graphs and provides a mechanism for attaching properties to the vertices and edges. Complete documentation for the ***adjacency_matrix*** class can be found in §14.1.2.

Note that although all of the examples in this book use relatively small graphs (to allow drawings of the graphs to fit on a single page), the BGL graph classes are robust and space efficient. They have been used to represent graphs with millions of vertices.

1.3.2 Graph Adaptors

The BGL also includes a large number of graph adaptors. This first group of classes adapts any BGL graph to provide new behavior.

- *reverse_graph* is an adaptor that reverses the edge directions of a directed graph on the fly, so that in-edges behave like out-edges, and vice versa.

- *filtered_graph* is an adaptor that creates a view of a graph where two predicate function objects control whether vertices and edges from the original graph appear in the adapted graph, or whether they are hidden.

BGL also provides support for objects and data structures that are not BGL graph classes. This support is provided via adaptor classes and overloaded functions. The following describes these interfaces.

- *edge_list* is an adaptor that creates a BGL graph out of an iterator range of edges.

- Stanford GraphBase is supported by overloaded functions in the header file *boost/-graph/stanford_graph.hpp*. As a result of these overloaded functions, the GraphBase type *Graph** satisfies the BGL graph interface.

- LEDA is a popular object-oriented package that includes graph data structures and algorithms. Overloaded functions in the header file *boost/graph/leda_graph.hpp* allow the LEDA graph type *GRAPH<vtype, etype>* to satisfy the BGL graph interface.

- The STL composite type *std::vector< std::list<int> >* is supported as a graph by overloaded functions in the header file *boost/graph/vector_as_graph.hpp*.

The BGL interface is described completely in the concept reference in Chapter 12. Each graph class implements some (or all) of these concepts. The *adjacency_list* class can be considered a canonical implementation (or model) of a BGL graph, since it illustrates all of the basic ideas and interfaces of the BGL graphs.

1.4   Generic Graph Algorithms

The BGL graph algorithms are generic algorithms. As such, they are highly flexible in terms of the types of graph data structures to which they can be applied and in terms of how the algorithms can be customized to solve a wide range of problems. First, we look at using the *topological_sort()* function with two different graph types, and then we demonstrate the power of the generic *depth_first_search()* function by showing how it can be used to implement *topological_sort()*.

1.4.1   The Topological Sort Generic Algorithm

A topological ordering of a directed graph is an ordering of its vertices such that if there is an edge (u, v) in the graph, then vertex u appears before vertex v in the ordering. The BGL *topological_sort*( ) function template takes two arguments: the graph to be ordered and an output iterator. The algorithm writes vertices to the output iterator in reverse topological order.

One use for topological orderings is for scheduling tasks. Figure 1.3 shows a graph where the vertices are errands that need to be accomplished and where the edges indicate dependencies between errands (e.g., getting cash at the ATM has to be done before buying groceries). In the next two sections we show how to apply the BGL topological sort algorithm to this problem. In each section a different type of graph representation is used to demonstrate the generic nature of the BGL function.

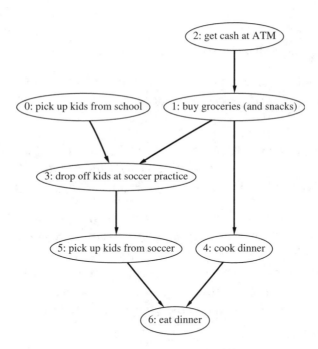

Figure 1.3 A graph representing scheduling dependencies between tasks. For now, an arbitrary vertex number is assigned to each task.

Using Topological Sort with a Vector of Lists

First we apply the topological sort to a graph built using *std::vector*<*std::list*<*int*>>. The following is the outline of the program.

⟨ *topo-sort1.cpp* 15a ⟩ ≡

```
#include <deque> // to store the vertex ordering
#include <vector>
#include <list>
#include <iostream>
#include <boost/graph/vector_as_graph.hpp>
#include <boost/graph/topological_sort.hpp>
int main()
{
  using namespace boost;
  ⟨Create labels for each of the tasks 15b⟩
  ⟨Create the graph 15c⟩
  ⟨Perform the topological sort and output the results 16⟩
  return EXIT_SUCCESS;
}
```

The vertices of the graph are represented using the integers from zero to six; storing the vertex labels in an array is therefore a convenient choice.

⟨ Create labels for each of the tasks 15b ⟩ ≡

```
const char* tasks[] = {
  "pick up kids from school",
  "buy groceries (and snacks)",
  "get cash at ATM",
  "drop off kids at soccer practice",
  "cook dinner",
  "pick up kids from soccer",
  "eat dinner" };
const int n_tasks = sizeof(tasks) / sizeof(char*);
```

The graph is realized as a vector of lists. Each vertex in the graph is associated with an index location in the vector. The size of the vector is thus the number of vertices in the graph. The list at that index location is used to represent the edges from that vertex to other vertices in the graph. Each edge (u, v) is added to the graph by pushing the integer for v onto the uth list. Figure 1.4 shows the resulting data structure. Due to the functions defined in *boost/graph/vector_as_graph.hpp* the vector of lists satisfies the requirements of the BGL VertexListGraph concept, and therefore can be used in the *topological_sort()* function.

⟨ Create the graph 15c ⟩ ≡

```
std::vector< std::list<int> > g(n_tasks);
g[0].push_back(3);
g[1].push_back(3);
g[1].push_back(4);
g[2].push_back(1);
g[3].push_back(5);
```

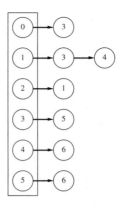

Figure 1.4 A vector of lists representation of the task dependency graph.

> *g*[**4**]*.push_back*(**6**);
> *g*[**5**]*.push_back*(**6**);

Before we call *topological_sort*() we need to create a place to store the results. The BGL algorithm for topological sort writes its output in reverse topological order (because it is more efficient to implement it that way). Recovering the topological order requires reversing the ordering computed by the algorithm. The following example uses *std::deque* as its output data structure because it supports constant time insertion at the front, which reverses the ordering. In addition, calling *topological_sort*() requires one of two things: (1) supply a color property map so that the algorithm can mark vertices to keep track of its progress through the graph, or (2) supply a mapping from vertices to integers so that the algorithm can create its own color map with an array.

Since in this example the vertices are already integers, we just pass *identity_property_map* in as the vertex index map. The *vertex_index_map*() function is used to specify a named parameter (see §2.7).

⟨ Perform the topological sort and output the results 16 ⟩ ≡

>   *std::deque*<*int*> *topo_order;*
>
>   *topological_sort*(*g,*
>   *std::front_inserter*(*topo_order*),
>   *vertex_index_map*(*identity_property_map*()));
>
>   *int n* = **1**;
>   *for* (*std::deque*<*int*>*::iterator i* = *topo_order.begin*();
>   *i* != *topo_order.end*(); ++*i,* ++*n*) {
>   *std::cout* << *tasks*[**i*] << *std::endl;*
>   }

The output shows an order in which the tasks could be carried out.

> *get cash at ATM*
> *buy groceries (and snacks)*
> *cook dinner*
> *pick up kids from school*
> *drop off kids at soccer practice*
> *pick up kids from soccer*
> *eat dinner*

Using Topological Sort with the *adjacency_list* **Class**

To demonstrate the flexibility of the generic algorithm *topological_sort()* we now change to using an altogether different graph type: the BGL *adjacency_list* class template. Since the *topological_sort()* function is a function template, graph structures of arbitrary type can be used. All that is required is that the type satisfies the concepts required by the algorithm.

The first two template parameters of the *adjacency_list* class determine the particular internal structure that is used. The first argument *listS* specifies that *std::list* is used for each out-edge list. The second argument *vecS* specifies that *std::vector* is used as the backbone of the adjacency list. This version of the *adjacency_list* class is similar in character to the vector of lists used in the previous section.

⟨ Create an adjacency list object 17a ⟩ ≡
> *adjacency_list<listS, vecS, directedS> g(n_tasks);*

The function *add_edge()* provides the interface for inserting edges into an *adjacency_list* (and all other graphs that support the EdgeMutableGraph concept). The vertex descriptor type for *adjacency_list* is an integer when *std::vector* is used for the backbone, which is why we can use integers to specify vertices. It is not always true for a given graph type that you can use integers to specify vertices.

⟨ Add edges to the adjacency list 17b ⟩ ≡
```
add_edge(0, 3, g);
add_edge(1, 3, g);
add_edge(1, 4, g);
add_edge(2, 1, g);
add_edge(3, 5, g);
add_edge(4, 6, g);
add_edge(5, 6, g);
```

The rest of the program is similar to the previous example, except that the *adjacency_list.hpp* header file is included instead of *vector_as_graph.hpp*. The following is the code for the program, with two of the parts reused from the previous section.

⟨ *topo-sort2.cpp* 18 ⟩ ≡

```
#include <vector>
#include <deque>
#include <boost/graph/topological_sort.hpp>
#include <boost/graph/adjacency_list.hpp>
int main()
{
  using namespace boost;
  ⟨Create labels for each of the tasks 15b⟩
  ⟨Create an adjacency list object 17a⟩
  ⟨Add edges to the adjacency list 17b⟩
  ⟨Perform the topological sort and output the results 16⟩
  return EXIT_SUCCESS;
}
```

1.4.2   The Depth-First Search Generic Algorithm

The BGL implementation of *topological_sort*() is only a few lines long because it can be implemented using the *depth_first_search*() function (and, in fact, the topological sort algorithm is typically presented this way in textbooks). The implementation consists of *depth_first_search*() used with a visitor that records the order in which vertices pass through the "finish vertex" event of the depth-first search. The explanation for why this computes a topological ordering is given in §3.3.

The following code creates an algorithm visitor that records vertices as they pass through the finish event point of a depth-first search. To make this class more generic the vertex ordering is recorded in an output iterator, allowing the user to choose the output method.

```
template <typename OutputIterator>
class topo_sort_visitor : public default_dfs_visitor { // inherit empty actions
public:
  topo_sort_visitor(OutputIterator iter) : m_iter(iter) { }
  template <typename Vertex, typename Graph>
  void finish_vertex(Vertex u, const Graph&) { *m_iter++ = u; }
private:
  OutputIterator m_iter;
};
```

Thus, *topological_sort*() is implemented by invoking *depth_first_search*() using the *topo_sort_visitor* as a parameter.

```
template <typename Graph, typename OutputIterator>
void topological_sort(Graph& g, OutputIterator result_iter) {
  topo_sort_visitor<OutputIterator> vis(result_iter);
  depth_first_search(g, visitor(vis));
}
```

Chapter 2

Generic Programming in C++

2.1   Introduction

Generic programming (GP) is a methodology for program design and implementation that separates data structures and algorithms through the use of abstract requirement specifications. In C++, generic programming is characterized by the use of parametric polymorphism through the use of templates, with an emphasis on efficiency.

Generic programming is the methodology that we used in the construction of the Boost Graph Library. To understand the organization and structure of the BGL, the reader needs a good understanding of generic programming. Because generic programming is a relatively new methodology (at least in the C++ community), we give an introduction to generic programming in this chapter. We also discuss the main techniques for generic programming in C++, which rely heavily on templates. These techniques are not just a collection of tricks; taken together, they form what one might consider a new sublanguage within C++.

The abstract requirement specifications in generic programming are similar to the older notion of abstract data types (ADTs). To review, an abstract data type is a type specification. It consists of a description of the applicable operations and gives the semantics of those operations, which often include preconditions, postconditions, and axioms (or invariants) [30]. A classic example of an abstract data type is a *stack* with methods to implement push and pop. There are numerous ways to implement a stack, such as using a resizable array or a linked list, but as long as the implementation meets the ADT specification, the implementation details can be ignored by the user of a stack.

In generic programming, we take the notion of an ADT a step further. Instead of writing down the specification for a single type, we describe a family of types that all have a common interface and semantic behavior. The set of requirements that describes the interface and semantic behavior is referred to as a *concept*. Algorithms constructed in the generic style are then applicable to *any* type that satisfies the requirements of the algorithm. This ability to use many different types with the same variable (or parameter of a function) is referred to as *polymorphism*.

2.1.1   Polymorphism in Object-Oriented Programming

In object-oriented programming (OOP), polymorphism is realized with virtual functions and inheritance, which is called *subtype polymorphism*. The interface requirements of a concept can be written as virtual functions in an abstract base class. The preconditions and invariants become assertions when possible. Concrete classes inherit from the abstract base class and provide the implementation of these functions. The concrete classes are said to be *subtypes* (or derived classes) of the base class. Generic functions are written in terms of the abstract base class and the function calls are dispatched at run-time based on the concrete type of the object (via virtual function tables in C++). Any *subtype* of the abstract base class can be interchanged and used in the generic function.

A classic example of a concept from mathematics is an *Additive Abelian Group*, which is a set of elements with an addition operator that obeys the associative law, has an inverse, and has an identity element (zero) [45]. We can represent this concept in C++ by defining an abstract base class as follows:

```
// The AdditiveAbelianGroup concept as an abstract base class:
class AdditiveAbelianGroup {
public:
  virtual void add (AdditiveAbelianGroup* y) = 0;
  virtual AdditiveAbelianGroup* inverse () = 0;
  virtual AdditiveAbelianGroup* zero () = 0;
};
```

Using this abstract base class we can write a reusable function such as *sum()*.

```
AdditiveAbelianGroup* sum (array<AdditiveAbelianGroup*> v)
{
  AdditiveAbelianGroup* total = v[0]->zero();
  for (int i = 0; i < v.size(); ++i)
    total->add(v[i]);
  return total;
}
```

The *sum()* function will work on any array as long as the element type derives from *Additive-AbelianGroup*. Examples of such types would be real numbers and vectors.

```
class Real : public AdditiveAbelianGroup {
  // ...
};
class Vector : public AdditiveAbelianGroup {
  // ...
};
```

2.1.2 Polymorphism in Generic Programming

In generic programming, polymorphism is realized through class or function templates. Templates provide *parametric polymorphism*. Below is ***sum()*** written as a function template. The ***AdditiveAbelianGroup*** base class is no longer needed, although by convention (and for documentation purposes) we use the name ***AdditiveAbelianGroup*** for the template parameter.

```
template <typename AdditiveAbelianGroup>
AdditiveAbelianGroup sum (array<AdditiveAbelianGroup> v)
{
  AdditiveAbelianGroup total = v[0].zero();
  for (int i = 0; i < v.size(); ++i)
    total.add(v[i]);
  return total;
}
```

In C++ a *concept* is a set of requirements that a template argument must meet so that the class template or function template can compile and execute properly.

Even though concepts exist only implicitly in generic programming, they are vitally important and must be carefully documented. Currently, such documentation is typically accomplished in the comments of the code or in books such as *Generic Programming and the STL* [3]. Consider again the example of an AdditiveAbelianGroup, but this time as a concept.

```
// concept AdditiveAbelianGroup
//      valid expressions:
//          x.add(y)
//          y = x.inverse()
//          y = x.zero()
//      semantics:
//          ...
```

Concrete types that satisfy the requirements of AdditiveAbelianGroup do not need to inherit from a base class. The types of the template argument are substituted into the function template during instantiation (at compile time). The term *model* is used to describe the relationship between concrete types and the concepts they satisfy. For example, ***Real*** and ***Vector*** model the AdditiveAbelianGroup concept.

```
struct Real { // no inheritance
  // ...
};
struct Vector { // no inheritance
  // ...
};
```

2.1.3   Comparison of GP and OOP

So far, we have loosely described generic programming as "programming with templates" and object-oriented programming as "programming with inheritance." This is somewhat misleading because the core semantics of these two methodologies are only indirectly related to templates and inheritance. More formally, generic programming is based on *parametric polymorphism*, whereas object-oriented programming is based on *subtype polymorphism*. In C++ these ideas are implemented with templates and inheritance, but other languages provide different mechanisms. For example, the signatures extension in GNU C++ [4] provides an alternate form of subtype polymorphism. Multimethods (in languages such as CLOS [21]) provide semantics closer to that of parametric polymorphism but with run-time dispatching (compared to the compile-time dispatching of templates).

Nevertheless, since Standard C++ is our language choice, it is useful to compare GP and OOP by comparing inheritance (and virtual functions) with templates in the context of C++.

Virtual Functions Are Slower than Function Templates

A virtual function call is slower than a call to a function template (which is the same speed as a call to a normal function). A virtual function call includes an extra pointer dereference to find the appropriate method in the virtual function table. By itself, this overhead may not be significant. Significant slowdowns can result indirectly in compiled code, however, because the indirection may prevent an optimizing compiler from inlining the function and from applying subsequent optimizations to the surrounding code after inlining.

Of course the overall impact of the overhead is entirely dependent on the amount of work done in the function—that is, how much the overhead will be amortized. For components at the level of the STL iterators and containers, or at the level of graph iterators, function call overhead is significant. Efficiency at this level is affected greatly by whether functions like *operator++()* are inlined. For this reason, templates are the only choice for implementing efficient, low-level, reusable components such as those you find in the STL or the BGL.

Run-time Dispatch versus Compile-time Dispatch

The run-time dispatch of virtual functions and inheritance is certainly one of the best features of object-oriented programming. For certain kinds of components, run-time dispatching is an absolute requirement; decisions need to be made based on information that is only available at run time. When this is the case, virtual functions and inheritance are needed.

Templates do not offer run-time dispatching, but they do offer significant flexibility at compile time. In fact, if the dispatching can be performed at compile time, templates offer more flexibility than inheritance because they do not require the template arguments types to inherit from some base class (more about this later).

Code Size: Virtual Functions Are Small, Templates Are Big

A common concern in template-based programs is *code bloat*, which typically results from naive use of templates. Carefully designed template components need not result in significantly larger code size than their inheritance-based counterparts. The main technique in controlling the code size is to separate out the functionality that depends on the template types and the functionality that is independent of the template types. An example of how to do this can be seen in the SGI STL implementation of *std::list*.

The Binary Method Problem

There is a serious problem that shows up when using subtyping (inheritance and virtual functions) to express operations that work on two or more objects. This problem is known as the binary method problem [8]. The classic example for this problem, which we illustrate next, is a point class interface (a coordinate in a plane) that has an *equal()* member function. This problem is particularly important for the BGL, since most of the types it defines (vertex and edge desriptors and iterators) require an *operator==()* much like a point class *equal()* function.

The following abstract base class describes the interface for a point class.

```
class Point {
public:
  virtual bool equal(const Point* p) const = 0;
};
```

Using this interface, a library writer could write a "generic" function that takes any class derived from *Point* and print out whether the two objects are equal.

```
void print_equal(const Point* a, const Point* b) {
  std::cout << std::boolalpha << a->equal(b) << std::endl;
}
```

Now consider an implementation of a particular point class, say the *ColorPoint* class. Suppose that in our application the only point class we will be using is the *ColorPoint* class. It is only necessary to define equality between two color point objects, and not between a color point and any other kind of point.

```
class ColorPoint : public Point {
public:
  ColorPoint(float x, float y, std::string c) : x(x), y(y), color(c) { }
  virtual bool equal(const ColorPoint* p) const
    { return color == p->color && x == p->x && y == p->y; }
protected:
  float x, y;
  std::string color;
};
```

However, when we try to use this class, we find out that the *ColorPoint::equal* ( ) function did not override the *Point::equal* ( ) function. When trying to instantiate a *ColorPoint* object we get the following error.

> error: object of abstract class type *"ColorPoint"* is not allowed:
> pure virtual function *"Point::equal"* has no overrider

It turns out that by the contravariance subtyping rule, the parameter type in the derived classes member function must be either the same type or a base class of the type as the parameter in the base class. In the case of the *ColorPoint* class, the parameter to *equal* ( ) must be *Point*, not *ColorPoint*. However, making this change causes another problem. Inside the *equal* ( ) function, the *Point* argument must be downcast to be able to check to determine if the data members are equal. The insertion of this downcast means that it is no longer known at compile time whether a program using the *ColorPoint* class is type safe. An object of a different point class could be passed to the *equal* ( ) function in error, causing an exception at run time. The following *ColorPoint2* class changes the parameter of the *equal* ( ) to *Point* and inserts the downcast.

```
class ColorPoint2 : public Point {
public:
  ColorPoint2 (float x, float y, std::string s) : x(x), y(y), color(s) { }
  virtual bool equal(const Point* p) const {
    const ColorPoint2* cp = dynamic_cast<const ColorPoint2*>(p);
    return color == cp−>color && x == cp−>x && y == cp−>y;
  }
protected:
  float x, y;
  std::string color;
};
```

Now suppose that we were using function templates instead of virtual functions to express polymorphism. Then the *print_equal* ( ) function could be written like this:

```
template <typename PointType>
void print_equal2 (const PointType* a, const PointType* b) {
  std::cout << std::boolalpha << a−>equal(b) << std::endl;
}
```

To use this function, the color point class does not need to inherit from *Point*, and the subtyping issues are irrelevant. When the *print_equal2* ( ) function is called with two objects of type *ColorPoint*, the *PointType* parameter is substituted for *ColorPoint* and the call to *equal* simply resolves to *ColorPoint::equal* ( ). Full compile-time type safety is therefore retained.

```
ColorPoint* a = new ColorPoint (0.0, 0.0, "blue");
ColorPoint* b = new ColorPoint (0.0, 0.0, "green");
print_equal2 (a, b);
```

Since the BGL is implemented in terms of function templates, we did not have to be concerned with the binary method problem. If instead the BGL had been implemented with virtual functions, the binary method problem would have been a constant source of trouble.

2.2 Generic Programming and the STL

The problem domain underlying the STL is that of basic algorithms for computer science (e.g., array and list structures, searching and sorting algorithms—the kind of things you dealt with in your data structure and algorithms classes). Now, there have been any number of "foundational" library collections that have attempted to provide some kind of comprehensive set of data structures and algorithms. What diffrerentiates the STL from the rest of these efforts is generic programming (process and practice).

As described by Musser and Stepanov [35], the GP process as it is applied to a particular problem domain consists of the following basic steps:

1. Identify useful and efficient algorithms

2. Find their generic representation (i.e., parameterize each algorithm such that it makes the fewest possible requirements of the data on which it operates)

3. Derive a set of (minimal) requirements that allow these algorithms to run and to run efficiently

4. Construct a framework based on classifications of requirements

This process is reflected in the structure and organization of the STL components.

In terms of programming *practice*, the minimization process and framework design imply a structure where algorithms are expressed independently of any particular data types on which they might operate. Rather, algorithms are written to generic specifications that are deduced from the algorithms' needs.

For instance, algorithms typically need the abstract functionality of being able to *traverse* through a data structure and to *access* its elements. If data structures provide a standard interface for traversal and access, generic algorithms can be freely mixed and matched with data structures (called *containers* in the terminology of the STL).

The main facilitator in the separation of algorithms and containers in the STL is the *iterator* (sometimes called a *generalized pointer*). Iterators provide a mechanism for traversing containers and accessing their elements. The interface between an algorithm and a container is in terms of iterator requirements that must be met by the type of iterators exported by the container. Generic algorithms are most flexible when they are written in terms of iterators and do not rely on a particular container.

Iterators are classified into broad categories, some of which are InputIterator, ForwardIterator, and RandomAccessIterator. Figure 2.1 depicts the relationship among containers, algorithms, and iterators.

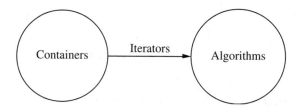

Figure 2.1 Separation of containers and algorithms using iterators.

The STL defines a set of requirements for each class of iterators. The requirements are in the form of which operations (valid expressions) are defined for each iterator, and what the meaning of the operation is. As an example of how these requirements are defined, a sample from the requirements for the STL random-access iterator (which includes those of the forward iterator) is listed in Table 2.1. In the table, type X is the iterator type, T is the pointed-to type, and U is the type of a member of T. The objects a, b, and r are iterators, m is a member of T, and n is an integer.

expression	return type	note
$a == b$	*bool*	$*a == *b$
$a \mathrel{!=} b$	*bool*	$!(a == b)$
$a < b$	*bool*	$b - a > 0$
$*a$	*T&*	dereference a
$a\mathrm{-}{>}m$	*U&*	$(*a).m$
$++r$	*X&*	$r == s \rightarrow ++r == ++s$
$--r$	*X&*	$r == s \rightarrow --r == --s$
$r += n$	*X&*	same as n of $++r$
$a + n$	*X*	$\{\ tmp = a;\ return\ tmp += n;\ \}$
$b - a$	Distance	$(a < b)\ ?\ distance(a, b)$ $\qquad\qquad : - distance(b, a)$
$a[n]$	convertible to *T*	$*(a + n)$

Table 2.1 A sample of the STL random-access iterator requirements.

Accumulate Example

For a concrete example of generic programming we look at the algorithm *accumulate ( )*, which successively applies a binary operator to an initial value and each element in a container. A typical use of *accumulate ( )* is to sum the elements of a container using the addition operator. The following code shows how one could implement the ***accumulate()*** algorithm in C++. The *first* and *last* arguments are iterators that mark the beginning and passed-the-end of the sequence. All of the arguments to the function are parameterized on type so that the algorithm can be used with any container that models the InputIterator concept. Iterator traversal uses the same notation as pointers; specifically, *operator++()* increments to the next position. Several other ways to move iterators (especially random access iterators) are listed in Table 2.1. To access the container element under the iterator, one uses the dereference operator, *operator*()*, or the subscript operator, *operator[]()*, to access at an offset from the iterator.

```
template <typename InputIterator, typename T, typename BinaryOperator>
T accumulate(InputIterator first, InputIterator last, T init, BinaryOperator binary_op)
{
  for (; first != last; ++first)
    init = binary_op(init, *first);
  return init;
}
```

To demonstrate the flexibility that the iterator interface provides, we use the ***accumulate()*** function template with a vector and with a linked list (both from the STL).

```
// using accumulate with a vector
std::vector<double> x(10, 1.0);
double sum1;
sum1 = std::accumulate(x.begin(), x.end(), 0.0, std::plus<double>());

// using accumulate with a linked list
std::list<double> y;
double sum2;
// copy vector's values into the list
std::copy(x.begin(), x.end(), std::back_inserter(y));
sum2 = std::accumulate(y.begin(), y.end(), 0.0, std::plus<double>());
assert(sum1 == sum2); // they should be equal
```

2.3 Concepts and Models

The previous section showed an example of the RandomAccessIterator requirements. It also showed how InputIterator was used as a requirement for the ***accumulate()*** function and how both *std::list::iterator* and *std::vector::iterator* could be used with this function. In this section, we define the terms for describing relationships among sets of requirements, functions, and types.

In the context of generic programming, the term *concept* is used to describe the collection of requirements that a template argument must meet for the function or class template to compile and operate properly. In the text, the sans-serif font is used to distinguish concept names.

Examples of concept definitions can be found in the C++ Standard, many of which deal with the requirements for iterators. In addition, Matthew Austern's book *Generic Programming and the STL* [3] and the SGI STL Web site provide comprehensive documentation on the concepts used in the STL. These concepts are used heavily in the definition of the BGL concepts. The SGI STL Web site is at the following URL:

http://www.sgi.com/tech/stl/

2.3.1   Sets of Requirements

The requirements for a concept consist of a set of valid expressions, associated types, invariants, and complexity guarantees. A type *models* a concept if it meets the set of requirements. A concept can also extend the requirements of another concept, which is called *refinement*.

Valid Expressions are C++ expressions that must compile successfully for the types involved in the expression to be considered models of the concept.

Associated Types are auxiliary types that have some relation to the type *T* modeling the concept. The requirements in a concept typically make statements about associated types. For example, iterator requirements typically include an associated type called the *value_type* and the requirement that objects returned by the iterator's dereference operator must be of the *value_type*. In C++ it is common to use a traits class to map from the type *T* to the associated types of the concept.

Invariants are run-time characteristics of types that must always be true. The invariants often take the form of preconditions and postconditions. When a precondition is not fulfilled, the behavior of the operation is, in general, undefined and can lead to a segmentation fault. This is the case for the Boost Graph Library. Some libraries provide debugging versions that use assertions or throw exceptions when a precondition is violated. A future version of the Boost Graph Library may do this.

Complexity Guarantees are maximum limits on how long the execution of one of the valid expressions will take, or how much of the various resources its computation will use.

2.3.2   Example: InputIterator

In this section, we take a closer look at InputIterator as an example of a concept. First, the InputIterator concept is a refinement of TrivialIterator which, in turn, is a refinement of Assignable and EqualityComparable. Thus, the InputIterator meets all the requirements of a TrivialIterator (which meets all of the requirements of Assignable and EqualityComparable).

The result is that a type that models InputIterator will have a dereference operator, it can be copied and assigned, and it can be compared with other iterator objects using == and *!=*.

The InputIterator concept adds the requirement for pre-increment and post-increment operators. These requirements are denoted by the following *valid expressions*. Objects *i* and *j* are instances of a type *T* that models InputIterator.

i = j   *// assignment (from Assignable)*
T i(j); *// copy (from Assignable)*
i == j *// equality test (from EqualityComparable)*
i != j   *// inequality test (from EqualityComparable)*
*i   *// dereference (from TrivialIterator)*
++i   *// pre-increment operator*
i++   *// post-increment operator*

The *std::iterator_traits* class provides access to the *associated types* of an iterator type. The type of an object that is pointed to by an iterator type (call it *X*) can be determined via the *value_type* of the traits class. The other associated types are *reference*, *pointer*, *difference_type*, and *iterator_category*. Associated types and traits classes are discussed in more detail in §2.4. In the following function template we show the use of the *iterator_traits* class to obtain the *value_type* of the iterator and dereference the iterator.

```
template <typename Iterator> void dereference_example (Iterator i)
{
  typename iterator_traits<Iterator>::value_type t;
  t = *i;
}
```

As for complexity guarantees, all of the InputIterator operations are required to be constant time. Some types that *model* InputIterator are *std::list<int>::iterator*, *double**, and *std::istream_iterator<char>*.

The purpose of defining concepts becomes clear when considering the implementation of generic algorithms. The implementation of the *std::for_each()* function follows. Inside the function precisely four operations are applied to the iterator objects *first* or *last*: comparison using *operator!=()*, increment with *operator++()*, dereference with *operator*()*, and copy construction. For this function to compile and operate properly the iterator arguments must support at least these four operations. The concept InputIterator includes these operations (and not many more), so it is a reasonable choice for succinctly describing the requirements of *for_each()*.

```
template <typename InputIterator, typename Function>
Function for_each (InputIterator first, InputIterator last, Function f)
{
  for ( ; first != last; ++first)
    f (*first);
  return f;
}
```

2.4   Associated Types and Traits Classes

One of the most important techniques used in generic programming is the traits class, which was introduced by Nathan Myers [36]. The traits class technique may seem somewhat un-natural when first encountered (due to the syntax) but the essence of the idea is simple. It is essential to learn how to use traits classes, for they are used regularly in generic libraries such as the STL and the BGL.

2.4.1   Associated Types Needed in Function Template

A traits class is basically a way of determining information about a type that you would otherwise know nothing about. For example, consider a generic *sum*() function:

```
template <typename Array>
X sum(const Array& v, int n)
{
  X total = 0;
  for (int i = 0; i < n; ++i)
    total += v[i];
  return total;
}
```

From the point of view of this function template, not much is known about the template type *Array*. For instance, the type of the elements that are inside the array is not given. However, this information is necessary in order to declare the local variable *total*, which should be the same type as the elements of *Array*. The *X* that is there now is just a placeholder that needs to be replaced by something else to produce a correct *sum*() function.

2.4.2   Typedefs Nested in Classes

One way to access information out of a type is to use the scope operator *::* to access *typedef*s that are nested inside the class. For example, an array class might look like the following:

```
class my_array {
public:
  // the type for elements in the array
  typedef double value_type;
  double& operator[](int i) {
    return m_data[i];
  };
private:
  double* m_data;
};
```

The type of the elements in the array can be accessed via *my_array::value_type*. The generic *sum()* function can be realized using this technique as follows (note that the *X* placeholders have been replaced with *typename Array::value_type*[1]):

```
template <typename Array>
typename Array::value_type sum(const Array& v, int n)
{
  typename Array::value_type total = 0;
  for (int i = 0; i < n; ++i)
    total += v[i];
  return total;
}
```

In the *sum()* function above, the technique of using a nested typedef works as long as *Array* is a class type that has such a nested typedef. However, there are important cases for which having a nested typedef is neither practical nor possible. For instance, one might want to use the generic *sum()* function with a class from a third party that did not provide the required typedef. Or, one might want to use the *sum()* function with a built-in type such as *double**.

```
int n = 100;
double* x = new double[n];
sum(x, n);
```

In both of these cases, it is quite likely that the functional requirements of our desired use are met; that is, the *operator[]()* works with *double** and with our imaginary third-party array. The limitation to reuse is in how to communicate the type information from the classes we want to use to the *sum()* function.

2.4.3 Definition of a Traits Class

The solution to this is a *traits class*, which is a class template whose sole purpose is to provide a mapping from a type to other types, functions, or constants. The language mechanism that allows a class template to create a mapping is *template specialization*. The mapping is accomplished by creating different versions of the traits class for specific type parameters. We show how this works by creating an *array_traits* class that can be used in the *sum()* function.

The *array_traits* class is templated on the *Array* type and allows us to determine the *value_type* (the type of the element) of the array. The default (fully templated) case assumes that the array is a class with a nested typedef such as *my_array*:

```
template <typename Array>
struct array_traits {
  typedef typename Array::value_type value_type;
};
```

---

[1]When the type on the left hand side of the *::* scope operator somehow depends on a template argument then use the *typename* keyword in front of the type.

We can then create a specialization of the *array_traits* template to handle when the *Array* template argument is a built-in type like *double**:

```
template  <>  struct  array_traits<double*>  {
  typedef  double  value_type;
};
```

Third-party classes, say *johns_int_array*, can be similarly accommodated:

```
template  <>  struct  array_traits<johns_int_array>  {
  typedef  int  value_type;
};
```

The *sum()* function, written with *array_traits* class, is shown below. To access the type for the *total* variable we extract the *value_type* from *array_traits*.

```
template  <typename  Array>
typename  array_traits<Array>::value_type  sum(const  Array&  v,  int  n)
{
  typename  array_traits<Array>::value_type  total = 0;
  for  (int  i = 0;  i < n;  ++i)
    total += v[i];
  return  total;
}
```

2.4.4   Partial Specialization

Writing a traits class for every pointer type is not practical or desirable. The following shows how to use partial specialization to provide array traits for all pointer types. The C++ compiler will attempt a pattern match between the template argument provided at the instantiation of the traits class and all the specializations defined, picking the specialization that is the best match. The partial specialization for *T** will match whenever the type is a pointer. The previous complete specializations for *double** would still match first for that particular pointer type.

```
template  <typename  T>
struct  array_traits<T*>  {
  typedef  T  value_type;
};
```

Partial specialization can also be used to create a version of *array_traits* for a third-party class template.

```
template  <typename  T>
struct  array_traits< johns_array<T> >  {
  typedef  T  value_type;
};
```

The most well-known use of a traits class is the *iterator_traits* class used in the STL. The BGL also uses traits classes such as *graph_traits* and the *property_traits* classes. Typically, a traits class is used with a particular concept or family of concepts. The *iterator_traits* class is used with the family of iterator concepts. The *graph_traits* class is used with the family of BGL graph concepts.

2.4.5 Tag Dispatching

A technique that often goes hand in hand with traits classes is *tag dispatching*, which is a way of using function overloading to dispatch based on properties of a type. A good example of this is the implementation of the *std::advance()* function in the STL, which, in the default case, increments an iterator *n* times. Depending on the kind of iterator, there are different optimizations that can be applied in the implementation. If the iterator is random access, then the *advance()* function can simply be implemented with *i += n* and is very efficient; that is, it is in constant time. If the iterator is bidirectional, then it may be the case that *n* is negative, so we can decrement the iterator *n* times. The relation between external polymorphism and traits classes is that the property to be exploited for dispatch (in this case, the *iterator_category*) is accessed through a traits class.

In the following example, the *advance()* function uses the *iterator_traits* class to determine the *iterator_category*. It then makes a call to the overloaded *advance_dispatch()* function. The appropriate *advance_dispatch()* is selected by the compiler based on whatever type the *iterator_category* resolves to (one of the tag classes in the following code). A *tag* is simply a class whose only purpose is to convey some property for use in tag dispatching. By convention, the name of a tag class ends in *_tag*. We do not define a function overload for the *forward_iterator-_tag* because that case is handled by the function overloaded for *input_iterator_tag*.

```
struct input_iterator_tag {};
struct output_iterator_tag {};
struct forward_iterator_tag : public input_iterator_tag {};
struct bidirectional_iterator_tag : public forward_iterator_tag {};
struct random_access_iterator_tag : public bidirectional_iterator_tag {};

template <typename InputIterator, typename Distance>
void advance_dispatch(InputIterator& i, Distance n, input_iterator_tag)
  { while (n--) ++i; }

template <typename BidirectionalIterator, typename Distance>
void advance_dispatch(BidirectionalIterator& i, Distance n, bidirectional_iterator_tag)
{
  if (n >= 0)
    while (n--) ++i;
  else
    while (n++) --i;
}
```

```
template <typename RandomAccessIterator, typename Distance>
void advance_dispatch (RandomAccessIterator& i, Distance n, random_access_iterator_tag)
{
  i += n;
}
template <typename InputIterator, typename Distance>
void advance (InputIterator& i, Distance n)
{
  typedef typename iterator_traits<InputIterator>::iterator_category Cat;
  advance_dispatch (i, n, Cat());
}
```

The BGL *graph_traits* class includes three categories: *directed_category*, *edge_parallel-
_category*, and *traversal_category*. The tags for these categories can be used for dispatching
similarly to *iterator_category*.

2.5   Concept Checking

An important aspect of using a generic library is using appropriate classes as template arguments to algorithms (using classes that model the concepts specified by the requirements of
the algorithm). If an improper class is used, the compiler will emit error messages, but deci-
phering these messages can present a significant hurdle to the user of a template library [2, 41].
The compiler may produce literally pages of difficult-to-decipher error messages for even a
small error.

The following is an example of a typical mistake, where the *std::sort ( )* function is applied
to an array of objects. In this case, *operator< ( )* is not implemented for the object type *foo*,
which means that *foo* violates the requirements for LessThanComparable (as given in the
documentation for *std::sort ( )*).

```
#include <algorithm>
class foo { };
int main (int, char* [ ])
{
  foo array_of_foo [10];
  std::sort (array_of_foo, array_of_foo + 10);
  return 0;
}
```

The resulting error message is difficult to understand and all but the most experienced
of C++ programmers would be hard pressed to deduce the actual programming error from
the error message. The error message does not mention the concept that was violated
(LessThanComparable) and it exposes many of the internal functions used in *std::sort ( )*.
In addition, the error message fails to indicate the line at which the error occurs—in this case,
the call to *std::sort ( )*. The error looks like this:

stl_heap.h: In function void __adjust_heap<foo*,int,foo>(foo*,int,int,foo):
stl_heap.h:214:   *instantiated from __make_heap<foo*,foo,ptrdiff_t>(foo*,*
    foo*,foo*,ptrdiff_t*)
stl_heap.h:225:   *instantiated from make_heap<foo*>(foo*,foo*)*
stl_algo.h:1562:   *instantiated from __partial_sort<foo*,foo>(foo*,foo*,*
    foo*,foo*)
stl_algo.h:1574:   *instantiated from partial_sort<foo*>(foo*,foo*,foo*)*
stl_algo.h:1279:   *instantiated from __introsort_loop<foo*,foo,int>(foo*,*
    foo*,foo*,int)
stl_algo.h:1320:   *instantiated from here*
stl_heap.h:115: no match for foo & < foo &

2.5.1 Concept-Checking Classes

To overcome this problem we have developed a C++ idiom for up-front enforcement of concept compliance, which we call *concept checking* [39]. The supporting code for this idiom is available as the Boost Concept Checking Library (BCCL) [6]. For each concept, the BCCL provides a concept-checking class, such as the following concept-checking class for LessThanComparable. The required valid expressions for the concept are exercised in the *constraints*() member function.

```
template <typename T>
struct LessThanComparableConcept {
  void constraints() {
    (bool)(a < b);
  }
  T a, b;
};
```

The concept-checking class is instantiated with the user's template arguments at the beginning of the generic algorithm using the BCCL *function_requires*().

```
#include <boost/concept_check.hpp>
template <typename Iterator>
void safe_sort(Iterator first, Iterator last)
{
  typedef typename std::iterator_traits<Iterator>::value_type T;
  function_requires< LessThanComparableConcept<T> >();
  // other requirements ...
  std::sort(first, last);
}
```

Now when *safe_sort*() is misused the error message (listed on the next page) is much more comprehensible: the message is shorter, the point of error is indicated, the violated concept is listed, and the internal functions of the algorithm are not exposed.

> *boost/concept_check.hpp: In method*
>   *void boost::LessThanComparableConcept<foo>::constraints ( ):*
> *boost/concept_check.hpp:31:   instantiated from*
>   *boost::function_requires<boost::LessThanComparableConcept<foo> > ( )*
> *sort_eg.cpp:11:   instantiated from safe_sort<foo*> (foo*, foo*)*
> *sort_eg.cpp:21:   instantiated from here*
>   *boost/concept_check.hpp:260: no match for foo & < foo &*

The Boost Graph Library uses concept checks to provide better error messages to users. For each graph concept there is a corresponding concept-checking class defined in the ***boost/graph/graph_concepts.hpp*** header file. At the beginning of each BGL algorithm there are concept checks for each of the parameters. Error messages originating from ***graph_concepts.hpp*** are a likely indication that one of the argument types given to an algorithm does not meet the algorithm's requirements for a concept.

2.5.2   Concept Archetypes

The complementary problem to concept checking is verifying whether the documented requirements for a generic algorithm actually cover the algorithm's implementation, a problem we refer to as *concept covering*. Typically, library implementors check for covering by manual inspection, which of course is error prone. We have also developed a C++ idiom that exploits the C++ compiler's type checker [39] to automate this task. The code for concept covering is also available as part of the Boost Concept Checking Library.

The BCCL provides an *archetype class* for each concept used in the Standard Library. An archetype class provides a minimal implementation of a concept. To check whether a concept covers an algorithm, the archetype class for the concept is instantiated and passed to the algorithm.

The following example program attempts to verify that the requirements of *std::sort ( )* are covered by an iterator that models RandomAccessIterator having a value type modeling LessThanComparable.

```
#include <algorithm>
#include <boost/concept_archetype.hpp>
int main ( )
{
  using namespace boost;
  typedef less_than_comparable_archetype<> T;
  random_access_iterator_archetype<T> ri;
  std::sort (ri, ri);
}
```

In fact, this program will not successfully compile because those concepts do not cover the requirements that *std::sort ( )* makes of its template parameters. The resulting error message indicates that the algorithm also requires that the value type be CopyConstructible.

null_archetype (const null_archetype<int> &) is private

Not only is the copy constructor needed, but the assignment operator is needed as well. These requirements are summarized in the Assignable concept. The following code shows the implementation of the archetype class for Assignable. The **Base** template parameter is provided so that archetypes can be combined. For checking *std::sort()*, we would need to combine the archetype classes for Assignable and LessThanComparable.

```
template <typename Base = null_archetype<> >
class assignable_archetype : public Base {
   typedef assignable_archetype self;
public:
   assignable_archetype (const self&) { }
   self& operator= (const self&) { return *this; }
};
```

The Boost Graph Library includes an archetype class for every graph concept in the header file *boost/graph/graph_archetypes.hpp*. Test programs to verify the specification of each BGL algorithm using the graph archetypes are located in the *libs/graph/test/* directory.

2.6 The Boost Namespace

Like all other Boost libraries, every component of the BGL is defined in the *boost* namespace to avoid name clashes with other libraries or application programs. In this section we describe how to access BGL classes and functions in the *boost* namespace.

2.6.1 Classes

There are several ways to access BGL classes. The following code shows three ways to access the *adjacency_list* class that is in the *boost* namespace.

```
{ // Apply namespace prefix to access BGL classes
   boost::adjacency_list<> g;
}
{ // Bring BGL class into current scope with using statement
   using boost::adjacency_list;
   adjacency_list<> g;
}
{ // Bring all Boost components into current scope
   using namespace boost;
   adjacency_list<> g;
}
```

For brevity and clarity of presentation, the example code in this book omits the *boost::* prefix (the code is presented as if *using namespace boost;* already appears in an enclosing scope). For code using Boost libraries, we recommend using the explicit **boost::** prefix in header files, and either the namespace prefix or specific *using* statements in source files. We caution against the blanket **using namespace boost;** statement because this eliminates the protection against name clashes that is introduced by the **boost** namespace. It is useful, however, to write using statements in function scope because the danger of introducing name clashes in such a limited scope is much reduced.

2.6.2   Koenig Lookup

Graph Operations

The BGL interface consists of overloaded functions defined for each graph type. For example, the **num_vertices()** function has a single argument, the graph object, and returns the number of vertices. This function is overloaded for each BGL graph class. Interestingly (and fortunately, as we will see), overloaded functions may be called without qualifying the function name with the namespace. Using a process called *Koenig lookup* the C++ compiler examines the argument type and looks for overloaded functions *in the namespace of the argument type.*[2]

The following example illustrates Koenig lookup. Consider the case of someone using graph classes that are supplied by two different graph libraries. Each library has its own namespace, inside of which is defined a graph class and a **num_vertices()** function.

```
namespace lib_jack {
  class graph { /* ... */ };
  int num_vertices(const graph&) { /* ... */ }
}
namespace lib_jill {
  class graph { /* ... */ };
  int num_vertices(const graph&) { /* ... */ }
}
```

Suppose the user wants to apply some generic graph algorithm, say **boost::pail()**, to both of these graph types.

```
int main()
{
  lib_jack::graph g1;
  boost::pail(g1);
  lib_jill::graph g2;
  boost::pail(g2);
}
```

---

[2]Koenig lookup is named after its inventor, Andrew Koenig. It is sometimes called "argument dependent lookup."

Inside of the *boost::pail*() there is a call to *num_vertices*(). The desired behavior in this situation is that if a graph from *lib_jack* is used, then *lib_jack::num_vertices*() gets called, but if the graph from *lib_jill*() is used, then *lib_jill::num_vertices*() gets called. *Koenig lookup* is the C++ language feature that provides this behavior. Provided the function call is not qualified with a namespace, the C++ compiler will search the namespace of the arguments to find the correct function to call.

```
namespace boost {
  template <typename Graph>
  void pail (Graph& g)
  {
    typename graph_traits<Graph>::vertices_size_type
      N = num_vertices (g); // Koenig lookup will resolve
    // ...
  }
} // namespace boost
```

Graph Algorithms

The BGL graph algorithms differ from the graph operations in that they are function templates, not overloaded functions. Therefore, Koenig lookup does *not* apply to BGL graph algorithms. As a result, BGL graph algorithms must be accessed using the *boost::* namespace prefix, or by using one of the other methods described in §2.6.1. For example, to call the *breadth_first_search*() algorithm, the *boost::* prefix is required, as shown:

```
boost::breadth_first_search (g, start, visitor (vis));
```

2.7 Named Function Parameters

Many BGL algorithms have long parameter lists to provide the maximum amount of flexibility. However, in many situations this flexibility is not needed, and one would like to use defaults for many of the parameters. For example, consider the following function template having three parameters.

```
template <typename X, typename Y, typename Z>
void f (X x, Y y, Z z);
```

The user should be able to pass in zero or more arguments and the unspecified parameters would use the defaults. The user might want to pass an argument for parameter y but not x or z. Some languages provide direct support for this with a feature called *named parameters* (also sometimes called *keyword parameters*). Using named parameters, a label is used with each argument to indicate to which parameter it is bound, replacing the normal convention

of binding arguments to parameters according to their order in the parameter list. If C++
supported named parameters, then one could call function $f()$ in the following way.

```
int a;
int b;
f(z=b, x=a); // bind b to parameter z, a to parameter x,
             // and y gets its default argument
```

Of course, C++ does not support named parameters, but this feature can be approximated
using a little trickery. The BGL includes a class named *bgl_named_params* that mimics named
parameters by allowing lists of parameters to be built up.[3] The following code shows an example of calling *bellman_ford_shortest_paths()* using the named parameter technique. Each
of the arguments is passed to a function whose name indicates to which parameter the argument should be bound. Note that named parameters are delimited by a *period*, not a comma.
bgl_named_params class is not explicitly referred to; it is created implicitly by the call to
weight_map(), and then the argument list is extended by the calls to *distance_map()* and *pre-
decessor_map()*.

```
bool r = boost::bellman_ford_shortest_paths (g, int(N),
    boost::weight_map (weight) .
    distance_map (&distance[0]) .
    predecessor_map (&parent[0]) );
```

The order in which the arguments are provided is not important as long as each argument
is matched with the correct parameter function. The following is a call to *bellman_ford_-
shortest_paths()* that is equivalent to the one just shown.

```
bool r = boost::bellman_ford_shortest_paths (g, int(N),
    boost::predecessor_map (&parent[0]) .
    distance_map (&distance[0]) .
    weight_map (weight) );
```

---

[3]This is a generalization of idiom described in D&E [41].

Chapter 3

A BGL Tutorial

As discussed in the previous chapter, *concepts* play a central role in generic programming. Concepts are the interface definitions that allow many different components to be used with the same algorithm. The Boost Graph Library defines a large collection of concepts that cover various aspects of working with a graph, such as traversing a graph or modifying its structure. In this chapter, we introduce these concepts and also provide some motivation for the choice of concepts in the BGL.

From the description of the generic programming process (see page 19), concepts are derived from the algorithms that are used to solve problems in particular domains. In this chapter we examine the problem of tracking file dependencies in a build system. For each subproblem, we examine generalizations that can be made to the solutions, with the goal of increasing the reusability (the genericity) of the solution. The result, at the end of the chapter, is a generic graph algorithm and its application to the file-dependency problem.

Along the way, we also cover some of the more mundane but necessary topics, such as how to create a graph object and fill in the vertices and edges.

3.1   File Dependencies

A common use of the graph abstraction is to represent dependencies. One common type of dependency that we programmers deal with on a routine basis is that of compilation dependencies between files in programs that we write. Information about these dependencies is used by programs such as *make*, or by IDEs such as Visual C++, to determine which files must be recompiled to generate a new version of a program (or, in general, of some target) after a change has been made to a source file.

Figure 3.1 shows a graph that has a vertex for each source file, object file, and library that is used in the *killerapp* program. An edge in the graph shows that a target depends on another target in some way (such as a dependency due to inclusion of a header file in a source file, or due to an object file being compiled from a source file).

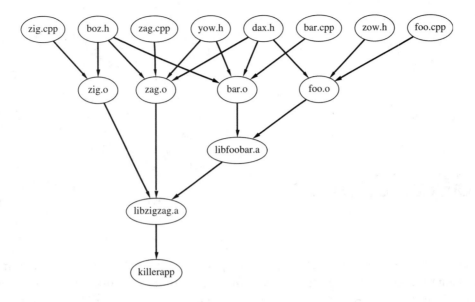

Figure 3.1 A graph representing file dependencies.

Answers to many of the questions that arise in creating a build system such as make can be formulated in terms of the dependency graph. We might ask these questions:

- If all of the targets need to be made, in what order should that be accomplished?

- Are there any cycles in the dependencies? A dependency cycle is an error, and an appropriate message should be emitted.

- How many steps are required to make all of the targets? How many steps are required to make all of the targets if independent targets are made simultaneously in parallel (using a network of workstations or a multiprocessor, for example)?

In the following sections these questions are posed in graph terms, and graph algorithms are developed to provide solutions. The graph in Figure 3.1 is used in all of the examples.

3.2   Graph Setup

Before addressing these questions directly, we must first find a way to represent the file-dependency graph of Figure 3.1 in memory. That is, we need to construct a BGL graph object.

Deciding Which Graph Class To Use

There are several BGL graph classes from which to choose. Since BGL algorithms are generic, they can also be used with any conforming user-defined graph class, but in this chapter we restrict our discussion to BGL graph classes. The principle BGL graph classes are the *adjacency_list* and *adjacency_matrix* classes. The *adjacency_list* class is a good choice for most situations, particularly for representing sparse graphs. The file-dependencies graph has only a few edges per vertex, so it is sparse. The *adjacency_matrix* class is a good choice for representing dense graphs, but a very bad choice for sparse graphs.

The *adjacency_list* class is used exclusively in this chapter. However, most of what is presented here also applies directly to the *adjacency_matrix* class because its interface is almost identical to that of the *adjacency_list* class. Here we use the same variant of *adjacency_list* as was used in §1.4.1.

```
typedef adjacency_list<
    listS,       // Store out-edges of each vertex in a std::list
    vecS,        // Store vertex set in a std::vector
    directedS    // The file dependency graph is directed
    > file_dep_graph;
```

Constructing a Graph Using Edge Iterators

In §1.2.4 we showed how the *add_vertex()* and *add_edge()* functions can be used to create a graph. Those functions add vertices and edges one at a time, but in many cases one would like to add them all at once. To meet this need the *adjacency_list* graph class has a constructor that takes two iterators that define a range of edges. The edge iterators can be any InputIterator that dereference to a *std::pair* of integers (i, j) that represent an edge in the graph. The two integers i and j represent vertices where $0 \le i < |V|$ and $0 \le j < |V|$. The *n* and *m* parameters say how many vertices and edges will be in the graph. These parameters are optional, but providing them improves the speed of graph construction. The graph properties parameter *p* is attached to the graph object. The function prototype for the constructor that uses edge iterators is as follows:

```
template <typename EdgeIterator>
adjacency_list(EdgeIterator first, EdgeIterator last,
    vertices_size_type n = 0, edges_size_type m = 0,
    const GraphProperties& p = GraphProperties())
```

The following code demonstrates the use of the edge iterator constructor to create a graph. The *std::istream_iterator* is used to make an input iterator that reads the edges in from the file. The file contains the number of vertices in the graph, followed by pairs of numbers that specify the edges. The second default-constructed input iterator is a placeholder for the end of the input. The *std::istream_iterator* is passed directly into the constructor for the graph.

```
std::ifstream file_in ( "makefile-dependencies.dat ") ;
typedef graph_traits<file_dep_graph>::vertices_size_type size_type;
size_type n_vertices;
file_in >> n_vertices; // read in number of vertices
std::istream_iterator<std::pair<size_type, size_type> > input_begin (file_in) , input_end;
file_dep_graph g (input_begin, input_end, n_vertices);
```

Since the value type of the *std::istream_iterator* is *std::pair*, an input operator needs to be defined for *std::pair*.

```
namespace std {
  template <typename T>
  std::istream& operator>>(std::istream& in, std::pair<T,T>& p) {
    in >> p.first >> p.second;
    return in;
  }
}
```

3.3   Compilation Order

The first question that we address is that of specifying an order in which to build all of the targets. The primary consideration here is ensuring that before building a given target, all the targets that it depends on are already built. This is, in fact, the same problem as in §1.4.1, scheduling a set of errands.

3.3.1   Topological Sort via DFS

As mentioned in §1.4.2, a topological ordering can be computed using a depth-first search (DFS). To review, a DFS visits all of the vertices in a graph by starting at any vertex and then choosing an edge to follow. At the next vertex another edge is chosen to follow. This process continues until a dead end (a vertex with no out-edges that lead to a vertex not already discovered) is reached. The algorithm then backtracks to the last discovered vertex that is adjacent to a vertex that is not yet discovered. Once all vertices reachable from the starting vertex are explored, one of the remaining unexplored vertices is chosen and the search continues from there. The edges traversed during each of these separate searches form a *depth-first tree*; and all the searches form a *depth-first forest*. A depth-first forest for a given graph is not unique; there are typically several valid DFS forests for a graph because the order in which the adjacent vertices are visited is not specified. Each unique ordering creates a different DFS tree.

Two useful metrics in a DFS are the *discover time* and *finish time* of a vertex. Imagine that there is an integer counter that starts at zero. Every time a vertex is first visited, the value of the counter is recorded as the discover time for that vertex and the value of the counter is incremented. Likewise, once all of the vertices reachable from a given vertex have been visited, then that vertex is finished. The current value of the counter is recorded as the finish time for that vertex and the counter is incremented. The discover time of a parent in a DFS tree is always earlier than the discover time of a child. Similarly, the finish time of a parent is always later than the finish time of a child. Figure 3.2 shows a depth-first search of the file dependency graph, with the tree edges marked with black lines and with the vertices labeled with their discover and finish times (written as discover/finish).

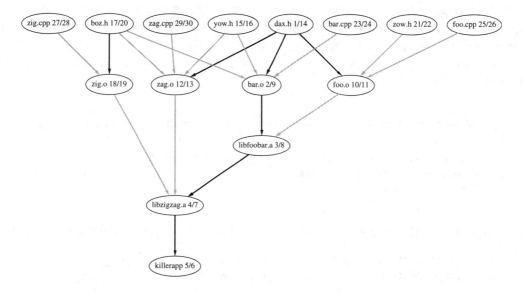

Figure 3.2 A depth-first search of the file dependency graph. Edges in the DFS tree are black and non-tree edges are gray. Each vertex is labeled with its discover and finish time.

The relationship between topological ordering and DFS can be explained by considering three different cases at the point in the DFS when an edge (u, v) is examined. For each case, the finish time of v is always earlier than the finish time of u. Thus, the finish time is simply the topological ordering (in reverse).

1. Vertex v is not yet discovered. This means that v will become a descendant of u and will therefore end up with a finish time earlier than u because DFS finishes all descendants of u before finishing u.

2. Vertex v was discovered in an earlier DFS tree. Therefore, the finish time of v must be earlier than that of u.

3. Vertex v was discovered earlier in the current DFS-tree. If this case occurs, the graph contains a cycle and a topological ordering of the graph is not possible. A *cycle* is a path of edges such that the first vertex and last vertex of the path are the same vertex.

The main part of the depth-first search is a recursive algorithm that calls itself on each adjacent vertex. We will create a function named ***topo_sort_dfs*** ( ) that will implement a depth-first search modified to compute a topological ordering. This first version of the function will be a straightforward, nongeneric function. In the following sections we will make modifications that will finally result in a generic algorithm.

The parameters to ***topo_sort_dfs*** ( ) include the graph, the starting vertex, a pointer to an array to record the topological order, and an array for recording which vertices have been visited. The ***topo_order*** pointer starts at the end of the array and then decrements to obtain the topological ordering from the reverse topological ordering. Note that ***topo_order*** is passed by reference so that the decrement made to it in each recursive call modifies the original object (if ***topo_order*** were instead passed by value, the decrement would happen instead to a copy of the original object).

```
void
topo_sort_dfs (const file_dep_graph& g, vertex_t u, vertex_t*& topo_order, int* mark)
{
  mark[u] = 1; // 1 means visited, 0 means not yet visited
  ⟨For each adjacent vertex, make recursive call 47⟩
  *−−topo_order = u;
}
```

The ***vertex_t*** type and ***edge_t*** types are the vertex and edge descriptors for the ***file_dep_graph***.

```
typedef graph_traits<file_dep_graph>::vertex_descriptor vertex_t;
typedef graph_traits<file_dep_graph>::edge_descriptor edge_t;
```

3.3.2   Marking Vertices Using External Properties

Each vertex should be visited only once during the search. To record whether a vertex has been visited, we can mark it by creating an array that stores the mark for each vertex. In general, we use the term *external property storage* to refer to the technique of storing vertex or edge properties (marks are one such property) in a data structure like an array or hash table that is separate from the graph object (i.e., that is *external* to the graph). Property values are looked up based on some key that can be easily obtained from a vertex or edge descriptor. In this example, we use a version of ***adjacency_list*** where the the vertex descriptors are integers from zero to ***num_vertices(g) - 1***. As a result, the vertex descriptors themselves can be used as indexes into the mark array.

3.3.3   Accessing Adjacent Vertices

In the ***topo_sort_dfs*** ( ) function we need to access all the vertices adjacent to the vertex ***u***. The BGL concept AdjacencyGraph defines the interface for accessing adjacent vertices. The function ***adjacent_vertices*** ( ) takes a vertex and graph object as arguments and returns a pair of iterators whose value type is a vertex descriptor. The first iterator points to the first adjacent vertex, and the second iterator points past the end of the last adjacent vertex. The adjacent vertices are not necessarily ordered in any way. The type of the iterators is the ***adjacency_iterator*** type obtained from the ***graph_traits*** class. The reference section for ***adjacency_list*** (§14.1.1) reveals that the graph type we are using, ***adjacency_list***, models the AdjacencyGraph concept. We may therefore correctly use the function ***adjacent_vertices()*** with our file dependency graph. The code for traversing the adjacent vertices in ***topo_sort_dfs()*** follows.

⟨ For each adjacent vertex, make recursive call 47 ⟩ ≡

```
graph_traits<file_dep_graph>::adjacency_iterator vi, vi_end;
for (tie(vi, vi_end) = adjacent_vertices(u, g); vi != vi_end; ++vi)
  if (mark[*vi] == 0)
    topo_sort_dfs(g, *vi, topo_order, mark);
```

3.3.4 Traversing All the Vertices

One way to ensure that an ordering is obtained for every vertex in the graph (and not just those vertices reachable from a particular starting vertex) is to surround the call to ***topo_sort_dfs()*** with a loop through every vertex in the graph. The interface for traversing all the vertices in a graph is defined in the VertexListGraph concept. The ***vertices()*** function takes a graph object and returns a pair of vertex iterators. The loop through all the vertices and the creation of the mark array is encapsulated in a function called ***topo_sort()***.

```
void topo_sort(const file_dep_graph& g, vertex_t* topo_order)
{
  std::vector<int> mark(num_vertices(g), 0);
  graph_traits<file_dep_graph>::vertex_iterator vi, vi_end;
  for (tie(vi, vi_end) = vertices(g); vi != vi_end; ++vi)
    if (mark[*vi] == 0)
      topo_sort_dfs(g, *vi, topo_order, &mark[0]);
}
```

To make the output from ***topo_sort()*** more user friendly, we need to convert the vertex integers to their associated target names. We have the list of target names stored in a file (in the order that matches the vertex number) so we read in this file and store the names in an array, which we then use when printing the names of the vertices.

```
std::vector<std::string> name(num_vertices(g));
std::ifstream name_in("makefile-target-names.dat");
graph_traits<file_dep_graph>::vertex_iterator vi, vi_end;
for (tie(vi, vi_end) = vertices(g); vi != vi_end; ++vi)
  name_in >> name[*vi];
```

Now we create the order array to store the results and then apply the topological sort function.

```
std::vector<vertex_t> order(num_vertices(g));
topo_sort(g, &order[0] + num_vertices(g));
for (int i = 0; i < num_vertices(g); ++i)
  std::cout << name[order[i]] << std::endl;
```

The output is

```
zag.cpp
zig.cpp
foo.cpp
bar.cpp
zow.h
boz.h
zig.o
yow.h
dax.h
zag.o
foo.o
bar.o
libfoobar.a
libzigzag.a
killerapp
```

3.4   Cyclic Dependencies

One important assumption in the last section is that the file dependency graph does not have any cycles. As stated in §3.3.1, a graph with cycles does not have a topological ordering. A well-formed makefile will have no cycles, but errors do occur, and our build system should be able to catch and report such errors.

Depth-first search can also be used for the problem of detecting cycles. If DFS is applied to a graph that has a cycle, then one of the branches of a DFS tree will loop back on itself. That is, there will be an edge from a vertex to one of its ancestors in the tree. This kind of edge is called a *back edge*. This occurrence can be detected if we change how we mark vertices. Instead of marking each vertex as visited or not visited, we use a three-way coloring scheme: white means undiscovered, gray means discovered but still searching descendants, and black means the vertex and all of its descendants have been discovered. Three-way coloring is useful for several graph algorithms, so the header file *boost/graph/properties.hpp* defines the following enumerated type.

```
enum default_color_type { white_color, gray_color, black_color };
```

A cycle in the graph is identified by an adjacent vertex that is gray, meaning that an edge loops back to an ancestor. The following code is a version of DFS instrumented to detect cycles.

```
bool has_cycle_dfs (const file_dep_graph& g, vertex_t u, default_color_type* color)
{
  color[u] = gray_color;
  graph_traits<file_dep_graph>::adjacency_iterator vi, vi_end;
  for (tie(vi, vi_end) = adjacent_vertices(u, g); vi != vi_end; ++vi)
    if (color[*vi] == white_color)
      if (has_cycle_dfs(g, *vi, color))
        return true; // cycle detected, return immediately
    else if (color[*vi] == gray_color) // *vi is an ancestor!
      return true;
  color[u] = black_color;
  return false;
}
```

As with the topological sort, in the *has_cycle*() function the recursive DFS function call is placed inside of a loop through all of the vertices so that we catch all of the DFS trees in the graph.

```
bool has_cycle (const file_dep_graph& g)
{
  std::vector<default_color_type> color(num_vertices(g), white_color);
  graph_traits<file_dep_graph>::vertex_iterator vi, vi_end;
  for (tie(vi, vi_end) = vertices(g); vi != vi_end; ++vi)
    if (color[*vi] == white_color)
      if (has_cycle_dfs(g, *vi, &color[0]))
        return true;
  return false;
}
```

3.5 Toward a Generic DFS: Visitors

At this point we have completed two functions, *topo_sort*() and *has_cycle*(), each of which is implemented using depth-first search, although in slightly different ways. However, the fundamental similarities between the two functions provide an excellent opportunity for code reuse. It would be much better if we had a single generic algorithm for depth-first search that expresses the commonality between *topo_sort*() and *has_cycle*() and then used parameters to customize the DFS for each of the different problems.

The design of the STL gives us a hint for how to create a suitably parameterized DFS algorithm. Many of the STL algorithms can be customized by providing a user-defined function object. In the same way, we would like to parameterize DFS in such a way that *topo_sort*() and *has_cycle*() can be realized by passing in a function object.

Unfortunately, the situation here is a little more complicated than in typical STL algorithms. In particular, there are several different locations in the DFS algorithm where customized actions must occur. For instance, the *topo_sort*() function records the ordering at the bottom of the recursive function, whereas the **has_cycle()** function needs to insert an operation inside the loop that examines the adjacent vertices.

The solution to this problem is to use a function object with more than one callback member function. Instead of a single **operator()** function, we use a class with several member functions that are called at different locations (we refer to these places as *event points*). This kind of function object is called an *algorithm visitor*. The DFS visitor will have five member functions: *discover_vertex()*, *tree_edge()*, *back_edge()*, *forward_or_cross_edge()*, and *finish_vertex()*. Also, instead of iterating over the adjacent vertices, we iterator over out-edges to allow passing edge descriptors to the visitor functions and thereby provide more information to the user-defined visitor. This code for a DFS function has a template parameter for a visitor:

```
template <typename Visitor>
void dfs_v1 (const file_dep_graph& g, vertex_t u, default_color_type* color, Visitor vis)
{
  color[u] = gray_color;
  vis.discover_vertex(u, g);
  graph_traits<file_dep_graph>::out_edge_iterator ei, ei_end;
  for (tie(ei, ei_end) = out_edges(u, g); ei != ei_end; ++ei) {
    if (color[target(*ei, g)] == white_color) {
      vis.tree_edge(*ei, g);
      dfs_v1(g, target(*ei, g), color, vis);
    } else if (color[target(*ei, g)] == gray_color)
      vis.back_edge(*ei, g);
    else
      vis.forward_or_cross_edge(*ei, g);
  }
  color[u] = black_color;
  vis.finish_vertex(u, g);
}


template <typename Visitor>
void generic_dfs_v1 (const file_dep_graph& g, Visitor vis)
{
  std::vector<default_color_type> color(num_vertices(g), white_color);
  graph_traits<file_dep_graph>::vertex_iterator vi, vi_end;
  for (tie(vi, vi_end) = vertices(g); vi != vi_end; ++vi) {
    if (color[*vi] == white_color)
      dfs_v1(g, *vi, &color[0], vis);
  }
}
```

The five member functions of the visitor provide the flexibility we need, but a user that only wants to add one action should not have to write four empty member functions. This is easily solved by creating a default visitor from which user-defined visitors can be derived.

```
struct default_dfs_visitor {
  template <typename V, typename G>
  void discover_vertex(V, const G&) { }

  template <typename E, typename G>
  void tree_edge(E, const G&) { }

  template <typename E, typename G>
  void back_edge(E, const G&) { }

  template <typename E, typename G>
  void forward_or_cross_edge(E, const G&) { }

  template <typename V, typename G>
  void finish_vertex(V, const G&) { }
};
```

To demonstrate that this generic DFS can solve our problems, we reimplement the *topo_sort()* and *has_cycle()* functions. First we need to create a visitor that records the topological ordering on the "finish vertex" event point. The code for this visitor follows.

```
struct topo_visitor : public default_dfs_visitor {
  topo_visitor(vertex_t*& order) : topo_order(order) { }
  void finish_vertex(vertex_t u, const file_dep_graph&) {
    *--topo_order = u;
  }
  vertex_t*& topo_order;
};
```

Only two lines of code are required in the body of *topo_sort()* when implemented using generic DFS. One line creates the visitor object and one line calls the generic DFS.

```
void topo_sort(const file_dep_graph& g, vertex_t* topo_order)
{
  topo_visitor vis(topo_order);
  generic_dfs_v1(g, vis);
}
```

To reimplement the *has_cycle()* function, we use a visitor that records that the graph has a cycle whenever the back edge event point occurs.

```
struct cycle_detector : public default_dfs_visitor {
  cycle_detector(bool& cycle) : has_cycle(cycle) { }
  void back_edge(edge_t, const file_dep_graph&) {
    has_cycle = true;
  }
  bool& has_cycle;
};
```

The new *has_cycle()* function creates a cycle detector object and passes it to the generic DFS.

```
bool has_cycle (const file_dep_graph& g)
{
  bool has_cycle = false;
  cycle_detector vis (has_cycle);
  generic_dfs_v1 (g, vis);
  return has_cycle;
}
```

3.6   Graph Setup: Internal Properties

Before addressing the next question about file dependencies, we are going to take some time out to switch to a different graph type. In the previous sections we used arrays to store information such as vertex names. When vertex or edge properties have the same lifetime as the graph object, it can be more convenient to have the properties somehow embedded in the graph itself (we call these *internal properties*). If you were writing your own graph class you might add data members for these properties to a vertex or edge struct.

The *adjacency_list* class has template parameters that allow arbitrary properties to be attached to the vertices and edge: the *VertexProperties* and *EdgeProperties* parameters. These template parameters expect the argument types to be the *property<Tag, T>* class, where *Tag* is a type that specifies the property and *T* gives the type of the property object. There are a number of predefined property tags (see §15.2.3) such as *vertex_name_t* and *edge_weight_t*. For example, to attach a *std::string* to each vertex use the following property type:

```
property<vertex_name_t, std::string>
```

If the predefined property tags do not meet your needs, you can create a new one. One way to do this is to define an enumerated type named *vertex_xxx_t* or *edge_xxx_t* that contains an enum value with the same name minus the *_t* and give the enum value a unique number. Then use *BOOST_INSTALL_PROPERTY* to create the required specializations of the *property_kind* and *property_num* traits classes.[1] Here we create compile-time cost property that we will use in the next section to compute the total compile time.

```
namespace boost {
  enum vertex_compile_cost_t { vertex_compile_cost = 111 }; // a unique #
  BOOST_INSTALL_PROPERTY (vertex, compile_cost);
}
```

The *property* class has an optional third parameter that can be used to nest multiple *property* classes thereby attaching multiple properties to each vertex or edge. Here we create a new typedef for the graph, this time adding two vertex properties and an edge property.

---

[1] Defining new property tags would be much simpler if more C++ compilers were standards conformant.

```
typedef adjacency_list<
  listS,        // Store out-edges of each vertex in a std::list
  listS,        // Store vertex set in a std::list
  directedS, // The file dependency graph is directed
  // vertex properties
  property<vertex_name_t, std::string,
    property<vertex_compile_cost_t, float,
      property<vertex_distance_t, float,
        property<vertex_color_t, default_color_type> > > >,
  // an edge property
  property<edge_weight_t, float>
  > file_dep_graph2;
```

We have also changed the second template argument to *adjacency_list* from *vecS* to *listS*. This has some important implications. If we were to remove a vertex from the graph it would happen in constant time (with *vecS* the vertex removal time is linear in the number of vertices and edges). On the down side, the vertex descriptor type is no longer an integer, so storing properties in arrays and using the vertex as an offset will no longer work. However, the separate storage is no longer needed because we now have the vertex properties stored in the graph.

In §1.2.2 we introduced the notion of a property map. To review, a property map is an object that can be used to map from a key (such as a vertex) to a value (such as a vertex name). When properties have been specified for an *adjacency_list* (as we have just done), property maps for these properties can be obtained using the PropertyGraph interface. The following code shows an example of obtaining two property maps: one for vertex names and another for compile-time cost. The *property_map* traits class provides the type of the property map.

```
typedef property_map<file_dep_graph2, vertex_name_t>::type name_map_t;
typedef property_map<file_dep_graph2, vertex_compile_cost_t>::type
  compile_cost_map_t;
typedef property_map<file_dep_graph2, vertex_distance_t>::type distance_map_t;
typedef property_map<file_dep_graph2, vertex_color_t>::type color_map_t;
```

The *get()* function returns a property map object.

```
name_map_t name_map = get(vertex_name, g);
compile_cost_map_t compile_cost_map = get(vertex_compile_cost, g);
distance_map_t distance_map = get(vertex_distance, g);
color_map_t color_map = get(vertex_color, g);
```

There will be another file containing the estimated compile time for each makefile target. We read this file using a *std::ifstream* and write the properties into the graph using the property maps, *name_map* and *compile_cost_map*. These property maps are models of *LvaluePropertyMap* so they have an *operator[]()* that maps from vertex descriptors to a reference to the appriopriate vertex property object.

```
std::ifstream  name_in ( "makefile-target-names.dat " ) ;
std::ifstream  compile_cost_in ( "target-compile-costs.dat " ) ;
graph_traits<file_dep_graph2>::vertex_iterator  vi ,  vi_end;
for  (tie(vi,  vi_end)  =  vertices(g) ;  vi != vi_end;  ++vi)  {
    name_in  >>  name_map[*vi] ;
    compile_cost_in  >>  compile_cost_map[*vi] ;
}
```

In the following sections we will modify the topological sort and DFS functions to use the property map interface to access vertex properties instead of hard-coding access with a pointer to an array.

3.7   Compilation Time

The next questions we need to answer are, "How long will a compile take?" and "How long will a compile take on a parallel computer?" The first question is easy to answer. We simply sum the compile time for all the vertices in the graph. Just for fun, we do this computation using the *std::accumulate* function. To use this function we need iterators that, when dereferenced, yield the compile cost for the vertex. The vertex iterators of the graph do not provide this capability. When dereferenced, they yield vertex descriptors. Instead, we use the *graph_property_iter_range* class (see §16.8) to generate the appropriate iterators.

```
graph_property_iter_range<file_dep_graph2,  vertex_compile_cost_t>::iterator  ci ,  ci_end;
tie(ci,  ci_end)  =  get_property_iter_range(g,  vertex_compile_cost) ;
std::cout  <<  "total (sequential) compile time: "
           <<  std::accumulate(ci,  ci_end,  0.0)  <<  std::endl;
```

The output of the code sequence is

total (sequential) compile time: **21.3**

Now suppose we have a parallel super computer with hundreds of processors. If there are build targets that do not depend on each other, then they can be compiled at the same time on different processors. How long will the compile take now? To answer this, we need to determine the critical path through the file dependency graph. Or, to put it another way, we need to find the longest path through the graph.

The black lines in Figure 3.3 show the file dependency of *libfoobar.a*. Suppose that we have already determined when *bar.o* and *foo.o* will finish compiling. Then the compile time for *libfoobar.a* will be the longer of the times for *bar.o* and *foo.o* plus the cost for linking them together to form the library file.

Now that we know how to compute the "distance" for each vertex, in what order should we go through the vertices? Certainly if there is an edge (u, v) in the graph, then we better compute the distance for u before v because computing the distance to v requires the distance to u. This should sound familiar. We need to consider the vertices in topological order.

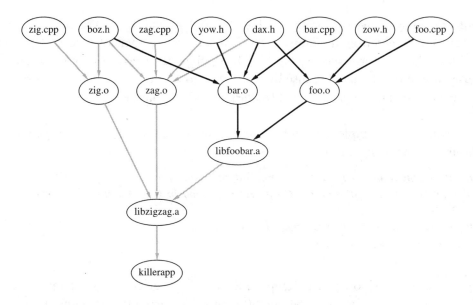

Figure 3.3 Compile time contributions to *libfoobar.a*.

3.8 A Generic Topological Sort and DFS

Due to the change in graph type (from *file_dep_graph* to *file_dep_graph2*) we can no longer use the *topo_sort()* function that we developed in §3.4. Not only does the graph type not match, but also the *color* array used inside of *generic_dfs_v1()* relies on the fact that vertex descriptors are integers (which is not true for *file_dep_graph2*). These problems give us an opportunity to create an even more generic version of topological sort and the underlying DFS. We parameterize the *topo_sort()* function in the following way.

- The specific type *file_dep_graph* is replaced by the template parameter *Graph*. Merely changing to a template parameter does not help us unless there is a standard interface shared by all the graph types that we wish to use with the algorithm. This is where the BGL graph traversal concepts come in. For *topo_sort()* we need a graph type that models the VertexListGraph and IncidenceGraph concepts.

- Using a *vertex_t** for the ordering output is overly restrictive. A more generalized way to output a sequence of elements is to use an output iterator, just as the algorithms in the C++ Standard Library do. This gives the user much more options in terms of where to store the results.

- We need to add a parameter for the color map. To make this as general as possible, we only want to require what is *essential*. In this case, the *topo_sort()* function needs to be able to map from a vertex descriptor to a marker object for that vertex. The Boost Property Map Library (see Chapter 15) defines a minimalistic interface for performing this mapping. Here we use the LvaluePropertyMap interface. The internal *color_map* that we obtained from the graph in §3.6 implements the LvaluePropertyMap interface, as does the color array we used in §3.3.4. A pointer to an array of color markers can be used as a property map because there are function overloads in *boost/property_map.hpp* that adapt pointers to satisfy the LvaluePropertyMap interface.

The following is the implementation of our generic *topo_sort()*. The *topo_visitor* and *generic_dfs_v2()* are discussed next.

```
template <typename Graph, typename OutputIterator, typename ColorMap>
void topo_sort(const Graph& g, OutputIterator topo_order, ColorMap color)
{
  topo_visitor<OutputIterator> vis(topo_order);
  generic_dfs_v2(g, vis, color);
}
```

The *topo_visitor* class is now a class template to accommodate the output iterator. Instead of decrementing, we now increment the output iterator (decrementing an output iterator is not allowed). To get the same reversal behavior as in the first version of *topo_sort()*, the user can pass in a reverse iterator or something like a front insert iterator for a list.

```
template <typename OutputIterator>
struct topo_visitor : public default_dfs_visitor {
  topo_visitor(OutputIterator& order) : topo_order(order) { }
  template <typename Graph>
  void finish_vertex(typename graph_traits<Graph>::vertex_descriptor u, const Graph&)
    { *topo_order++ = u; }
  OutputIterator& topo_order;
};
```

The generic DFS changes in a similar fashion, with the graph type and color map becoming parameterized. In addition, we do not *a priori* know the color type, so we must get the color type by asking the *ColorMap* for its value type (though the *property_traits* class). Instead of using constants such as *white_color*, we use the color functions defined in *color_traits*.

```
template <typename Graph, typename Visitor, typename ColorMap>
void generic_dfs_v2(const Graph& g, Visitor vis, ColorMap color)
{
  typedef color_traits<typename property_traits<ColorMap>::value_type> ColorT;
  typename graph_traits<Graph>::vertex_iterator vi, vi_end;
  for (tie(vi, vi_end) = vertices(g); vi != vi_end; ++vi)
    color[*vi] = ColorT::white();
  for (tie(vi, vi_end) = vertices(g); vi != vi_end; ++vi)
    if (color[*vi] == ColorT::white())
      dfs_v2(g, *vi, color, vis);
}
```

The logic from the *dfs_v1* does not need to change; however, there are a few small changes required due to making the graph type parameterized. Instead of hard-coding *vertex_t* as the vertex descriptor type, we extract the appropriate vertex descriptor from the graph type using *graph_traits*. The fully generic DFS function follows. This function is essentially the same as the BGL *depth_first_visit()*.

```
template <typename Graph, typename ColorMap, typename Visitor>
void dfs_v2 (const Graph& g,
    typename graph_traits<Graph>::vertex_descriptor u,
    ColorMap color, Visitor vis)
{
    typedef typename property_traits<ColorMap>::value_type color_type;
    typedef color_traits<color_type> ColorT;
    color[u] = ColorT::gray();
    vis.discover_vertex(u, g);
    typename graph_traits<Graph>::out_edge_iterator ei, ei_end;
    for (tie(ei, ei_end) = out_edges(u, g); ei != ei_end; ++ei)
        if (color[target(*ei, g)] == ColorT::white()) {
            vis.tree_edge(*ei, g);
            dfs_v2(g, target(*ei, g), color, vis);
        } else if (color[target(*ei, g)] == ColorT::gray())
            vis.back_edge(*ei, g);
        else
            vis.forward_or_cross_edge(*ei, g);
    color[u] = ColorT::black();
    vis.finish_vertex(u, g);
}
```

The real BGL *depth_first_search()* and *topological_sort()* functions are quite similar to the generic functions that we developed in this section. We give a detailed example of using the BGL *depth_first_search()* function in §4.2, and the documentation for *depth_first_search()* is in §13.2.3. The documentation for *topological_sort()* is in §13.2.5.

3.9   Parallel Compilation Time

Now that we have a generic topological sort and DFS, we are ready to solve the problem of finding how long the compilation will take on a parallel computer. First, we perform a topological sort, storing the results in the *topo_order* vector. We pass the reverse iterator of the vector into *topo_sort()* so that we end up with the topological order (and not the reverse topological order).

```
std::vector<vertex_t> topo_order(num_vertices(g));
topo_sort(g, topo_order.rbegin(), color_map);
```

Before calculating the compile times we need to set up the distance map (which we are using to store the compile time totals). For vertices that have no incoming edges (we call these source vertices), we initialize their distance to zero because compilation of these makefile targets can start right away. All other vertices are given a distance of infinity. We find the source vertices by marking all vertices that have incoming edges.

```
graph_traits<file_dep_graph2>::vertex_iterator i, i_end;
graph_traits<file_dep_graph2>::adjacency_iterator vi, vi_end;

// find source vertices with zero in-degree by marking all vertices with incoming edges
for (tie(i, i_end) = vertices(g); i != i_end; ++i)
  color_map[*i] = white_color;
for (tie(i, i_end) = vertices(g); i != i_end; ++i)
  for (tie(vi, vi_end) = adjacent_vertices(*i, g); vi != vi_end; ++vi)
    color_map[*vi] = black_color;

// initialize distances to zero, or for source vertices to the compile cost
for (tie(i, i_end) = vertices(g); i != i_end; ++i)
  if (color_map[*i] == white_color)
    distance_map[*i] = compile_cost_map[*i];
  else
    distance_map[*i] = 0;
```

Now we are ready to compute the distances. We go through all of the vertices stored in *topo_order*, and for each one we update the distance (total compile time) for each adjacent vertex. What we are doing here is somewhat different than what was described earlier. Before, we talked about each vertex looking "up" the graph to compute its distance. Here, we have reformulated the computation so that instead we are pushing distances "down" the graph. The reason for this change is that looking "up" the graph requires access to in-edges, which our graph type does not provide.

```
std::vector<vertex_t>::iterator ui;
for (ui = topo_order.begin(); ui != topo_order.end(); ++ui) {
  vertex_t u = *ui;
  for (tie(vi, vi_end) = adjacent_vertices(u, g); vi != vi_end; ++vi)
    if (distance_map[*vi] < distance_map[u] + compile_cost_map[*vi])
      distance_map[*vi] = distance_map[u] + compile_cost_map[*vi];
}
```

The maximum distance value from among all the vertices tells us the total parallel compile time. Again we use *graph_property_iter_range* to create property iterators over vertex distances. The *std::max_element()* function does the work of locating the maximum.

```
graph_property_iter_range<file_dep_graph2, vertex_distance_t>::iterator ci, ci_end;
tie(ci, ci_end) = get_property_iter_range(g, vertex_distance);
std::cout << "total (parallel) compile time: "
          << *std::max_element(ci, ci_end) << std::endl;
```

The output is

total (*parallel*) *compile time:* **11.9**

Figure 3.4 shows two numbers for each makefile target: the compile cost for the target and the time at which the target will finish compiling during a parallel compile.

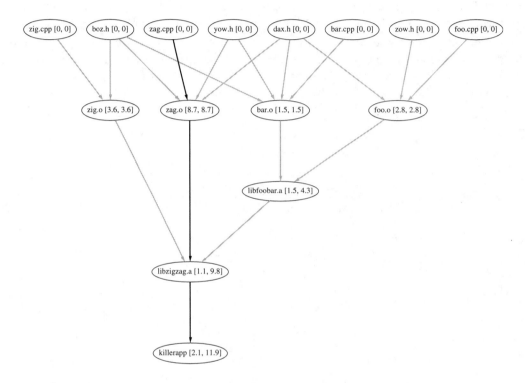

Figure 3.4 For each vertex there are two numbers: compile cost and accumulated compile time. The critical path consists of black lines.

3.10 Summary

In this chapter we have applied BGL to answer several questions that would come up in constructing a software build system: In what order should targets be built? Are there any cyclic dependencies? How long will compilation take? In answering these questions we looked at topological ordering of a directed graph and how this can be computed via a depth-first search.

To implement the solutions we used the BGL *adjacency_list* to represent the file dependency graph. We wrote straightforward implementations of topological sort and cycle detection. We then identified common pieces of code and factored them out into a generic implementation of depth-first search. We used algorithm visitors to parameterize the DFS and then wrote specific visitors to implement the topological sort and the cycle detection.

We then looked at using a different variation of the *adjacency_list* class that allowed properties such as vertex name and compile cost to be attached to the vertices of the graph. We then further generalized the generic DFS by parameterizing the graph type and the property access method. The chapter finished with an application of the generic topological sort and DFS to compute the time it would take to compile all the targets on a parallel computer.

Chapter 4

Basic Graph Algorithms

4.1 Breadth-First Search

Breadth-first search (BFS) is a fundamental technique for discovering information about a graph that can be applied to many different problems. The BGL provides a generic implementation of BFS in the *breadth_first_search()* algorithm. This function template is parameterized so that it can be used in many situations. In this section, we describe breadth-first search and show how to use BFS to calculate Bacon numbers.

4.1.1 Definitions

Breadth-first search is a traversal through a graph that discovers all of the vertices reachable from a given source vertex. The order in which the vertices are discovered is determined by the distance from the source vertex to each vertex, with closer vertices being discovered before more distant vertices.

One way to think of breadth-first search is that it expands like the wave that emanates from a stone dropped into a pool of water. Vertices in the same "wave" are at the same distance from the source vertex. Figure 4.1 illustrates the application of BFS to a simple graph. The BFS discovery order for the vertices in Figure 4.1 is $\{d\}\{f,g\}\{c,h,b,e\}\{a\}$ (the vertices are grouped according to their distance from the source vertex d).

When a vertex v is discovered, the edge (u,v) that led to its discovery is called a *tree edge*. All of the tree edges together form a *breadth-first tree* with the source vertex as the root of the tree. Given a tree edge (u,v), vertex u is called the *predecessor* or *parent* of v. The tree edges in Figure 4.1 are indicated by the black lines, and non-tree edges are the gray lines.

The vertices in Figure 4.1 are labeled with their *shortest-path distance* from the source vertex d. The shortest-path distance $\delta(s,v)$ from some vertex s to vertex v is the the minimum number of edges in any path connecting s to v. A *shortest path* is a path whose length is equal to $\delta(s,v)$ (there can be more than one shortest path between two vertices). The main

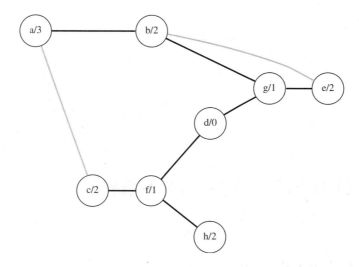

Figure 4.1 Breadth-first search spreading through a graph. The BFS tree consists of the black lines.

characteristic of breadth-first search is that vertices with smaller shortest-path distances are discovered before vertices with large distances.

Chapter 5 presents shortest-path computations where the path length is determined by the sum of weights assigned to edges in the path, not simply by the number of edges in the path.

4.1.2   Six Degrees of Kevin Bacon

An amusing application of breadth-first search comes up in the popular game "Six Degrees of Kevin Bacon." The idea of the game is to connect an actor[1] to Kevin Bacon through a trail of actors who appeared together in movies, and do so in fewer than six steps. For example, Theodore Hesburgh (President Emeritus of the University of Notre Dame) was in the movie *Rudy* with the actor Gerry Becker, who was in the movie *Sleepers* with Kevin Bacon. Why Kevin Bacon? For some reason, the three students who invented the game, Mike Ginelli, Craig Fass, and Brian Turtle, decided that Kevin Bacon was the center of the entertainment world. Mathematicians play a similar game; they keep track of their Erdös number, which is the number of co-authored publications that separate them from the famous Paul Erdös.

The "Six Degrees of Kevin Bacon" game is really a graph problem. The graph representing the problem can be modeled by assigning a vertex for each actor and creating an edge between two vertices if the corresponding actors have appeared together in a movie. Since the relationship between actors appearing together in a movie is symmetric, edges between actors can be undirected, resulting in an undirected graph.

---

[1]We use the term *actor* generically to mean both actors and actresses.

The problem of finding a trail of actors to Kevin Bacon becomes a traditional graph problem—that of finding a *path* between two vertices. Since we wish to find a path that is shorter than six steps, ideally we would like to find the *shortest path* between the vertices. As mentioned in the previous section, breadth-first search can be used to find shortest paths. Similar to the Erdös number, we use the term *Bacon number* to mean the shortest path length from a given actor to Kevin Bacon. In the following example we show how to use the BGL *breadth_first_search* ( ) function to calculate Bacon numbers for a collection of actors.

Input File and Graph Setup

For this example, we use a small subset of the movies and actors from the Internet Movie Database.[2] The file *example/kevin_bacon.dat* contains a list of actor pairs who appeared in the same movie. As shown in the following excerpt, each line of the file contains an actor's name, a movie, and another actor that appeared in the movie. A semicolon is used as a separator.

> *Patrick Stewart;Prince of Egypt, The* (**1998**)*;Steve Martin*

Our first task is to read the file using a *std::ifstream* and to create a graph from it.

```
std::ifstream datafile ( "./kevin-bacon.dat ") ;
if ( ! datafile) {
   std::cerr << "No ./kevin-bacon.dat file " << std::endl;
   return EXIT_FAILURE;
}
```

An *adjacency_list* is used to represent the graph, and *undirectedS* is used to indicate that it is undirected. As in §3.6, to attach the actors' names to the vertices and the movie names to the edges, the *property* class is used to specify the addition of these vertex and edge properties.

```
typedef adjacency_list<vecS, vecS, undirectedS, property<vertex_name_t, std::string>,
   property<edge_name_t, std::string> > Graph;
Graph g;
```

To access the properties, property map objects need to be obtained from the graph. The following code establishes these maps, which are used later with vertex and edge descriptors to access the associated vertex or edge name.

```
typedef property_map<Graph, vertex_name_t>::type actor_name_map_t;
actor_name_map_t actor_name = get(vertex_name, g) ;
typedef property_map<Graph, edge_name_t>::type  movie_name_map_t;
movie_name_map_t connecting_movie = get(edge_name, g) ;
```

The file is read one line at a time and parsed into a list of tokens separated by semicolons. The Boost Tokenizer Library is used to create a "virtual" container of tokens.

---

[2]The Internet Movie Database is used by the CS department at the University of Virginia to supply the graph for their Oracle of Bacon.

```
for (std::string line; std::getline(datafile, line); ) {
  char_delimiters_separator<char> sep(false, "", ";");
  tokenizer<> line_toks(line, sep);
  tokenizer<>::iterator i = line_toks.begin();
  ⟨Get first actor name and add vertex to graph 64⟩
  ⟨Store the movie name to a variable 65a⟩
  ⟨Get second actor and add to graph 65b⟩
  ⟨Add edge connecting the two actors to the graph 65c⟩
}
```

Each line of the input corresponds to an edge in the graph that is incident to the two vertices specified by the names of two actors. The name of the movie is attached to the edge as a property. One issue in creating the graph from this file format is that it is a stream of edges. Although it is therefore a straightforward matter to insert edges into the graph based on the input stream, it is slightly less straightforward to insert vertices. The vertices appear only in the context of the edges that connect them, and a given vertex can appear multiple times in the input stream. To ensure that each vertex is only added once to the graph, a map from actor names to their vertices is used. As vertices are added to the graph, subsequent appearances of the same vertex (as part of a different edge) can be linked with the correct vertex already in the graph. This mapping is readily accomplished using *std::map*.

```
typedef graph_traits<Graph>::vertex_descriptor Vertex;
typedef std::map<std::string, Vertex> NameVertexMap;
NameVertexMap actors;
```

The first token of each line is an actor's name. If the actor is not already in the actor map, a vertex is added to the graph, the name property of the vertex is set to the name of the actor, and the vertex descriptor is recorded in the map. If the actor is already in the map, the *std::map::insert()* function returns an iterator pointing to the location of the corresponding vertex in the graph.

⟨ Get first actor name and add vertex to graph 64 ⟩ ≡

```
std::string actors_name = *i++;
NameVertexMap::iterator pos;
bool inserted;
Vertex u, v;
tie(pos, inserted) = actors.insert(std::make_pair(actors_name, Vertex()));
if (inserted) {
  u = add_vertex(g);
  actor_name[u] = actors_name;
  pos->second = u;
} else {
  u = pos->second;
}
```

The second token is the name of the movie, which is attached to the edge connecting the two actors. However, the edge cannot be created until there is a vertex descriptor for both actors. Therefore, the movie name is stored for later use.

⟨ Store the movie name to a variable 65a ⟩ ≡

```
std::string movie_name = *i++;
```

The third token is the second actor, and the same technique is used to insert the corresponding vertex into the graph.

⟨ Get second actor and add to graph 65b ⟩ ≡

```
tie (pos, inserted) = actors.insert (std::make_pair (*i, Vertex ( ) ) );
if (inserted) {
  v = add_vertex (g);
  actor_name [v] = *i;
  pos->second = v;
} else v = pos->second;
```

The final step is to add an edge connecting the two actors and to record the name of the connecting movie. Since *setS* is used for the *EdgeList* type of the *adjacency_list*, parallel edges in the input are not inserted into the graph.

⟨ Add edge connecting the two actors to the graph 65c ⟩ ≡

```
graph_traits<Graph>::edge_descriptor e;
tie (e, inserted) = add_edge (u, v, g);
if (inserted) connecting_movie [e] = movie_name;
```

Computing Bacon Numbers with Breadth-First Search

With our approach of computing Bacon numbers using BFS, we compute Bacon numbers for all actors in the graph and therefore require storage locations for those numbers. Since we are using an *adjacency_list* with *VertexList=vecS*, the vertex descriptors are integers and are in the range $[0, |V|)$. Therefore, the Bacon numbers can be stored in a *std::vector*, with the vertex descriptor used as an index.

```
std::vector<int> bacon_number (num_vertices (g));
```

Now the *breadth_first_search ( )* takes three arguments: the graph, the source vertex, and the named parameters. The source vertex should be the vertex corresponding to Kevin Bacon, which can be obtained from the *actors* name-to-vertex map. The Bacon number for Kevin Bacon himself is, of course, zero.

```
Vertex src = actors [ "Kevin Bacon" ];
bacon_number [src] = 0;
```

To calculate the Bacon numbers, the distances along the shortest paths are recorded. Specifically, when the BFS algorithm finds a tree edge (u, v), the distance for v can be computed with $d[v] \leftarrow d[u] + 1$. To insert this action into the BFS, a visitor class *bacon_number-_recorder* is defined that models the BFSVisitor concept and includes the distance computation in the *tree_edge()* event-point member function. The class *bacon_number_recorder* is derived from *default_bfs_visitor* to provide the default (empty) implementation of the remaining event-point member functions. The generic LvaluePropertyMap interface is used to access the distance of a vertex to make the visitor more reusable.

```
template <typename DistanceMap>
class bacon_number_recorder : public default_bfs_visitor {
public:
  bacon_number_recorder(DistanceMap dist) : d(dist) { }

  template <typename Edge, typename Graph>
  void tree_edge(Edge e, const Graph& g) const {
    typename graph_traits<Graph>::vertex_descriptor
      u = source(e, g), v = target(e, g);
    d[v] = d[u] + 1;
  }
private:
  DistanceMap d;
};

// Convenience function
template <typename DistanceMap>
bacon_number_recorder<DistanceMap>
record_bacon_number(DistanceMap d)
{
  return bacon_number_recorder<DistanceMap>(d);
}
```

We are now ready to call *breadth_first_search()*. The visitor argument is a named parameter, so the argument must be passed using the *visitor()* function. Here a pointer to the beginning of the *bacon_number* array is used as the distance map.

```
breadth_first_search(g, src, visitor(record_bacon_number(&bacon_number[0])));
```

The Bacon number for each actor is output by looping through all the vertices in the graph and looking up the corresponding Bacon number.

```
graph_traits<Graph>::vertex_iterator i, end;
for (tie(i, end) = vertices(g); i != end; ++i) {
  std::cout << actor_name[*i] << " has a Bacon number of "
            << bacon_number[*i] << std::endl;
}
```

Here are some excerpts from the output of the program.

> *William Shatner has a Bacon number of* **2**
> *Denise Richards has a Bacon number of* **1**
> *Kevin Bacon has a Bacon number of* **0**
> *Patrick Stewart has a Bacon number of* **2**
> *Steve Martin has a Bacon number of* **1**
> **. . .**

4.2 Depth-First Search

Depth-first search is a fundamental building block for many graph algorithms. The strongly connected component algorithm (§13.5.2) and topological sort algorithm (§13.2.5) both rely on depth-first search. Depth-first search is also useful on its own—for instance, it can be used to compute reachability and to detect cycles in a graph (see §3.4).

This last capability makes DFS useful as part of an optimizing compiler that may need to identify loops in the control-flow graph of a program. This section describes how to use the *depth_first_search*() and *depth_first_visit*() functions by walking through an example of detecting and determining the extent of loops in the control-flow graph.

4.2.1 Definitions

A depth-first search visits all the vertices in a graph exactly once. When choosing which edge to explore next, DFS always chooses to go "deeper" into the graph (hence the name "depth-first"). That is, DFS will pick the next adjacent undiscovered vertex until reaching a vertex that has no undiscovered adjacent vertices. The algorithm then backtracks to the previous vertex and continues along any as-yet unexplored edges from that vertex. After DFS has visited all the reachable vertices from a particular source vertex, it chooses one of the remaining undiscovered vertices and continues the search. This process creates a set of *depth-first trees* that together form the *depth-first forest*. Figure 4.2 shows DFS applied to an undirected graph, with the edges labeled in the order they were explored.

Similar to BFS, the DFS algorithm marks vertices with colors to keep track of the progress of the search through the graph. Initially, all vertices are white. When a vertex is discovered, it is made gray; after all descendants of the vertex have been discovered, it is made black.

A depth-first search assigns the edges of the graph into three categories: tree edges, back edges, and forward or cross edges. A *tree edge* is an edge in the depth-first search forest constructed (implicitly or explicitly) by running DFS traversal over a graph. More specifically, an edge (u, v) is a tree edge if v was first discovered while exploring edge (u, v). During the DFS, tree edges can be identified because vertex v of the examined edge will be colored white. Vertex u is called the *predecessor* or *parent* of vertex v in the search tree if edge (u, v) is a tree edge. A *back edge* connects a vertex to one of its ancestors in a search

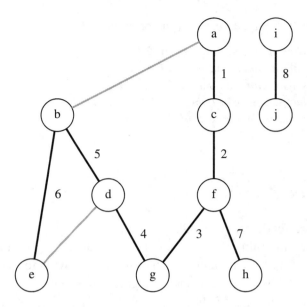

Figure 4.2 Depth-first search spreading through a graph. The DFS tree consists of the solid lines. The edges are labeled in the order that they were added to the DFS tree.

tree. This kind of edge is identified when the target vertex v of the examined edge is gray. Self loops are considered to be back edges. A *forward edge* is a non-tree edge (u, v) that connects a vertex u to a descendant v in a search tree. A *cross edge* is an edge that does not fall into the other three categories. If the target vertex v of an examined edge is colored black, then it is either a forward or cross edge (though we do not know which it is).

There are typically many valid depth-first forests for a given graph, and therefore many different (and equally valid) ways to categorize the edges. One way to implement DFS is to use first-in, last-out stack. DFS pushes its adjacenct vertices into a stack on processing a vertex and pops one vertex up for the next vertex to process. Another way to implement DFS is to use recursive functions. The two approaches are conceptually equivalent.

One interesting property of depth-first search is that the discover and finish times for each vertex form a parenthetical structure. If we output an open parenthesis when a vertex is discovered and a close parenthesis when a vertex is finished, then the result is a properly nested set of parentheses. Here we show the parenthetical structure for DFS applied to the graph of Figure 4.2. DFS is used as the kernel for several other graph algorithms, including topological sort and two of the connected component algorithms. It can also be used to detect cycles (see §3.4).

(a (c (f (g (d (b (e e) b) d) g) (h h) f) c) a) (i (j j) i)

4.2.2 Finding Loops in Program-Control-Flow Graphs

Our task for this section is to use DFS to find all the loops in a control-flow graph of a program. Figure 4.3 shows an example of a flow graph. Each box represents a *basic block*, which is a maximal sequence of instructions with a single entry and exit point. If there is an edge between two blocks, such as (B_1, B_6), then B_1 is a *predecessor* of B_6 and B_6 is a *successor* to B_1. A *loop* is defined as a set of blocks where all blocks are reachable from one another along some path in the flow graph [32].

Finding the loops in the flow graph consists of two steps. The first is to find all the back edges in the graph. Each back edge (u, v) identifies a loop, since v is the ancestor of u in the DFS tree and adding (u, v) completes the loop. The vertex v is called the *loop head*. DFS is used to identify the back edges of the flow graph. In Figure 4.3, (B_7, B_1) is an example of a back edge. The second step is to determine which vertices belong to each loop.

These two steps are combined in the function template ***find_loops()***. This function has three parameters: the ***entry*** vertex, the graph ***g***, and a container to store the vertices for each loop. The ***Graph*** type is required be a model of BidirectionalGraph so that both the in-edges and out-edges of the graph can be accessed in code part b. The ***Loops*** type is a container whose elements are sets of vertices. The back edges from the first step are stored in the ***back_edges*** vector and the ***color_map*** is used during the DFS to mark the algorithm's progress.

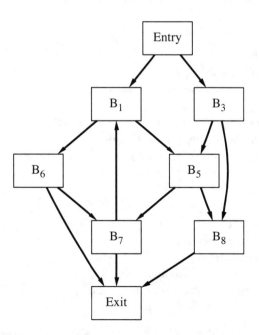

Figure 4.3 A control-flow graph for a program. Each box represents a basic block of instructions. The edge (B_7, B_1) is a back edge.

⟨ Find loops function template 70a ⟩ ≡

```
template <typename Graph, typename Loops>
void find_loops (
  typename graph_traits<Graph>::vertex_descriptor entry,
  const Graph& g,
  Loops& loops) // A container of sets of vertices
{
  function_requires< BidirectionalGraphConcept<Graph> >();
  typedef typename graph_traits<Graph>::edge_descriptor Edge;
  typedef typename graph_traits<Graph>::vertex_descriptor Vertex;
  std::vector<Edge> back_edges;
  std::vector<default_color_type> color_map (num_vertices (g));
  ⟨Find all back edges in the graph 71a⟩
  ⟨Find all the vertices in each loop 71b⟩
}
```

For the first step a DFSVisitor, *back_edge_recorder*, is created that will record the back edges during a depth-first search. To make this class more reusable, the storage mechanism for back edges is not given, but rather parameterized as an OutputIterator. The *back_edge_recorder* inherits from *default_dfs_visitor* to use default (empty) versions of event-point functions not provided by *back_edge_recorder*. Only the *back_edge*() member function needs to be implemented. The following is the code for the *back_edge_recorder* class template and its object generator function.

⟨ Back-edge recorder class 70b ⟩ ≡

```
template <typename OutputIterator>
class back_edge_recorder : public default_dfs_visitor {
public:
  back_edge_recorder (OutputIterator out) : m_out (out) { }
  template <typename Edge, typename Graph>
  void back_edge (Edge e, const Graph&) { *m_out++ = e; }
private:
  OutputIterator m_out;
};
// object generator function
template <typename OutputIterator>
back_edge_recorder<OutputIterator>
make_back_edge_recorder (OutputIterator out) {
  return back_edge_recorder<OutputIterator> (out);
}
```

We are now ready to call the DFS function. We choose *depth_first_visit*() instead of *depth_first_search*() because all the vertices in the flow graph are reachable from the entry vertex. The *entry* vertex is therefore passed in as the starting point of the DFS. The third argument is the visitor, which will be the back edge recorder. The argument to **make_back_-edge_recorder()** needs to be an output iterator, the **std::back_insert_iterator** adaptor is used to store into the **back_edges** vector. The last parameter of **depth_first_visit()** is the color property map that DFS will use to keep track of its progress through the graph. The color property map is created from an iterator to the **color_map** vector (see §15.2.2).

⟨ Find all back edges in the graph 71a ⟩ ≡

```
depth_first_visit(g, entry,
    make_back_edge_recorder(std::back_inserter(back_edges)),
    make_iterator_property_map(color_map.begin(), get(vertex_index, g)));
```

For the second step of our loop detection process, we determine which vertices belong to each loop. To accomplish this, for each of the back edges discovered in step one, **compute_loop_extent()** is called to find all the vertices in the loop.

⟨ Find all the vertices in each loop 71b ⟩ ≡

```
for (std::vector<Edge>::size_type i = 0; i < back_edges.size(); ++i) {
    loops.push_back(typename Loops::value_type());
    compute_loop_extent(back_edges[i], g, loops.back());
}
```

For a vertex v to belong to a loop indicated by a back edge (t, h), v must be reachable from h and t must be reachable from v. Therefore, the **compute_loop_extent()** function consists of three steps: compute all the vertices reachable from the head, compute all the vertices from which you can reach the tail, and intersect these two sets of vertices.

⟨ Compute loop extent 71c ⟩ ≡

```
template <typename Graph, typename Set>
void compute_loop_extent(typename graph_traits<Graph>::edge_descriptor back_edge,
    const Graph& g, Set& loop_set)
{
    function_requires< BidirectionalGraphConcept<Graph> >();
    typedef typename graph_traits<Graph>::vertex_descriptor Vertex;
    typedef color_traits<default_color_type> Color;

    Vertex loop_head, loop_tail;
    loop_tail = source(back_edge, g);
    loop_head = target(back_edge, g);

    ⟨Compute loop extent: reachable from head 72⟩
    ⟨Compute loop extent: reachable to tail 73a⟩
    ⟨Compute loop extent: intersect the reachable sets 73b⟩
}
```

To compute which vertices are reachable from the head of the loop, we use ***depth_first_visit*** ( )
again.   In this case, a new visitor does not need to be defined, since we only need to know
which vertices were discovered, and this can be determined by examining the color property
map after running DFS. Vertices that are colored gray or black (but not white) were discovered
during DFS. The color properties are stored in a vector ***reachable_from_head***. Figure 4.4 shows
all the vertices reachable from block B_1.

⟨ Compute loop extent: reachable from head 72 ⟩ ≡

> *std::vector<default_color_type>*
>> *reachable_from_head* (*num_vertices* (*g*) **,** *Color::white* ( )) **;**
>> *depth_first_visit* (*g* **,** *loop_head* **,** *default_dfs_visitor* ( ) **,**
>>> *make_iterator_property_map* (*reachable_from_head* **.** *begin* ( ) **,**
>>>> *get* (*vertex_index* **,** *g*))) **;**

For the second step, we need to compute all the vertices from which block B_7 is reachable.   This can be done by performing an "upstream" depth-first search. That is, instead
of exploring along the out-edges of each vertex, we explore along the in-edges. The BGL
depth_first_visit ( ) function uses the ***out_edges*** ( ) function to access the next vertices to explore, however it can still be applied to this situation by using the ***reverse_graph*** adaptor. This
adaptor takes a BidirectionalGraph and provides a view of the graph where the meanings of
out-edges and in-edges are swapped.

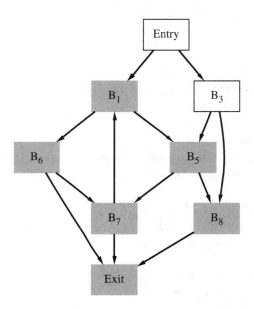

Figure 4.4 Vertices reachable from block B_1.

The following code shows how this is done. Figure 4.5 shows all the vertices from which block B_7 is reachable.

⟨ Compute loop extent: reachable to tail 73a ⟩ ≡

```
std::vector<default_color_type> reachable_to_tail(num_vertices(g));
reverse_graph<Graph> reverse_g(g);
depth_first_visit(reverse_g, loop_tail, default_dfs_visitor(),
  make_iterator_property_map(reachable_to_tail.begin(),
    get(vertex_index, g)));
```

The last step in computing all the vertices in a loop is intersecting the two reachable sets. We output a vertex to the *loop_set* if it was reachable from the head *and* if the tail can be reached from it.

⟨ Compute loop extent: intersect the reachable sets 73b ⟩ ≡

```
typename graph_traits<Graph>::vertex_iterator vi, vi_end;
for (tie(vi, vi_end) = vertices(g); vi != vi_end; ++vi)
  if (reachable_from_head[*vi] != Color::white()
      && reachable_to_tail[*vi] != Color::white())
    loop_set.insert(*vi);
```

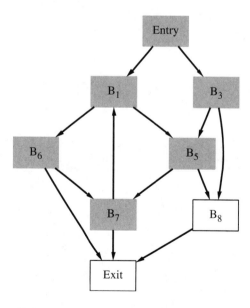

Figure 4.5 Vertices from which block B_7 can be reached.

Chapter 5

Shortest-Paths Problems

In this chapter we solve some Internet packet-routing problems using shortest-paths algorithms included in BGL. The first section explains the shortest-paths problem in general and
reviews some definitions. The second section gives a brief introduction to packet routing. The
third and fourth sections describe two commonly used packet-routing protocols and present
their implementations using BGL.

5.1 Definitions

A *path* is a sequence of vertices $\langle v_0, v_1, \ldots, v_k \rangle$ in a graph $G = (V, E)$ such that each of
the edges (v_i, v_{i+1}) is in the edge set E (each vertex is connected to the next vertex in the
sequence). In the shortest-path problem, each edge (u, v) is given a weight $w(u, v)$. The
weight of a path (or path length), is the sum of the weights for each edge in the path:

$$w(p) = \sum_{i=0}^{k-1} w(v_i, v_{i+1})$$

The *shortest-path weight* from vertex u to v is the minimum of all possible path weights:

$$\delta(u, v) = \begin{cases} \min\{w(p) : u \rightsquigarrow v\} & \text{if there is a path from } u \text{ to } v \\ \infty & \text{otherwise.} \end{cases}$$

A *shortest path* is any path whose path weight is equal to the shortest-path weight. Figure 5.1
shows an example of a shortest path.

The *single-pair shortest-path problem* is to find a shortest path that connects a given pair
of vertices. The *single-source shortest-paths problem* is to find a shortest path from a source
vertex to every other vertex in the graph. The set of shortest paths emanating from the source
vertex is called a *shortest-path tree*. The *all-pairs shortest-paths problem* is to find a shortest
path from every vertex to every other vertex in the graph.

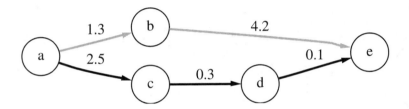

Figure 5.1 The shortest path from vertex a to e is denoted by the black lines.

It turns out that there are no algorithms for solving the single-pair problem that are asymptotically faster than algorithms that solve the single-source problem. The BGL includes two classical methods for solving the single-source problem: Dijkstra's algorithm and the Bellman–Ford algorithm. The BGL also includes Johnson's algorithm for all-pairs shortest paths.

Shortest-path algorithms have a wide variety of uses and are applied in many areas. One important application of current interest is Internet packet routing. The protocols that control how packets of information are transmitted through the Internet use shortest-path algorithms to reduce the amount of time it takes for a packet to reach its destination.

5.2   Internet Routing

When a computer sends a message to another using the Internet Protocol (IP), the message contents are put into a *packet*. Each packet, in addition to its message data (payload), includes meta-data such as source and destination addresses, length of the data, sequence number, and so on. If the message is large, the data are split into smaller parts, each of which is packetized. The individual parts are given sequence numbers so that the original message can be reassembled by the receiver.

If the destination address for the packet is outside of the local network, the packet is sent from the originating machine to an internet *router*. The router directs packets that it receives to other routers based on its *routing table*, which is constructed based on a *routing protocol*. After traveling from one router to the next (each step is called a *hop*), the packets arrive at their destination. If the network is congested, some packets may be dropped *en route*. Higher-level reliable protocols such as the Transmission Control Protocol (TCP) use handshaking between sender and receiver so that dropped packets are retransmitted. The UNIX program *traceroute* (or the Windows program *tracert*) can be used to show the route taken from your computer to other sites around the Internet.

The ultimate goal of a routing process is to deliver packets to their destinations as quickly as possible. There are a number of factors that determine how long a packet takes to arrive (e.g., the number of hops along the path, transmission delay within a router, transmission delay between routers, network bandwidth). The routing protocol must choose the best paths between routers; this information is stored in a routing table.

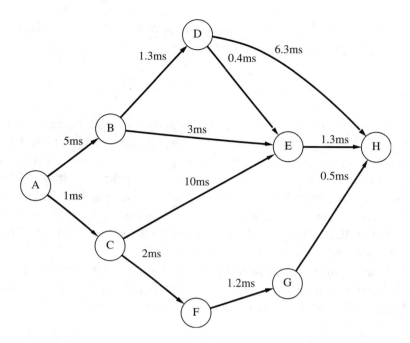

Figure 5.2 A set of Internet routers connected to one another, with the connections labeled with the mean transmission delay.

The routing problem can be modeled as a graph by associating a vertex with each router and an edge for each direct connection between two routers. Information such as delay and bandwidth are attached to each edge. Figure 5.2 shows a graph model for a simple router network. The routing problem is now transformed into a shortest-paths graph problem.

5.3 Bellman–Ford and Distance Vector Routing

Some of the first Internet routing protocols, such as the Routing Information Protocol (RIP) [19], used a distance-vector protocol. The basic idea behind RIP is for each router to maintain an estimate of distance to all other routers and to periodically compare notes with its neighbors. If a router learns of a shorter path to some destination from one of its neighbors, it will update its distance record to that destination and change its routing table to send packets to that destination via that neighbor. After enough time, the estimated distances maintained in this distributed fashion by multiple routers are guaranteed to converge to the true distance, therefore giving the routers accurate information about the best path.

The RIP is a distributed form of the Bellman–Ford single-source shortest-paths algorithm [5, 13]. The principle step in the Bellman–Ford algorithm, called *edge relaxation*, corresponds to the notion of "comparing notes with your neighbor." The relaxation operation applied to edge (u, v) performs the following update:

$$d[v] = \min(w(u, v) + d[u], d[v])$$

The Bellman–Ford algorithm loops through all of the edges in a graph, applying the relaxation operation to each. The algorithm repeats this loop $|V|$ times, after which it is guaranteed that the distances to each vertex have been reduced to the minimum possible (unless there is a negative cycle in the graph). If there is a negative cycle, then there will be edges in the graph that were not properly minimized. That is, there will be edges (u, v) such that $w(u, v) + d[u] < d[v]$ where w is weight and d is distance. To verify that all edges are minimized, the algorithm loops over all of the edges in the graph a final time, returning true if they are minimized, and returning false otherwise.

The BGL *bellman_ford_shortest_paths()* function implements the Bellman–Ford algorithm. The following sections show how to use this function to solve the routing problem depicted in Figure 5.2. The following is the outline for the program.

⟨ *bellman-ford-internet.cpp* 78 ⟩ ≡

```
#include <iostream>
#include <boost/array.hpp>
#include <boost/graph/edge_list.hpp>
#include <boost/graph/bellman_ford_shortest_paths.hpp>

int main()
{
    using namespace boost;
    ⟨Setup router network 79a⟩
    ⟨Assign edge weights 79b⟩
    ⟨Create vertex property storage 80b⟩
    ⟨Call the Bellman–Ford algorithm 80c⟩
    ⟨Output distances and parents 81⟩
    return EXIT_SUCCESS;
}
```

The first argument to *bellman_ford_shortest_paths()* is the graph object. The type of the graph object must model the EdgeListGraph concept. Many of the BGL graph classes model EdgeListGraph and can therefore be used with this algorithm. One such class is the *edge_list* class template used here. The *edge_list* class template is an adaptor that allows an iterator range to be viewed as a graph. The value type of the iterator must be a *std::pair* pair of vertex descriptors. The vertex descriptors can be of just about any type, although here integers are used to allow indexing into arrays.

For this example, the edges are stored in a **boost::array**, where each edge is a **std::pair**. Each vertex is given an ID number that is specified using an **enum**. The template parameters for **edge_list** are the iterator type, the iterator's value type, and the iterator's difference type.[1]

⟨ Setup router network 79a ⟩ ≡

```
// ID numbers for the routers (vertices).
enum { A, B, C, D, E, F, G, H, n_vertices };
const int n_edges = 11;
typedef std::pair<int, int> Edge;

// The list of connections between routers stored in an array.
array<Edge, n_edges> edges = { { Edge(A, B), Edge(A, C),
  Edge(B, D), Edge(B, E), Edge(C, E), Edge(C, F), Edge(D, H),
  Edge(D, E), Edge(E, H), Edge(F, G), Edge(G, H) } };

// Specify the graph type and declare a graph object
typedef edge_list<array<Edge, n_edges>::iterator> Graph;
Graph g(edges.begin(), edges.end());
```

To communicate the edge weight (transmission delays) to the algorithm, an edge weight property map that models the ReadablePropertyMap concept must be provided. The default for the **weight_map()** parameter is the internal edge weight property map of the graph, which is accessed via the call **get(edge_weight, g)**. Since the **edge_list** class does not support user-defined internal property maps, edge weights must be stored externally and a property map argument must be explicitly passed to the function. The **edge_list** class does provide an edge-to-index property map, so the edge indices can be used as offsets into an array where the edge properties. In this case the transmission delays are stored. The code below creates the array of transmission delay values.

⟨ Assign edge weights 79b ⟩ ≡

```
// The transmission delay values for each edge.
array<float, n_edges> delay =
  { { 5.0, 1.0, 1.3, 3.0, 10.0, 2.0, 6.3, 0.4, 1.3, 1.2, 0.5 } };
```

The **delay** array provides storage for the edge weights, but it does not provide the property map interface required by the algorithm for mapping from edge descriptors to the weight properties. The necessary property map interface is provided by the **iterator_property_map** class adaptor from the Boost Property Map Library. This class turns an iterator (such as the iterator for the array of delay values) into an LvaluePropertyMap. The helper function **make_iterator_property_map()** is a convenient mechanism for creating the adaptor. The first argument is the iterator, the second argument is a mapping from edges to edge indices, and the third argument

---

[1]For compilers with a working version of **std::iterator_traits**, the value type and difference type template parameters for **edge_list** are not necessary because correct default parameters are provided.

is an object of the iterator's value type, which is only needed for type deduction purposes. The following is an example of calling the ***make_iterator_property_map*** **( )** function (the return value of the function is the created adaptor object, which is passed directly to the Bellman–Ford function). The ***get*** **( )** function retrieves the edge index map from the graph object and is part of the PropertyGraph interface.

⟨ Create property map for delays 80a ⟩ ≡
> ***make_iterator_property_map*** **(** *delay* **.** *begin* **( ) ,** *get* **(** *edge_index* **,** *g* **) ,** *delay* **[0])**

Several properties are attached to vertices in the graph. As in Figure 5.2, the vertices are labeled with letters (their names). Distance labels are required to record the lengths of the shortest paths. Finally, a predecessor map ***parent*** is used to record the shortest-paths tree. For each vertex in the graph, the predecessor map records the parent of that vertex with respect to the shortest-paths tree. That is, each of the edges *(parent[u],u)* is an edge in the shortest-paths tree.

The ***edge_list*** class does not provide a way to attach properties to vertices (the vertices are only integers). The properties are stored in separate arrays indexed by vertex number. The distances are initialized to infinity and the parent of each vertex is initially set to itself.

⟨ Create vertex property storage 80b ⟩ ≡
> *// Declare some storage for some "external" vertex properties.*
> **char** *name* **[ ] =** *"ABCDEFGH"* **;**
> *array*<*int,* *n_vertices*> *parent* **;**
> **for** **(int** *i* **= 0;** *i* < *n_vertices* **; ++i)**
>   *parent* **[i] =** *i* **;**
> *array*<*float,* *n_vertices*> *distance* **;**
> *distance* **.** *assign* **(** *std::numeric_limits*<*float*>*::max* **( )) ;**
> *// Specify A as the source vertex*
> *distance* **[A] = 0;**

Since the vertex descriptors of the ***edge_list*** graph are integers, pointers to the property arrays qualify as property maps because the Boost Property Map Library includes specializations for built-in pointer types (see §15.2.1).

The following shows the call to ***bellman_ford_shortest_paths*** **( )**. The shortest-path distances are recorded in the distance vector and the parent of each vertex (with respect to the shortest-paths tree) is recorded in the parent vector.

⟨ Call the Bellman–Ford algorithm 80c ⟩ ≡
> **bool** *r* **=** *bellman_ford_shortest_paths* **(** *g* **, int (** *n_vertices* **) ,**
>   *weight_map* **(** ⟨ *Create property map for delays 80a* ⟩ **) .**
>   *distance_map* **(&** *distance* **[0]) .**
>   *predecessor_map* **(&** *parent* **[0])) ;**

The program concludes by printing out the predecessors and distances for each router in the network, or by notifying the user that there was a negative cycle in the network.

⟨ Output distances and parents 81 ⟩ ≡

```
if (r)
  for (int i = 0; i < n_vertices; ++i)
    std::cout << name[i] << ": " << distance[i]
        << " " << name[parent[i]] << std::endl;
else
  std::cout << "negative cycle" << std::endl;
```

Applied to the example input, the program output is as follows:

```
A: 0    A
B: 5    A
C: 1    A
D: 6.3  B
E: 6.7  D
F: 3    C
G: 4.2  F
H: 4.7  G
```

Thus, by working backward through the predecessors, we can see that the shortest path from router A to router H is $\langle A, C, F, G, H \rangle$.

5.4 Dijkstra and Link-State Routing

By the early 1980s there began to be concerns about the scalability of distance-vector routing. Two particular aspects caused problems:

- In environments where the topology of the network changes frequently, distance-vector routing would converge too slowly to maintain accurate distance information.

- Update messages contain distances to all nodes, so the message size grows with the size of the entire network.

As a result of these problems, *link-state routing* was developed [28, 37]. With link-state routing each router stores a graph representing the topology of the entire network and computes its routing table based on the graph using Dijkstra's single-source shortest-paths algorithm. To keep the graph up to date, routers share information about which links are "up" and which are "down" (the link state). When connectivity changes are detected, the information is "flooded" throughout the network in what is called a *link-state advertisement*.

Since only local information (neighbor connectivity) has to be shared, link-state routing does not have the message-size problems of distance vector routing. Also, since each router computes its own shortest paths, it takes much less time to react to changes in the network and recalculate accurate routing tables. One disadvantage of link-state routing is that it places more of a burden on each router in terms of computation and memory use. Even so, it has proved to be an effective protocol, and is now formalized in the Open Shortest Path First protocol (OSPF) [33], which is currently one of the preferred interior gateway routing protocols.

Dijkstra's algorithm finds all the shortest paths from the source vertex to every other vertex by iteratively growing the set of vertices S to which it knows the shortest path. At each step of the algorithm, the vertex in $V - S$ with the smallest distance label is added to S. Then the out-edges of the vertex are relaxed using the same technique from the Bellman–Ford algorithm, $d[v] = \min(w(u, v) + d[u], d[v])$. The algorithm then loops back, processing the next vertex in $V - S$ with the lowest distance label. The algorithm finishes when S contains all vertices reachable from the source vertex.

In the rest of this section we will show how to use the BGL *dijkstra_shortest_paths* ( ) function to solve the single-source shortest-paths problem for a network of routers and how this information is used to compute a routing table. Figure 5.3 shows the example network described in RFC 1583. In the figure, RT stands for router, N stands for network (which is a group of addresses treated as a single destination entity), and H stands for host.

To demonstrate Dijkstra's algorithm, we will compute the shortest-path tree for router six. The main steps of our program are as follows:

⟨ *ospf-example.cpp* 82 ⟩ ≡

```
#include <fstream> // for file I/O
#include <boost/graph/graphviz.hpp> // for read/write_graphviz()
#include <boost/graph/dijkstra_shortest_paths.hpp>
#include <boost/lexical_cast.hpp>
int main ( )
{
  using namespace boost;
  ⟨Read directed graph in from Graphviz dot file 84a⟩
  ⟨Copy the directed graph, converting string labels to integer weights 84b⟩
  ⟨Find router six 84c⟩
  ⟨Setup parent property map to record the shortest-paths tree 85a⟩
  ⟨Run the Dijkstra algorithm 85b⟩
  ⟨Set the color of the edges in the shortest-paths tree to black 85c⟩
  ⟨Write the new graph to a Graphviz dot file 85d⟩
  ⟨Write the routing table for router six 87a⟩
  return EXIT_SUCCESS;
}
```

The first step is to create the graph. The graph from Figure 5.3 is represented as a Graphviz dot file. The Graphviz package provides tools that automatically lay out and draw graphs. It is available at *www.graphviz.org*. The Graphviz tools use a special file format for graphs, called dot files. BGL includes a parser for reading this file format into a BGL graph. The parser can be accessed through the *read_graphviz* ( ) function defined in *boost/graph/graphviz.hpp*. Since the graph is directed, we use the *GraphvizDigraph* type. For an undirected graph we would use the *GraphvizGraph* type.

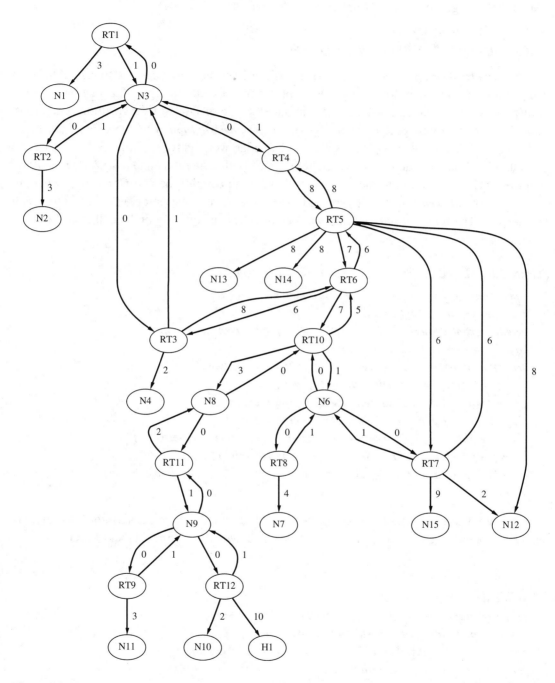

Figure 5.3 A directed graph representing a group of Internet routers using the same routing protocol. The edges are weighted with the cost of transmission.

⟨ Read directed graph in from Graphviz dot file 84a ⟩ ≡

> *GraphvizDigraph g_dot;*
> *read_graphviz ("figs/ospf-graph.dot ", g_dot) ;*

The *GraphvizDigraph* type stores the properties of vertices and edges as strings. Although strings may be convenient for file I/O and display purposes, edge weights must be represented as integers so that they can be easily manipulated inside of Dijkstra's algorithm. Therefore, *g_dot* is copied to a new graph. Each edge in the *GraphvizDigraph* type has a set of attributes stored in a *std::map<std::string, std::string>*. The edge weights from Figure 5.3 are stored in the "label" attribute of each edge. The label is converted to an *int* using *boost::lexical_cast* and then the edge is inserted into the new graph. Since the *Graph* type and *GraphvizDigraph* are both based on *adjacency_list* with *VertexList=vecS*, the vertex descriptor types for both graph are integers. The result of *source(*ei, g_dot)* can thus be used directly in the call to *add_edge ( )* on graph *g*.

⟨ Copy the directed graph, converting string labels to integer weights 84b ⟩ ≡

> *typedef adjacency_list<vecS, vecS, directedS, no_property,*
>   *property<edge_weight_t, int> > Graph;*
> *typedef graph_traits<Graph>::vertex_descriptor vertex_descriptor;*
> *Graph g (num_vertices (g_dot)) ;*
> *property_map<GraphvizDigraph, edge_attribute_t>::type*
>   *edge_attr_map = get (edge_attribute, g_dot) ;*
> *graph_traits<GraphvizDigraph>::edge_iterator ei, ei_end;*
> *for (tie (ei, ei_end) = edges (g_dot) ; ei != ei_end; ++ei) {*
>   *int weight = lexical_cast<int> (edge_attr_map [*ei] ["label"]) ;*
>   *property<edge_weight_t, int> edge_property (weight) ;*
>   *add_edge (source (*ei, g_dot) , target (*ei, g_dot) , edge_property, g) ;*
> *}*

To use router six as the source of the shortest-paths search, the vertex descriptor for router six must be located. The program searches for the vertex with an attribute label of "RT6."

⟨ Find router six 84c ⟩ ≡

> *vertex_descriptor router_six;*
> *property_map<GraphvizDigraph, vertex_attribute_t>::type*
>   *vertex_attr_map = get (vertex_attribute, g_dot) ;*
> *graph_traits<GraphvizDigraph>::vertex_iterator vi, vi_end;*
> *for (tie (vi, vi_end) = vertices (g_dot) ; vi != vi_end; ++vi)*
>   *if ("RT6 " == vertex_attr_map [*vi] ["label"]) {*
>   *router_six = *vi; break;*
>   *}*

Together, the shortest paths from router six to all other routers form a shortest-paths tree. An efficient way to represent such a tree is to record the parent of each node in the tree. Here we simply use a *std::vector* to record the parents.

⟨ Setup parent property map to record the shortest-paths tree 85a ⟩ ≡

```
std::vector<vertex_descriptor> parent(num_vertices(g));
// All vertices start out as their own parent
typedef graph_traits<Graph>::vertices_size_type size_type;
for (size_type p = 0; p < num_vertices(g); ++p)
  parent[p] = p;
```

We are now ready to invoke Dijkstra's algorithm. We pass in the parent array as the argument to the *predecessor_map()* named parameter.

⟨ Run the Dijkstra algorithm 85b ⟩ ≡

```
dijkstra_shortest_paths(g, router_six, predecessor_map(&parent[0]));
```

Next we set the color attribute of the tree edges to black in preparation for printing the graph to a Graphviz dot file. The tree edges have been recorded in the *parent* array. For every vertex i in the graph, edge $(parent[i], i)$ is a tree edge, unless $parent[i] = i$, in which case i is the root vertex or an unreachable vertex.

⟨ Set the color of the edges in the shortest-paths tree to black 85c ⟩ ≡

```
graph_traits<GraphvizDigraph>::edge_descriptor e;
for (size_type i = 0; i < num_vertices(g); ++i)
  if (parent[i] != i) {
    e = edge(parent[i], i, g_dot).first;
    edge_attr_map[e]["color"] = "black";
  }
```

Now we write the graph to a dot file. The default color for the edges is set to gray (for non-tree edges). Figure 5.4 shows the computed shortest-paths tree for router six.

⟨ Write the new graph to a Graphviz dot file 85d ⟩ ≡

```
graph_property<GraphvizDigraph, graph_edge_attribute_t>::type&
  graph_edge_attr_map = get_property(g_dot, graph_edge_attribute);
graph_edge_attr_map["color"]="gray";
write_graphviz("figs/ospf-sptree.dot", g_dot);
```

The last step is to compute the routing table for router six. The routing table has three columns: the destination, the next hop that should be taken to get to the destination, and the total cost to reach the destination. To populate the routing table, entries are created for each destination in the network. The information for each entry can be created by following the shortest path backward from the destination to router six using the parent map. A node that is its own parent is skipped because the node is either router six or the node is not reachable from router six.

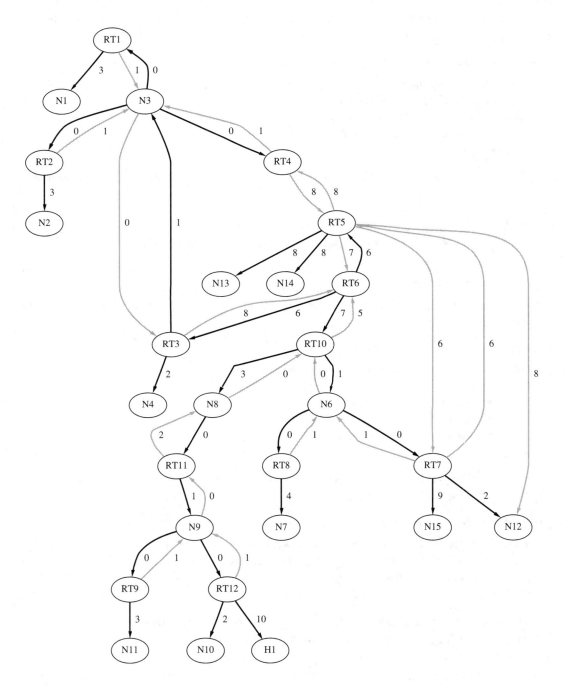

Figure 5.4 The shortest-paths tree for router six.

⟨ Write the routing table for router six 87a ⟩ ≡

```
std::ofstream rtable ("routing-table.dat");
rtable << "Dest     Next Hop    Total Cost" << std::endl;
for (tie(vi, vi_end) = vertices(g_dot); vi != vi_end; ++vi)
  if (parent[*vi] != *vi) {
    rtable << vertex_attr_map[*vi]["label"] << "     ";
    ⟨Follow path backward to router six using parents 87b⟩
  }
```

While following the path from each destination to router six, the edge weights are accumulated into the total *path_cost*. We also record the child of the current vertex because at loop termination this is the vertex to use as the next hop.

⟨ Follow path backward to router six using parents 87b ⟩ ≡

```
vertex_descriptor v = *vi, child;
int path_cost = 0;
property_map<Graph, edge_weight_t>::type
weight_map = get(edge_weight, g);
do {
  path_cost += get(weight_map, edge(parent[v], v, g).first);
  child = v;
  v = parent[v];
} while (v != parent[v]);
rtable << vertex_attr_map[child]["label"] << "       ";
rtable << path_cost << std::endl;
```

The resulting routing table is as follows.

Dest	Next Hop	Total Cost
RT1	RT3	7
RT2	RT3	7
RT3	RT3	6
RT4	RT3	7
RT5	RT5	6
RT7	RT10	8
RT8	RT10	8
RT9	RT10	11
RT10	RT10	7
RT11	RT10	10
RT12	RT10	11
N1	RT3	10
N2	RT3	10
N3	RT3	7

N4	*RT3*	**8**
N6	*RT10*	**8**
N7	*RT10*	**12**
N8	*RT10*	**10**
N9	*RT10*	**11**
N10	*RT10*	**13**
N12	*RT10*	**10**
N13	*RT5*	**14**
N14	*RT5*	**14**
N15	*RT10*	**17**
H1	*RT10*	**21**

Chapter 6

Minimum-Spanning-Tree Problem

The Boost Graph Library implements two classical algorithms for solving the minimum-spanning-tree problem: Kruskal's [23] and Prim's [38]. The minimum-spanning-tree problem shows up in many application domains such as telephone network planning, electronic circuit layout, and data storage compression. In this chapter we apply the BGL algorithms to the telephone network planning problem.

6.1 Definitions

The *minimum-spanning-tree problem* is defined as follows. Given an undirected graph $G = (V, E)$, find an acyclic subset of the edges $T \subseteq E$ that connects all of the vertices in the graph and whose total weight is minimized. The total weight is the sum of the weight of the edges in T:

$$w(T) = \sum_{(u,v) \in T} w(u, v).$$

An acyclic subset of edges that connects all the vertices in the graph is called a *spanning tree*. A tree T with minimum total weight is a *minimum spanning tree*.

6.2 Telephone Network Planning

Suppose that you are responsible for setting up the telephone lines for a remote region. The region consists of several towns and a network of roads. Setting up a telephone line requires access for the trucks, and hence, a road alongside the route for the line. Your budget is quite small, so building new roads is out of the question and the telephone lines have to go in along existing roads. Also, you would like to minimize the total length of wire required to connect all the towns in the region.

Since the region is sparsely populated, considerations such as bandwidth are not important. Figure 6.1 shows the network of roads connecting the towns abstracted into a weighted graph. Our goal is to find an optimal layout for the telephone lines. First we solve the problem using Kruskal's algorithm, then we solve it with Prim's algorithm.

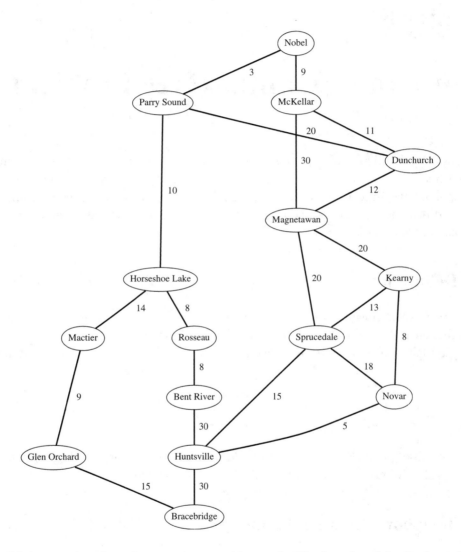

Figure 6.1 A remote region of towns connected by roads. The lengths of the roads are labeled in miles.

6.3 Kruskal's Algorithm

Kruskal's algorithm starts with each vertex in a tree by itself and with no edges in the set T, which becomes the minimum spanning tree. The algorithm then examines each edge in the graph in order of increasing edge weight. If an edge connects two vertices in different trees, the algorithm merges the two trees into a single tree and adds the edge to T. Once all of the edges have been examined, the tree T will span the graph (assuming the graph is connected) and the tree will be a minimum spanning tree.

Following is the outline of a program that applies the ***kruskal_minimum_spanning_tree( )*** function to compute the best layout for the telephone lines.

⟨ ***kruskal-telephone.cpp* 91a** ⟩ ≡

```
#include <iostream>
#include <fstream>
#include <boost/lexical_cast.hpp>
#include <boost/graph/graphviz.hpp>
#include <boost/graph/kruskal_min_spanning_tree.hpp>

int main()
{
  using namespace boost;
  ⟨Read undirected graph in from Graphviz dot file 91b⟩
  ⟨Copy the undirected graph, converting string labels to integer weights 91c⟩
  ⟨Call Kruskal's algorithm and store MST in a vector 92a⟩
  ⟨Compute the weight of the spanning tree 92b⟩
  ⟨Mark tree edges with black lines and output to a dot file 92c⟩
  return EXIT_SUCCESS;
}
```

The graph for Figure 6.1 is stored in a Graphviz dot file so it is read into memory using the ***read_graphviz( )*** function from ***boost/graph/graphviz.hpp***. The ***GraphvizGraph*** type is used since this example uses an undirected graph.

⟨ Read undirected graph in from Graphviz dot file 91b ⟩ ≡

```
GraphvizGraph g_dot;
read_graphviz("figs/telephone-network.dot", g_dot);
```

As in §5.4, the edge labels need to be converted from strings to integers. This is accomplished by copying the ***GraphvizGraph*** to a new graph and by using ***lexical_cast*** to perform the string to integer conversion.

⟨ Copy the undirected graph, converting string labels to integer weights 91c ⟩ ≡

```
typedef adjacency_list<vecS, vecS, undirectedS, no_property,
  property<edge_weight_t, int> > Graph;
```

```
Graph g (num_vertices (g_dot) ) ;
property_map<GraphvizGraph, edge_attribute_t>::type
    edge_attr_map = get (edge_attribute, g_dot) ;
graph_traits<GraphvizGraph>::edge_iterator ei, ei_end;
for (tie (ei, ei_end) = edges (g_dot) ; ei != ei_end; ++ei) {
    int weight = lexical_cast<int> ( edge_attr_map [*ei] ["label"] ) ;
    property<edge_weight_t, int> edge_property (weight) ;
    add_edge (source (*ei, g_dot) , target (*ei, g_dot) , edge_property, g) ;
}
```

The call to Kruskal's algorithm requires that the graph type used be both a VertexListGraph and a EdgeListGraph. The "Model Of" section in the documentation for adjacency_list shows that the selected *Graph* type should work fine. To store the output of the algorithm (the edges of the minimum spanning tree), we use a *std::vector mst* and apply *std::back_inserter ()* to create an output iterator from it. There are a number of named parameters for Kruskal's algorithm; for this example, defaults are used for all of them. The weight map and vertex index map are, by default, obtained from the graph (they are internal properties). *edge_weight_t* is declared as a property for the *Graph* type and the vertex index map is automatically there for an *adjacency_list* with *VertexList=vecS*. The rank and predecessor maps (which are only used internal to Kruskal's algorithm) are by default created inside the algorithm.

⟨ Call Kruskal's algorithm and store MST in a vector 92a ⟩ ≡

```
std::vector<graph_traits<Graph>::edge_descriptor> mst;
kruskal_minimum_spanning_tree (g, std::back_inserter (mst) ) ;
```

When the call to the algorithm returns, the minimum spanning tree is now stored in *mst*. The total weight of the tree is computed by summing the weights of the edges in *mst*. The total edge weight computed for this minimum spanning tree is 145 miles.

⟨ Compute the weight of the spanning tree 92b ⟩ ≡

```
property_map<Graph, edge_weight_t>::type weight = get (edge_weight, g) ;
int total_weight = 0;
for (int e = 0; e < mst.size () ; ++e)
    total_weight += get (weight, mst [e] ) ;
std::cout << "total weight: " << total_weight << std::endl;
```

The tree edges are then colored black and the graph is saved to a dot file.

⟨ Mark tree edges with black lines and output to a dot file 92c ⟩ ≡

```
typedef graph_traits<Graph>::vertex_descriptor Vertex;
for (int i = 0; i < mst.size () ; ++i) {
    Vertex u = source (mst [i] , g) , v = target (mst [i] , g) ;
    edge_attr_map [edge (u, v, g_dot) .first] ["color"] = "black";
}
```

```
std::ofstream out ( "figs/telephone-mst-kruskal.dot ") ;
graph_property<GraphvizGraph, graph_edge_attribute_t>::type&
   graph_edge_attr_map = get_property (g_dot, graph_edge_attribute) ;
graph_edge_attr_map [ "color "] = "gray ";
graph_edge_attr_map [ "style "] = "bold ";
write_graphviz (out, g_dot) ;
```

The resulting minimum spanning tree is shown in Figure 6.2.

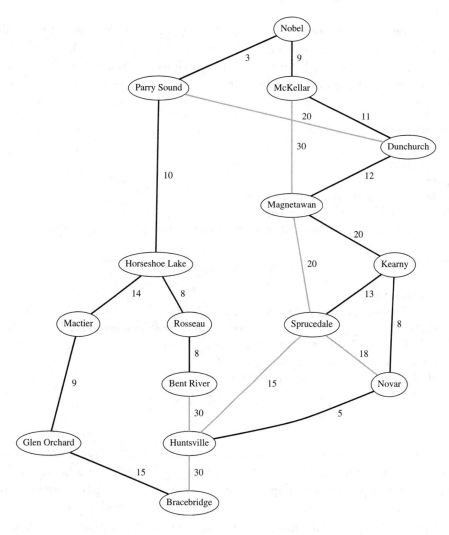

Figure 6.2 The minimum spanning tree, which is the optimal layout for the telephone lines, is indicated by the black lines.

6.4   Prim's Algorithm

Prim's algorithm grows the minimum spanning tree one vertex at a time (instead of one edge at a time, as in Kruskal's algorithm). The basic idea of Prim's algorithm is to add vertices to the minimum spanning tree based on which of the remaining vertices shares an edge having minimum weight with any of the vertices already in the tree. Prim's algorithm is similar to Dijkstra's algorithm. (In fact, the BGL implementation of Prim's algorithm is simply a call to Dijkstra's algorithm, with a special choice for the distance comparison and combine functions.)

In this section, the BGL *prim_minimum_spanning_tree* **( )** algorithm is applied to the same telephone network planning problem from Figure 6.1. The main outline of the program is similar to the use of Kruskal's algorithm in the previous section, although there are some differences in how Prim's algorithm outputs the spanning tree edges.

⟨ *prim-telephone.cpp* 94 ⟩ ≡

```
#include <iostream>
#include <fstream>
#include <vector>
#include <boost/lexical_cast.hpp>
#include <boost/graph/graphviz.hpp>
#include <boost/graph/prim_minimum_spanning_tree.hpp>

int main ( )
{
  using namespace boost;
  ⟨Read undirected graph in from Graphviz dot file 91b⟩
  ⟨Copy the undirected graph, converting string labels to integer weights 91c⟩
  ⟨Call Prim's algorithm and record MST in predecessors 95a⟩
  ⟨Calculate the weight of the spanning tree 95b⟩
  ⟨Mark the tree edges and output to a dot file 95c⟩
  return EXIT_SUCCESS;
}
```

The first two steps, reading from the dot file and copying the graph, are the same as in the previous section. In the call to Prim's algorithm, the first parameter is the graph and the second parameter is a predecessor map. The predecessor map records the minimum spanning tree. For each vertex v in the graph, $parent[v]$ is the parent of v with respect to the minimum spanning tree. Inside the algorithm, $parent[v]$ may be assigned to multiple times, but the last assignment is guaranteed to set the correct parent. A number of named parameters for *prim_minimum_spanning_tree* **( )** can be used to fine-tune various aspects of the function, but default values for all named parameters are used here. The edge weight and vertex index maps internal to the **Graph** type are used, and the color and distance utility maps are constructed inside of the algorithm. The root vertex defaults to **vertices(g).first*, which is acceptable here because the choice of the root for the minimum spanning tree is arbitrary.

⟨ Call Prim's algorithm and record MST in predecessors 95a ⟩ ≡

```
typedef graph_traits<Graph>::vertex_descriptor Vertex;
std::vector<Vertex> parent(num_vertices(g));
prim_minimum_spanning_tree(g, &parent[0]);
```

With the minimum spanning tree recorded in the **parent** array, the total weight is calculated by looping through all the vertices in the graph and summing the weight of each edge $(parent[v], v)$. If $parent[v] = v$ we know that either v is the root of the tree or it was not in the same connected component as the rest of the vertices, so in either case $(parent[v], v)$ is not a spanning tree edge and should be skipped. Again, the calculation for the graph of Figure 6.1 results in a total edge weight of 145 miles.

⟨ Calculate the weight of the spanning tree 95b ⟩ ≡

```
property_map<Graph, edge_weight_t>::type weight = get(edge_weight, g);
int total_weight = 0;
for (int v = 0; v < num_vertices(g); ++v)
  if (parent[v] != v)
    total_weight += get(weight, edge(parent[v], v, g).first);
std::cout << "total weight: " << total_weight << std::endl;
```

For display purposes, the edges of the minimum spanning tree are marked with black lines and then written to a dot file. The resulting minimum spanning tree is shown in Figure 6.3. Note that the tree here is slightly different than the one produced by Kruskal's algorithm. Instead of having an edge between Magnetawan and Kearny, there is an edge between Magnetawan and Sprucedale. This highlights the fact that minimum spanning trees are not unique; there can be more than one minimum spanning tree for a particular graph.

⟨ Mark the tree edges and output to a dot file 95c ⟩ ≡

```
for (int u = 0; u < num_vertices(g); ++u)
  if (parent[u] != u)
    edge_attr_map[edge(parent[u], u, g_dot).first]["color"] = "black";
std::ofstream out("figs/telephone-mst-prim.dot");
graph_property<GraphvizGraph, graph_edge_attribute_t>::type&
  graph_edge_attr_map = get_property(g_dot, graph_edge_attribute);
graph_edge_attr_map["color"] = "gray";
write_graphviz(out, g_dot);
```

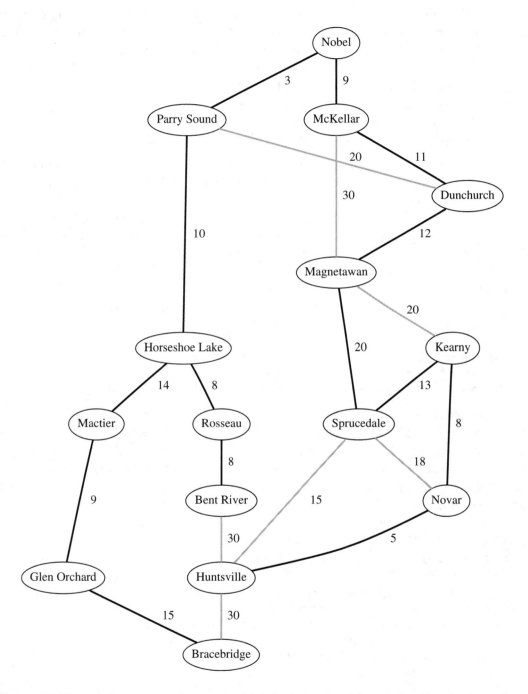

Figure 6.3 The minimum spanning tree, which is the optimal layout for the telephone lines, is indicated by the black lines.

Chapter 7

Connected Components

One basic question about a network is which vertices are reachable from one another. For example, a well designed Web site should have enough links between Web pages so that all pages can be reached from the home page. In addition, it is often nice to have links going back to the home page, or at least to the previous page in a sequence. In a directed graph, groups of vertices that are mutually reachable are called *strongly connected components*. In an undirected graph, groups of vertices that are reachable from one another are called *connected components*.

A study of 200 million Web pages has shown that 56 million of the Web pages on the Internet form one large strongly connected component [7]. The study also showed that when viewed as an undirected graph, there are 150 million pages in one large connected component and about 50 million pages that are disconnected from the large component (they reside in much smaller connected components of their own).

The BGL provides two functions for computing all the connected components of a graph, one for when the graph is unchanging (or if the connected components only need to be computed once) and one for when the graph is growing. The BGL also implements Tarjan's algorithm for computing the strongly connected components of a graph in linear time.

In the following sections, we start with some definitions and then apply the BGL connected components functions to World Wide Web networks.

7.1 Definitions

A *path* is a sequence of vertices where there is an edge connecting each vertex to the next vertex in the path. If there exists a path from vertex u to w, then we say that vertex w is *reachable* from vertex u. A *connected component* is a group of vertices in an undirected graph that are reachable from one another. A *strongly connected component* is a group of vertices in a directed graph that are mutually reachable from one another. The reachable relation for undirected graphs and the mutually reachable relation for directed graphs are

equivalence relations: they are reflexive, symmetric, and transitive. The objects for which
an equivalence relationship is true form an *equivalence class*. A connected component is
therefore an equivalence class with respect to the reachable relation, and likewise a strongly
connected component is an equivalence class under the mutually reachable relation. As a
result, these two reachable relations partition the vertices of a graph into disjoint subsets.

7.2   Connected Components and Internet Connectivity

Computing the connected components of an undirected graph is a straightforward application
of depth-first search. The idea is to run DFS on the graph and mark all vertices in the same
DFS tree as belonging to the same connected component. The BGL implementation of *connected_components* ( ) calls *depth_first_search* ( ) with a special visitor object that labels each
discovered vertex with the current component and increments the current component at the
"start vertex" event point.

The steps to computing the connected components of the network shown in Figure 7.1
are as follows: (1) read the network into memory, (2) represent it with a BGL graph, and
(3) call the *connected_components* ( ) function. Each vertex in the graph is assigned an integer
denoting the component to which the vertex belongs. The following gives an outline of the
program.

⟨ *cc-internet.cpp* 98a ⟩ ≡

```
#include <fstream>
#include <vector>
#include <string>
#include <boost/graph/connected_components.hpp>
#include <boost/graph/graphviz.hpp>

int main ( )
{
   using namespace boost;
   ⟨Read graph into memory 98b⟩
   ⟨Create storage for component assignments 100a⟩
   ⟨Call connected components function 100b⟩
   ⟨Color vertices by component and write to a dot file 100c⟩
}
```

The graph of Figure 7.1 is read in from the file *cc-internet.dot*, which is in Graphviz dot
format. The *GraphvizGraph* type was chosen (and not *GraphvizDigraph*) because the graph to
be represented is undirected.

⟨ Read graph into memory 98b ⟩ ≡

```
GraphvizGraph g;
read_graphviz ( "figs/cc-internet.dot", g);
```

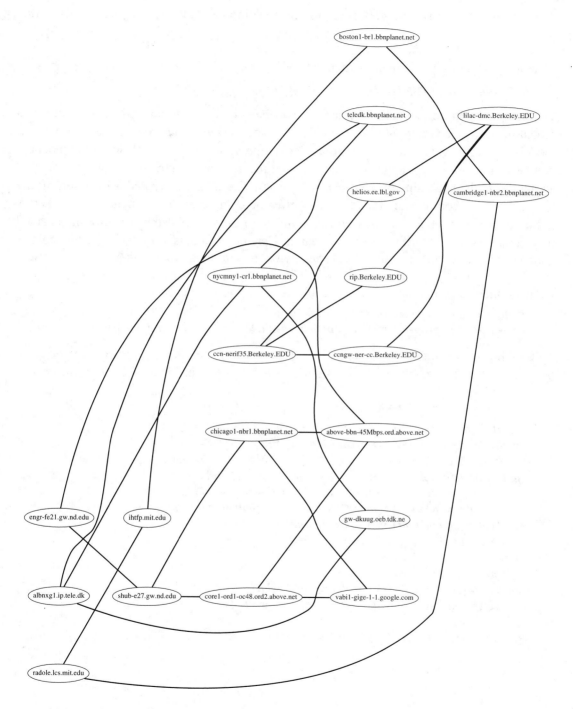

Figure 7.1 A collection of Internet routers with edges denoting direct connections.

A vector of size *num_vertices(g)* is used to store the component integer assigned to each vertex in the graph.

⟨ Create storage for component assignments 100a ⟩ ≡
    std::vector<int> component (num_vertices (g));

The first argument in the call to *connected_components* () is the graph type, which must be a model of VertexListGraph and IncidenceGraph. The *GraphvizGraph* type is suitable since it models these concepts. The second argument is a property map from vertices to component numbers. The property map is constructed using the *iterator_property_map* adaptor, wrapping an iterator to the beginning of the *component* vector. The *connected_components* () returns the total number of components found, and records the component assignment for each vertex in the *component* vector. The *connected_components* () algorithm also has a color map named parameter that is used for the depth-first search. Here the default is used; the algorithm creates the color map internally and uses the vertex index map of the graph to index into the array.

⟨ Call connected components function 100b ⟩ ≡
    int num_comp = connected_components (g,
      make_iterator_property_map (component.begin (), get (vertex_index, g)));

To visualize the results of the computation, colors are assigned to each vertex based on component number. The graph is then written to a Graphviz dot file. Figure 7.2 shows the results.

⟨ Color vertices by component and write to a dot file 100c ⟩ ≡
    property_map<GraphvizGraph, vertex_attribute_t>::type
      vertex_attr_map = get (vertex_attribute, g);
    std::string color[] = { "white", "gray", "black", "lightgray" };
    graph_traits<GraphvizGraph>::vertex_iterator vi, vi_end;
    for (tie (vi, vi_end) = vertices (g); vi != vi_end; ++vi) {
      *vertex_attr_map [*vi] ["color"] = color[component [*vi]];*
      *if (color[component [*vi]] == "white")*
        *vertex_attr_map [*vi] .erase ("color");*
      else
        *vertex_attr_map [*vi] ["style"] = "filled";*
      *if (vertex_attr_map [*vi] ["color"] == "black")*
        *vertex_attr_map [*vi] ["fontcolor"] = "white";*
    }
    write_graphviz ("figs/cc-internet-out.dot", g);

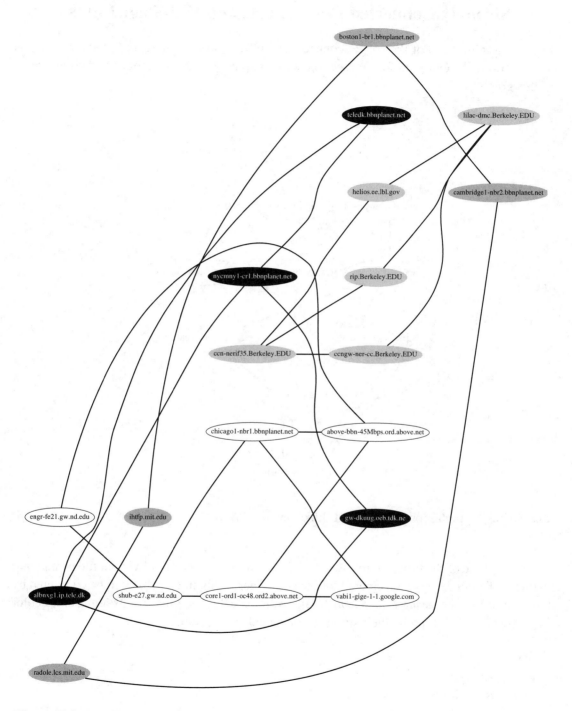

Figure 7.2 The connected components.

7.3   Strongly Connected Components and Web Page Links

Figure 7.3 shows a set of Web pages connected by URL links that are represented abstractly as a directed graph. Our goal for this section is to compute the strongly connected components of this graph.

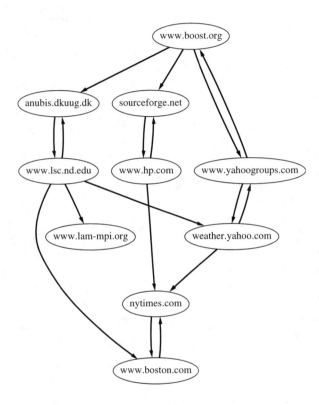

Figure 7.3 A graph representing URL links between Web sites.

The outline of the program follows. First, the graph from the Graphviz dot file is read into memory. The storage is then created for the component assignments that will be computed by the algorithm. The **strong_components ( )** algorithm is called and the results are used to color the vertices of the graph by their strongly connected component.

⟨ *scc.cpp* 102 ⟩ ≡

```
#include  <fstream>
#include  <map>
#include  <string>
#include  <boost/graph/strong_components.hpp>
#include  <boost/graph/graphviz.hpp>
```

```
int main ( )
{
  using namespace boost;
  ⟨Read directed graph into memory 103a⟩
  ⟨Allocate storage for component assignments 103b⟩
  ⟨Call strong components function 103c⟩
  ⟨Color vertices by component number and write to a dot file 104⟩
  return EXIT_SUCCESS;
}
```

The graph is read from the *scc.dot* file using the *GraphvizDigraph* type (because the graph is directed).

⟨ Read directed graph into memory 103a ⟩ ≡

```
GraphvizDigraph g;
read_graphviz ( "figs/scc.dot ", g ) ;
```

In the call to *strong_components* ( ), the *associative_property_map* adaptor is used to supply the property map interface required by the function. This adaptor creates a property map out of an AssociativeContainer such as *std::map*. The choice of *std::map* to implement the property map is rather inefficient in this case but demonstrates the flexibility of the property map interface. The vertex descriptor for *GraphvizDigraph* is an integer, so it has the required less-than operator required of *std::map*.

⟨ Allocate storage for component assignments 103b ⟩ ≡

```
typedef graph_traits<GraphvizDigraph>::vertex_descriptor vertex_t;
std::map<vertex_t, int> component;
```

The results of calling the *strong_components* ( ) algorithm are placed in the *component* array, assigning each vertex a component number. The component numbers are from zero to *num_comp - 1*. The graph passed to the *strong_components* ( ) function must be a model of the VertexListGraph and IncidenceGraph concepts—and indeed, the *GraphvizDigraph* meets these criteria. The second argument, the component map, must be a ReadWritePropertyMap. There are several more named parameters that can be specified, but they are all for utility property maps that are only used internally. By default, the algorithm creates arrays for these property maps and uses the vertex index property of the graph as an offset into them.

⟨ Call strong components function 103c ⟩ ≡

```
int num_comp = strong_components (g, make_assoc_property_map (component)) ;
```

The program finishes by coloring the vertices according to the component to which they belong. The output is written to a dot file, which produces the graph in Figure 7.4.

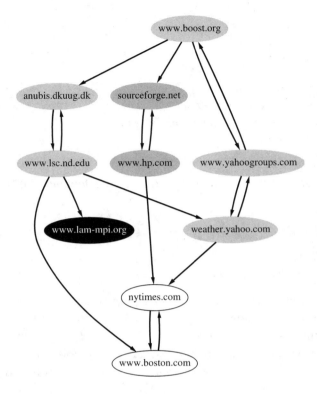

Figure 7.4 The strongly connected components.

⟨ Color vertices by component number and write to a dot file 104 ⟩ ≡

```
property_map<GraphvizDigraph, vertex_attribute_t>::type
  vertex_attr_map = get(vertex_attribute, g);
std::string color[] = { "white", "gray", "black", "lightgray" };
graph_traits<GraphvizDigraph>::vertex_iterator vi, vi_end;
for (tie(vi, vi_end) = vertices(g); vi != vi_end; ++vi) {
  vertex_attr_map[*vi]["color"] = color[component[*vi]];
  if (color[component[*vi]] == "white")
    vertex_attr_map[*vi].erase("color");
  else
    vertex_attr_map[*vi]["style"] = "filled";
  if (vertex_attr_map[*vi]["color"] == "black")
    vertex_attr_map[*vi]["fontcolor"] = "white";
}
write_graphviz("figs/scc-out.dot", g);
```

Chapter 8

Maximum Flow

The maximum-flow problem is the problem of determining how much of some quantity (say, water) can move through a network.

There is a long history of algorithms for solving the maximum-flow problem, with the first algorithm due to Ford and Fulkerson [12]. The best general-purpose algorithm known to date is the push-relabel algorithm of Goldberg [9, 16, 17], which is based on the notion of a *preflow* introduced by Karzanov [20].

The BGL contains two algorithms for computing maximum flows. The Edmunds–Karp algorithm (a refinement of the original Ford–Fulkerson) and the push-relabel algorithm.

8.1 Definitions

A *flow network* is a directed graph $G = (V, E)$ with a *source* vertex s and a *sink* vertex t. Each edge has a positive real-valued *capacity* and there is a *flow function* f defined over every vertex pair. The flow function must satisfy three contraints:

$$f(u, v) \leq c(u, v) \quad \forall\, (u, v) \in V \times V \qquad \text{(Capacity constraint)}$$
$$f(u, v) = -f(v, u) \quad \forall\, (u, v) \in V \times V \qquad \text{(Skew symmetry)}$$
$$\sum_{v \in V} f(u, v) = 0 \quad \forall\, u \in V - \{s, t\} \qquad \text{(Flow conservation)}$$

The *flow* of the network is the net flow entering the sink vertex t. The *residual capacity* of an edge is $r(u, v) = c(u, v) - f(u, v)$. The edges with $r(u, v) > 0$ are residual edges E_f that induce the residual graph $G_f = (V, E_f)$. An edge with $r(u, v) = 0$ is *saturated*.

$$|f| = \sum_{u \in V} f(u, t)$$

The maximum-flow problem is to determine the maximum possible value for $|f|$ and the corresponding flow values for every vertex pair in the graph.

An important property of a flow network is that the maximum flow is related to the capacity of the narrowest part of the network. According to the Max-Flow Min-Cut Theorem [12], the maximum value of the flow from a source vertex s to a sink vertex t in a flow network equals the minimum capacity among all (S, T) cuts. An (S, T) *cut* is a separation of the graph's vertices into two sets S and T, where $s \in S$ and $t \in T$. Any edge with its source vertex in S and its target vertex in T is a *forward edge* of the cut, and any edge with its source in T and target in S is a *backward edge* of the cut. The *capacity of a cut* is the sum of the capacities of the forward edges (backward edges are ignored). So if we look at the capacity for all the cuts that separate s and t, and select the cut with the minimum capacity, then its capacity will equal the maximum flow of the network.

8.2   Edge Connectivity

Whether an engineer is designing a telephone network, a LAN for a large company, or the router connections for the Internet backbone, an important consideration is how resilient the network is to damage. For example, if a cable gets cut during a storm, are there other cables through which the information can flow? In graph terminology, this is captured by the *edge connectivity* of a graph, which is the minimum number of edges that can be cut to produce a graph with two disconnected components (assuming the graph started as a single connected component). We use $\alpha(G)$ to represent the edge connectivity of a graph. The set of edges in the cut is called the *minimum disconnecting set*. The vertices of the graph are separated into two components, S^* and $\overline{S^*}$, so we use the notation $[S^*, \overline{S^*}]$ for representing the minimum cut. It turns out that calculating the edge connectivity of a graph can be reduced to a series of maximum-flow problems. In this section we take a look at the algorithm for computing the edge connectivity of an undirected graph [27].

Let $\alpha(u, v)$ represent the minimum number of edges that can be cut to disconnect the two vertices u and v from each other. If the two vertices are treated as source and sink and the capacity of every edge is set to one, then the minimum capacity cut (calculated by a maximum flow algorithm) is the same as the cut with the minimum number of edges. Therefore, by solving for the maximum flow we also determine the minimum number of edges that could be cut to disconnect the two vertices. Now, to find the edge connectivity of the whole graph, a maximum-flow algorithm can be run on every pair of vertices. The minimum of all these pair-wise min-cuts will be the min-cut for the graph.

Executing maximum flow for every pair of vertices is expensive, so it would be better to reduce the number of pairs that need to be examined. This can be achieved by exploiting a special property of the minimum disconnecting set $[S^*, \overline{S^*}]$. Let p be a vertex of minimum degree and δ be the minimum degree. If $\alpha(G) = \delta$, then S^* is just p. If $\alpha(G) \leq \delta - 1$, then it turns out that for any subset of S^*, call it S, the set of all nonneighbor vertices to the vertices in S has to be nonempty. This means that the minimum cut can be found by starting with

$S = p$, picking a vertex k from the set of nonneighbors of S, calculating $\alpha(p, k)$, and then adding k to S. This process is repeated until the set of nonneighbors of S is empty.

We implement the edge connectivity algorithm as a function template that uses the BGL VertexListGraph interface. The function returns the edge connectivity of the graph, and the edges in the disconnected set are written to the output iterator. The outline of the edge connectivity function follows.

⟨ Edge connectivity algorithm 107a ⟩ ≡

```
template <typename VertexListGraph, typename OutputIterator>
typename graph_traits<VertexListGraph>::degree_size_type
edge_connectivity (VertexListGraph& g, OutputIterator disconnecting_set)
{
    ⟨Type definitions 107b⟩
    ⟨Variable declarations 107c⟩
    ⟨Create a network-flow graph out of the undirected graph 108a⟩
    ⟨Find minimum-degree vertex and compute neighbors of S and nonneighbors of S 109b⟩
    ⟨Main loop 110a⟩
    ⟨Compute forward edges of the cut [S*, S̄*] 110b⟩
    return c;
}
```

The first section of the implementation creates some type definitions to provide shorter names for accessing types from the graph traits. A network-flow graph (a directed graph) is created based on the undirected input graph *g*, so the *adjacency_list* graph class is used.

⟨ Type definitions 107b ⟩ ≡

```
typedef typename graph_traits<VertexListGraph>::vertex_descriptor vertex_descriptor;
typedef typename graph_traits<VertexListGraph>::degree_size_type degree_size_type;
typedef color_traits<default_color_type> Color;
typedef typename adjacency_list_traits<vecS, vecS, directedS>::edge_descriptor
    edge_descriptor;
typedef adjacency_list<vecS, vecS, directedS, no_property,
    property<edge_capacity_t, degree_size_type,
        property<edge_residual_capacity_t, degree_size_type,
            property<edge_reverse_t, edge_descriptor> > > > FlowGraph;
```

We use *std::set* for the sets S and neighbors of S because uniqueness during insertion must be ensured. The sets S^* and nonneighbors of S are represented with *std::vector* because we know ahead of time that the inserted elements will be unique.

⟨ Variable declarations 107c ⟩ ≡

```
vertex_descriptor u, v, p, k;
edge_descriptor e1, e2;
bool inserted;
```

```
typename graph_traits<VertexListGraph>::vertex_iterator vi, vi_end;
degree_size_type delta, alpha_star, alpha_S_k;
std::set<vertex_descriptor> S, neighbor_S;
std::vector<vertex_descriptor> S_star, nonneighbor_S;
std::vector<default_color_type> color (num_vertices (g) );
std::vector<edge_descriptor> pred (num_vertices (g) );
```

The network flow graph is constructed based on the input graph. Each edge in the flow graph has three properties—capacity, residual capacity, and reverse edge—that are accessed through the property map objects *cap*, *res_cap*, and *rev_edge*, respectively.

⟨ Create a network-flow graph out of the undirected graph 108a ⟩ ≡

```
FlowGraph flow_g (num_vertices (g) );
typename property_map<FlowGraph, edge_capacity_t>::type
  cap = get (edge_capacity, flow_g);
typename property_map<FlowGraph, edge_residual_capacity_t>::type
  res_cap = get (edge_residual_capacity, flow_g);
typename property_map<FlowGraph, edge_reverse_t>::type
  rev_edge = get (edge_reverse, flow_g);

typename graph_traits<VertexListGraph>::edge_iterator ei, ei_end;
for (tie (ei, ei_end) = edges (g); ei != ei_end; ++ei) {
  u = source (*ei, g), v = target (*ei, g);
  tie (e1, inserted) = add_edge (u, v, flow_g);
  cap [e1] = 1;
  tie (e2, inserted) = add_edge (v, u, flow_g);
  cap [e2] = 1;
  rev_edge [e1] = e2;
  rev_edge [e2] = e1;
}
```

In the main algorithm, several pieces of functionality are divided into separate functions. The first is finding the minimum-degree vertex, which is implemented by looping through all of the vertices in the graph and comparing their degree.

⟨ Find minimum-degree vertex function 108b ⟩ ≡

```
template <typename Graph>
std::pair<typename graph_traits<Graph>::vertex_descriptor,
          typename graph_traits<Graph>::degree_size_type>
min_degree_vertex (Graph& g)
{
  typename graph_traits<Graph>::vertex_descriptor p;
  typedef typename graph_traits<Graph>::degree_size_type size_type;
  size_type delta = std::numeric_limits<size_type>::max ();
  typename graph_traits<Graph>::vertex_iterator i, iend;
```

```
    for (tie(i, iend) = vertices(g); i != iend; ++i)
      if (degree(*i, g) < delta) {
        delta = degree(*i, g);
        p = *i;
      }
    return std::make_pair(p, delta);
  }
```

We also need the ability to insert every neighbor of a vertex (and a set of vertices) into a set, which can be done by examining the *adjacent_vertices*(). We assume the output iterator is similar to a *std::insert_iterator* for a *std::set*.

⟨ Output neighbors helper functions 109a ⟩ ≡

```
    template <typename Graph, typename OutputIterator>
    void neighbors(const Graph& g, typename graph_traits<Graph>::vertex_descriptor u,
        OutputIterator result)
    {
      typename graph_traits<Graph>::adjacency_iterator ai, aend;
      for (tie(ai, aend) = adjacent_vertices(u, g); ai != aend; ++ai)
        *result++ = *ai;
    }
    template <typename Graph, typename VertexIterator, typename OutputIterator>
    void neighbors(const Graph& g, VertexIterator first, VertexIterator last,
        OutputIterator result)
    {
      for (; first != last; ++first)
        neighbors(g, *first, result);
    }
```

The intitial step of the algorithm is to find the minimum-degree vertex p, set $S = p$, and then calculate neighbors of S and nonneighbors of S. We use *std::set_difference*() to compute $V - S$ (where V is the vertex set of the graph).

⟨ Find minimum-degree vertex and compute neighbors of S and nonneighbors of S 109b ⟩ ≡

```
    tie(p, delta) = min_degree_vertex(g);
    S_star.push_back(p);
    alpha_star = delta;
    S.insert(p);
    neighbor_S.insert(p);
    neighbors(g, S.begin(), S.end(), std::inserter(neighbor_S, neighbor_S.begin()));
    std::set_difference(vertices(g).first, vertices(g).second,
        neighbor_S.begin(), neighbor_S.end(), std::back_inserter(nonneighbor_S));
```

The iterative portion of the algorithm is finished when nonneighbors of S becomes empty. In each step of the loop, the maximum flow between p and a nonneighbor k is calculated using the Edmunds–Karp algorithm (see § 13.7.1). The vertices labeled (colored nonwhite) during the max-flow algorithm correspond to all the vertices on one side of the minimum cut. Thus, if the size of the cut is the smallest so far, the labeled vertices are recorded in S^*, k is inserted into S, and neighbors of S and nonneighbors of S are recomputed.

⟨ Main loop 110a ⟩ ≡

```
while (!nonneighbor_S.empty()) {
  k = nonneighbor_S.front();
  alpha_S_k = edmunds_karp_max_flow
    (flow_g, p, k, capacity_map(cap).residual_capacity_map(res_cap).
      reverse_edge_map(rev_edge).color_map(&color[0]).predecessor_map(&pred[0]));
  if (alpha_S_k < alpha_star) {
    alpha_star = alpha_S_k;
    S_star.clear();
    for (tie(vi, vi_end) = vertices(flow_g); vi != vi_end; ++vi)
      if (color[*vi] != Color::white())
        S_star.push_back(*vi);
  }
  S.insert(k);
  neighbor_S.insert(k);
  neighbors(g, k, std::inserter(neighbor_S, neighbor_S.begin()));
  nonneighbor_S.clear();
  std::set_difference(vertices(g).first, vertices(g).second,
    neighbor_S.begin(), neighbor_S.end(), std::back_inserter(nonneighbor_S));
}
```

The last step is to find the edges in the cut, which are edges that have one vertex in S^* and the other vertex in $\overline{S^*}$. These edges are written to the output iterator named *disconnecting_set*, and the number of edges in the cut is returned.

⟨ Compute forward edges of the cut $[S^*, \overline{S^*}]$ 110b ⟩ ≡

```
std::vector<bool> in_S_star(num_vertices(g), false);
typename std::vector<vertex_descriptor>::iterator si;
for (si = S_star.begin(); si != S_star.end(); ++si)
  in_S_star[*si] = true;
degree_size_type c = 0;
for (si = S_star.begin(); si != S_star.end(); ++si) {
  typename graph_traits<VertexListGraph>::out_edge_iterator ei, ei_end;
  for (tie(ei, ei_end) = out_edges(*si, g); ei != ei_end; ++ei)
    if (!in_S_star[target(*ei, g)]) {
      *disconnecting_set++ = *ei;
      ++c;
    }
}
```

Figure 8.1 shows the example graph to which the edge connectivity algorithm is applied.

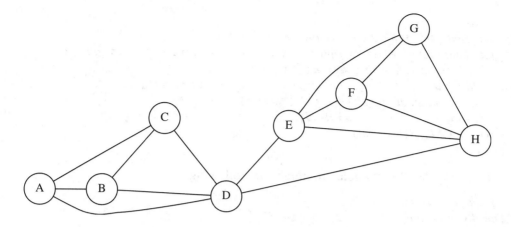

Figure 8.1 Example graph for edge connectivity.

⟨ *edge-connectivity.cpp* 111 ⟩ ≡

```
#include <algorithm>
#include <utility>
#include <boost/graph/edmunds_karp_max_flow.hpp>
#include <boost/graph/push_relabel_max_flow.hpp>
#include <boost/graph/adjacency_list.hpp>
#include <boost/graph/graphviz.hpp>

namespace boost {
  ⟨Find minimum-degree vertex function 108b⟩
  ⟨Output neighbors helper functions 109a⟩
  ⟨Edge connectivity algorithm 107a⟩
}

int main()
{
  using namespace boost;
  GraphvizGraph g;
  read_graphviz("figs/edge-connectivity.dot", g);

  typedef graph_traits<GraphvizGraph>::edge_descriptor edge_descriptor;
  typedef graph_traits<GraphvizGraph>::degree_size_type degree_size_type;
  std::vector<edge_descriptor> disconnecting_set;
  degree_size_type c = edge_connectivity(g, std::back_inserter(disconnecting_set));

  std::cout << "The edge connectivity is " << c << "." << std::endl;

  property_map<GraphvizGraph, vertex_attribute_t>::type
    attr_map = get(vertex_attribute, g);
```

```
std::cout << "The disconnecting set is {";
for (std::vector<edge_descriptor>::iterator i = disconnecting_set.begin();
        i != disconnecting_set.end(); ++i)
    std::cout << "(" << attr_map[source(*i, g)]["label"] << ","
        << attr_map[target(*i, g)]["label"] << ") ";
std::cout << "}." << std::endl;
return EXIT_SUCCESS;
}
```

The output from the example program is the following:

The edge connectivity is **2.**
The disconnecting set is $\{(D,E)\ (D,H)\ \}.$

Chapter 9

Implicit Graphs: A Knight's Tour

The knight's-tour problem is as follows: Find a path for a knight to touch all of the squares of an $n \times n$ chessboard exactly once. The knight's tour is an example of a *Hamiltonian path*—that is, a simple closed path that passes through each vertex of the graph exactly once (where each square of the chessboard is treated as a vertex in the graph). The edges of the graph are determined by the pattern in which a knight can jump (for example, up two and over one). In this section, we use a generic backtracking search algorithm to find the knight's tour. The backtracking algorithm is a brute-force algorithm and quite slow, so we also show an improvement to the algorithm using Warnsdorff's heuristic [46]. The Hamiltonian path problem is NP-complete [15] (for large problem sizes it cannot be solved in a reasonable amount of time). An example of a knight's tour on a regular 8×8 chessboard is shown in Figure 9.1.

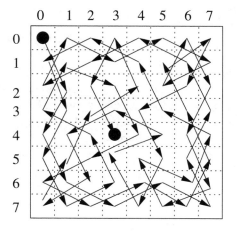

Figure 9.1 An example of a knight's tour.

One unique aspect of this example is that it does not use an explicit data structure (such as the *adjacency_list* class) to represent the graph. Rather, an *implicit* graph structure *knights_tour_graph* is deduced from the allowable moves of a knight on a chessboard.

9.1   Knight's Jumps as a Graph

The *knights_tour_graph* is a model of AdjacencyGraph, so we need to implement an *adjacent_vertices()* function that returns a pair of adjacency iterators. The adjacency iterator treats each of the squares that are legal moves from the current position as adjacent vertices.

The pattern of the knight's jumps are stored in an array, as follows.

```
typedef std::pair<int,int> Position;
Position knight_jumps[8] = { Position(2, -1), Position(1, -2),
    Position(-1, -2), Position(-2, -1), Position(-2, 1),
    Position(-1, 2), Position(1, 2), Position(2, 1) };
```

The *knight_adjacency_iterator* contains several data members: the current position on the chessboard *m_pos*, the current place in the *knight_jumps* array *m_i*, and a pointer to the graph *m_g*. Incrementing the adjacency iterator (using *operator++()*) increments *m_i*. The new position may be invalid (off the board), so *m_i* may need to be incremented further, which is handled in the *valid_position()* member function. The first jump may also be invalid, so the *valid_position()* function is also called in the constructor of the adjacency iterator. A pointer to the chessboard is needed so that its size can be accessed (chessboards of arbitrary size may be used). When the adjacency iterator is dereferenced (*operator*()*) the current position offset by the current jump vector is returned. The following code shows the implementation of the *knight_adjacency_iterator*. The *boost::forward_iterator_helper* is used to automatically implement *operator++(int)* in terms of *operator++()* and *operator!=()* in terms of *operator==()*.

```
struct knight_adjacency_iterator
  : public boost::forward_iterator_helper<
      knight_adjacency_iterator, Position, std::ptrdiff_t, Position*, Position>
{
  knight_adjacency_iterator() { }
  knight_adjacency_iterator(int ii, Position p, const knights_tour_graph& g)
    : m_pos(p), m_g(&g), m_i(ii) { valid_position(); }
  Position operator*() const { return m_pos + knight_jumps[m_i]; }
  void operator++() { ++m_i; valid_position(); }
  bool operator==(const knight_adjacency_iterator& x) const { return m_i == x.m_i; }
protected:
  void valid_position();
  Position m_pos;
  const knights_tour_graph* m_g;
  int m_i;
};
```

In the *valid_position()* member function, the jump counter is incremented until a position is found that is on the board, or until the end of the jump array is reached.

```
void knight_adjacency_iterator::valid_position() {
  Position new_pos = m_pos + knight_jumps[m_i];
  while (m_i < 8 && (new_pos.first < 0 || new_pos.second < 0
                     || new_pos.first >= m_g->m_board_size
                     || new_pos.second >= m_g->m_board_size)) {
    ++m_i;
    new_pos = m_pos + knight_jumps[m_i];
  }
}
```

The *adjacent_vertices()* function is implemented by creating a pair of adjacency iterators using *0* for the beginning iterator's jump position and *8* for the past-the-end iterator's jump position.

```
std::pair<knights_tour_graph::adjacency_iterator, knights_tour_graph::adjacency_iterator>
adjacent_vertices(knights_tour_graph::vertex_descriptor v, const knights_tour_graph& g) {
  typedef knights_tour_graph::adjacency_iterator Iter;
  return std::make_pair(Iter(0, v, g), Iter(8, v, g));
}
```

The *knights_tour_graph* class only contains the size of the chessboard (stored as a data member) and the typedefs required of an AdjacencyGraph. The *num_vertices()* function returns the number of squares in the chessboard.

```
struct knights_tour_graph
{
  typedef Position vertex_descriptor;
  typedef std::pair<vertex_descriptor, vertex_descriptor> edge_descriptor;
  typedef knight_adjacency_iterator adjacency_iterator;
  typedef void out_edge_iterator;
  typedef void in_edge_iterator;
  typedef void edge_iterator;
  typedef void vertex_iterator;
  typedef int degree_size_type;
  typedef int vertices_size_type;
  typedef int edges_size_type;
  typedef directed_tag directed_category;
  typedef disallow_parallel_edge_tag edge_parallel_category;
  typedef adjacency_graph_tag traversal_category;
  knights_tour_graph(int n) : m_board_size(n) { }
  int m_board_size;
};
int num_vertices(const knights_tour_graph& g)
  { return g.m_board_size * g.m_board_size; }
```

Now that the knight's moves are mapped to the Boost graph interface, we can look at some graph algorithms that can be used to solve the knight's tour problem.

9.2   Backtracking Graph Search

The idea of a backtracking graph search is similar to a depth-first search in that a path is explored until a dead end is reached. The backtracking graph search is different in that after a dead end is reached, the algorithm backs up, unmarking the dead-end path, before continuing along a different path. In the following code, the backtracking search is implemented using a stack (instead of the recursive method), and discovery time for each vertex is recorded using a property map. The stack contains timestamp-vertex pairs so that the proper timestamp is available after backtracking from a dead end. The search is completed once all of the vertices have been visited, or when all possible paths have been exhausted.

Although the graph defined in the previous section was implicit (and represents the knight's move on a chessboard in particular), it nevertheless models a BGL Graph. The backtracking algorithm is therefore implemented for a Graph, rather than only for a *knights-_tour_graph*. The resulting algorithm is reusable for any graph data structure that models Graph.

```
template <typename Graph, typename TimePropertyMap>
bool backtracking_search (Graph& g,
    typename graph_traits<Graph>::vertex_descriptor src, TimePropertyMap time_map)
{
  〈Create the stack and initialize time stamp 116〉
  S.push (std::make_pair (time_stamp, src));
  while (!S.empty()) {
    〈Get vertex from top of stack, record time, and check for finish 117a〉
    〈Push all of the adjacent vertices onto the stack 117b〉
    〈If at dead end, rollback 117c〉
  } // while (!S.empty())
  return false;
}
```

A *std::stack* is used to record the vertices that need to be explored. The timestamp of when the vertex was pushed on to the stack is also recorded.

〈 Create the stack and initialize time stamp 116 〉 ≡

```
typedef typename graph_traits<Graph>::vertex_descriptor Vertex;
typedef std::pair<int, Vertex> P;
std::stack<P> S;
int time_stamp = 0;
```

The next step is to record the timestamp for the vertex at the top of the stack and check to see if all the vertices in the graph have been recorded and thus the algorithm is finished.

⟨ Get vertex from top of stack, record time, and check for finish 117a ⟩ ≡

```
Vertex x;
tie(time_stamp, x) = S.top();
put(time_map, x, time_stamp);
// all vertices have been visited, success!
if (time_stamp == num_vertices(g) − 1)
  return true;
```

Now all the adjacent vertices are scanned, and if an adjacent vertex has not yet been visited it is added to the stack. No available adjacent vertices indicates a dead end.

⟨ Push all of the adjacent vertices onto the stack 117b ⟩ ≡

```
bool deadend = true;
typename graph_traits<Graph>::adjacency_iterator i, end;
for (tie(i, end) = adjacent_vertices(x, g); i != end; ++i)
  if (get(time_map, *i) == −1) {
    S.push(std::make_pair(time_stamp + 1, *i));
    deadend = false;
  }
```

If the algorithm reaches a dead end, vertices are popped from the stack until a vertex is found that has not yet been explored. As we roll back, the timestamps for each vertex are reset, because it is possible that those vertices can be reached along a better path.

⟨ If at dead end, rollback 117c ⟩ ≡

```
if (deadend) {
  put(time_map, x, −1);
  S.pop();
  tie(time_stamp, x) = S.top();
  while (get(time_map, x) != −1) { // unwind stack to last unexplored vertex
    put(time_map, x, −1);
    S.pop();
    tie(time_stamp, x) = S.top();
  }
}
```

9.3   Warnsdorff's Heuristic

Warnsdorff's heuristic for choosing the next place to jump is to look ahead at each of the possible jumps, and see how many jumps are possible from that square. We call this the *number of successors*. The square with the fewest number of successors is chosen as the next move. The reason this heuristic helps is that it visits the most constrained vertices first, thereby avoiding some potential dead ends. The following function calculates the number of successors of a vertex.

```
template <typename Vertex, typename Graph, typename TimePropertyMap>
int number_of_successors (Vertex x, Graph& g, TimePropertyMap time_map) {
  int s_x = 0;
  typename graph_traits<Graph>::adjacency_iterator i, end;
  for (tie(i, end) = adjacent_vertices(x, g); i != end; ++i)
    if (get(time_map, *i) == −1)
      ++s_x;
  return s_x;
}
```

To implement this algorithm, we start with the backtracking algorithm, but instead of pushing the adjacent vertices onto the stack, we first order the vertices according to the number of successors. The ordering is accomplished by putting the adjacent vertices in a priority queue. Once all of the adjacent vertices are in the queue, they are popped off the queue and pushed onto the stack. An empty priority queue denotes a dead end.

```
template <typename Graph, typename TimePropertyMap>
bool warnsdorff (Graph& g, typename graph_traits<Graph>::vertex_descriptor src,
    TimePropertyMap time_map)
{
  ⟨Create the stack and initialize time stamp 116⟩
  S.push(std::make_pair(time_stamp, src));
  while (!S.empty()) {
    ⟨Get vertex from top of stack, record time, and check for finish 117a⟩
    // Put adjacent vertices into a local priority queue
    std::priority_queue<P, std::vector<P>, compare_first> Q;
    typename graph_traits<Graph>::adjacency_iterator i, end;
    int num_succ;
    for (tie(i, end) = adjacent_vertices(x, g); i != end; ++i)
      if (get(time_map, *i) == −1) {
        num_succ = number_of_successors(*i, g, time_map);
        Q.push(std::make_pair(num_succ, *i));
      }
    bool deadend = Q.empty();
    // move vertices from local priority queue to the stack
    for (; !Q.empty(); Q.pop()) {
      tie(num_succ, x) = Q.top();
      S.push(std::make_pair(time_stamp + 1, x));
    }
    ⟨If at dead end, rollback 117c⟩
  } // while (!S.empty())
  return false;
}
```

Chapter 10

Interfacing with Other Graph Libraries

Although the main goal of BGL is to aid the development of new applications and graph algorithms, there are quite a few existing codes that can benefit from using BGL algorithms. One way to use the BGL algorithms with existing graph data structures is to copy data from the older graph format into a BGL graph, which is then used with the BGL algorithms. The problem with this approach is that it can be inconvenient and expensive to perform this copy. Another approach is to use the existing data structure directly by wrapping it with a BGL interface.

The Adaptor pattern [14] is one mechanism for providing a new interface to an existing class. This approach typically requires that the adapted object be contained inside a new class that provides the desired interface. Containment is not required when wrapping a graph for BGL because the BGL graph interface consists solely of free (global nonmember) functions. With this kind of interface, instead of creating a new graph class, adapting an interface requires only overloading of the free functions that make up the interface. In §10.3 we show in detail how this works.

The BGL includes overloads for the LEDA [29] *GRAPH* type, the Stanford Graph-Base [22] *Graph** type, and also for the STL *std::vector*. LEDA is a popular object-oriented library for combinatorial computing, including graph data structures and algorithms. The Stanford GraphBase, by Donald Knuth, is a collection of graph data sets, graph generators, and programs that run graph algorithms on these graphs.

In the following sections, we show examples of using LEDA and SGB graph data structures with BGL algorithms. We then look at the implementation of the BGL adapting functions for the LEDA graph, providing an example for how to implement adaptors for other graph libraries.

In §1.4.1 we demonstrated the flexibility of the BGL algorithms by applying *topological_sort()* to both a graph represented by a vector of lists, *std::vector<std::list<int>>*, and also a graph represented by an *boost::adjacency_list*. We continue that example—scheduling a set of interdependent tasks—in the following two sections, first using the LEDA *GRAPH* type and then using an Stanford GraphBase (SGB) *Graph* type.

10.1   Using BGL Topological Sort with a LEDA Graph

The header file *boost/graph/leda_graph.hpp* contains function overloads that adapt the LEDA parameterized *GRAPH* type to the BGL interface. The BGL interface for the LEDA *GRAPH* is documented in §14.3.5. The LEDA–BGL interface was tested with LEDA version 4.1, one of the last freely available versions of LEDA. In addition to including the *leda_graph.hpp* header file you must have LEDA installed, set the include and library paths of your compiler, and link in the LEDA libraries. See the LEDA documentation for details.

The following is the outline for the task-scheduling program, this time using a LEDA *GRAPH* to represent the task dependencies.

⟨ *topo-sort-with-leda.cpp* 120a ⟩ ≡

```
#include <vector>
#include <string>
#include <iostream>
#include <boost/graph/topological_sort.hpp>
#include <boost/graph/leda_graph.hpp>
// Undefine macros from LEDA that conflict with the C++ Standard Library.
#undef string
#undef vector

int main()
{
  using namespace boost;
  ⟨Create a LEDA graph with vertices labeled by task 120b⟩
  ⟨Add edges to the LEDA graph 121a⟩
  ⟨Perform the topological sort on the LEDA graph 121b⟩
  return EXIT_SUCCESS;
}
```

The LEDA *GRAPH* class allows the user to attach objects to the vertices and edges of the graph, so here we attach the task names (in the form of *std::string*) to the vertices. We use the usual BGL *add_vertex()* function to add vertices to *leda_g*, and pass in the task names as the property object to be attached to the vertex. We store the vertex descriptors returned from *add_vertex()* in a vector so that we have fast access to any vertex when adding the edges.

⟨ Create a LEDA graph with vertices labeled by task 120b ⟩ ≡

```
typedef GRAPH<std::string, char> graph_t;
graph_t leda_g;
typedef graph_traits<graph_t>::vertex_descriptor vertex_t;
```

```
std::vector<vertex_t> vert(7);
vert[0] = add_vertex(std::string("pick up kids from school"), leda_g);
vert[1] = add_vertex(std::string("buy groceries (and snacks)"), leda_g);
vert[2] = add_vertex(std::string("get cash at ATM"), leda_g);
vert[3] = add_vertex(std::string("drop off kids at soccer practice"),leda_g);
vert[4] = add_vertex(std::string("cook dinner"), leda_g);
vert[5] = add_vertex(std::string("pick up kids from soccer"), leda_g);
vert[6] = add_vertex(std::string("eat dinner"), leda_g);
```

The next step is adding edges to the graph. Again, we use the usual BGL function, in this case *add_edge()*.

⟨ Add edges to the LEDA graph 121a ⟩ ≡

```
add_edge(vert[0], vert[3], leda_g);
add_edge(vert[1], vert[3], leda_g);
add_edge(vert[1], vert[4], leda_g);
add_edge(vert[2], vert[1], leda_g);
add_edge(vert[3], vert[5], leda_g);
add_edge(vert[4], vert[6], leda_g);
add_edge(vert[5], vert[6], leda_g);
```

Now that we have the graph constructed, we can make the call to *topological_sort()*. Again, because of the LEDA–BGL interface, the LEDA *GRAPH* can be used as-is with the BGL function. We simply pass the *leda_g* object into the algorithm. The *topological_sort()* requires a color property map to mark the vertices, so we use the LEDA *node_array* to map from vertices to colors. The *make_leda_node_property_map()* function is also defined in *boost/-graph/leda_graph.hpp*, which creates an adaptor that satisfies the LvaluePropertyMap concept in terms of a *node_array*. The reverse topological ordering is written into the *topo_order* vector, which we then reverse. The ordering is then output. The *operator[]()* of the LEDA *GRAPH* is used to access the task label for each vertex.

⟨ Perform the topological sort on the LEDA graph 121b ⟩ ≡

```
std::vector<vertex_t> topo_order;
node_array<default_color_type> color_array(leda_g);

topological_sort(leda_g, std::back_inserter(topo_order),
  color_map(make_leda_node_property_map(color_array)));

std::reverse(topo_order.begin(), topo_order.end());
int n = 1;
for (std::vector<vertex_t>::iterator i = topo_order.begin();
    i != topo_order.end(); ++i, ++n)
  std::cout << n << ": " << leda_g[*i] << std::endl;
```

10.2   Using BGL Topological Sort with a SGB Graph

The SGB defines a *Graph* struct that implements an adjacency-list style data-structure. The overloaded functions in *boost/graph/stanford_graph.hpp* adapt the SGB *Graph* struct to the BGL interface. In addition to including the *stanford_graph.hpp* header file, you must have the Stanford GraphBase installed and you must apply the PROTOTYPES change file that is included in the SGB distribution. The reason for this is that the original SGB header files did not define ANSI standard prototypes for the functions, which is required by a C++ compiler. When compiling a program using the SGB–BGL interface, you need to set up the include and library paths to find the SGB, and you need to link in the SGB library. The SGB–BGL interface is documented in §14.3.4.

The following code shows the outline for a program that computes a topological ordering for a set of interdependent tasks.

⟨ *topo-sort-with-sgb.cpp* 122a ⟩ ≡

```
#include <vector>
#include <string>
#include <iostream>
#include <boost/graph/topological_sort.hpp>
#include <boost/graph/stanford_graph.hpp>

int main ()
{
  using namespace boost;
  ⟨Create an SGB graph 122b⟩
  ⟨Create labels for the tasks 122c⟩
  ⟨Add edges to the SGB graph 123a⟩
  ⟨Perform the topological sort on the SGB graph 123b⟩
  gb_recycle (sgb_g) ;
  return EXIT_SUCCESS;
}
```

We create a SGB graph with a call to the SGB function *gb_new_graph* ().

⟨ Create an SGB graph 122b ⟩ ≡

```
const int n_vertices = 7;
Graph* sgb_g = gb_new_graph (n_vertices) ;
```

Next we write down the labels for the tasks (the vertices) in the graph. It is easy to go from an SGB vertex descriptor to an integer using the *sgb_vertex_id_map* defined in *stanford_graph.hpp*, so storing the labels in an array is convenient.

⟨ Create labels for the tasks 122c ⟩ ≡

```
const char* tasks[] = {
```

> *"pick up kids from school",*
> *"buy groceries (and snacks)",*
> *"get cash at ATM",*
> *"drop off kids at soccer practice",*
> *"cook dinner",*
> *"pick up kids from soccer",*
> *"eat dinner" };*
> *const int n_tasks = sizeof(tasks) / sizeof(char*);*

The SGB graph stores the vertices of the graph in an array, so we can access any vertex by an offset into the array. The **gb_new_edge** function takes two **Vertex*** arguments and an edge weight (which we do not need).

⟨ Add edges to the SGB graph 123a ⟩ ≡

```
gb_new_arc(sgb_g->vertices + 0, sgb_g->vertices + 3, 0);
gb_new_arc(sgb_g->vertices + 1, sgb_g->vertices + 3, 0);
gb_new_arc(sgb_g->vertices + 1, sgb_g->vertices + 4, 0);
gb_new_arc(sgb_g->vertices + 2, sgb_g->vertices + 1, 0);
gb_new_arc(sgb_g->vertices + 3, sgb_g->vertices + 5, 0);
gb_new_arc(sgb_g->vertices + 4, sgb_g->vertices + 6, 0);
gb_new_arc(sgb_g->vertices + 5, sgb_g->vertices + 6, 0);
```

Next we perform the topological sort. We pass the SGB graph as is into the algorithm. This time instead of creating a color map we let the algorithm create one for itself. However, to do this the *topological_sort()* function needs a mapping from vertices to integers. The SGB–BGL interface provides this property map. The vertex to index property map is obtained by the call *get(vertex_index, sgb_g)*.

⟨ Perform the topological sort on the SGB graph 123b ⟩ ≡

```
typedef graph_traits<Graph*>::vertex_descriptor vertex_t;
std::vector<vertex_t> topo_order;
topological_sort(sgb_g, std::back_inserter(topo_order),
  vertex_index_map(get(vertex_index, sgb_g)));
int n = 1;
for (std::vector<vertex_t>::reverse_iterator i = topo_order.rbegin();
    i != topo_order.rend(); ++i, ++n)
  std::cout << n << ": " << tasks[get(vertex_index, sgb_g)[*i]] << std::endl;
```

10.3 Implementing Graph Adaptors

Implementing new adaptors for other graph libraries and data structures is not difficult. As an example of how to create new adaptors, this section provides a detailed explanation of the implementation of the BGL interface for the LEDA *GRAPH*.

The first issue in creating the adaptor is which BGL concepts should be implemented. The following concepts are straightforward to implement on top of LEDA: VertexListGraph, BidirectionalGraph, VertexMutableGraph, and EdgeMutableGraph.

All types associated with a BGL graph class are accessed though the *graph_traits* class. This traits class can be partially specialized for the LEDA *GRAPH* class in the following way.[1] The *node* and *edge* types are the LEDA equivalent of vertex and edge descriptors. The LEDA *GRAPH* is for directed graphs, so we choose *directed_tag* for the *directed_category*. The LEDA *GRAPH* does not automatically prevent the insertion of parallel edges, so we choose *allow_parallel_edge_tag* for the *edge_parallel_category*. The return type for the LEDA function *number_of_nodes* ( ) is *int*, so we choose that type for the *vertices_size_type* of the graph. The tag type used for the *traversal_category* must reflect which traversal concepts the graph type models. Therefore we create a tag class that inherits from *bidirectional_graph_tag*, *adjacency-_graph_tag*, and *vertex_list_graph_tag*. The iterator types are described later in this section.

⟨ Graph traits for LEDA graph 124 ⟩ ≡

```
namespace boost {
  struct leda_graph_traversal_category :
    public virtual bidirectional_graph_tag,
    public virtual adjacency_graph_tag,
    public virtual vertex_list_graph_tag { };

  template <typename V, typename E>
  struct graph_traits< GRAPH<V,E> > {
    typedef node vertex_descriptor;
    typedef edge edge_descriptor;
    typedef directed_tag directed_category;
    typedef allow_parallel_edge_tag edge_parallel_category;
    typedef int vertices_size_type;
    typedef leda_graph_traversal_category traversal_category;
    ⟨Out-edge iterator type 125c⟩
    // more iterator typedefs ...
  };
} // namespace boost
```

First we write the *source* ( ) and *target* ( ) functions of the IncidenceGraph concept, which is part of the BidirectionalGraph concept. We use the LEDA *GRAPH* type for the graph parameter, and *graph_traits* to specify the edge parameter and the vertex return type. Although the LEDA types *node* and *edge* could be used, it is better practice to always use *graph_traits*. If there is a need to change the associated vertex or edge type, it will only need to be done in

---

[1]Some nonconformant compilers such as Visual C++ 6.0 do not support partial specialization. To access associated types in this situation, the traits class must be fully specialized for particular vertex and edge types. Alternatively a wrapper class containing the LEDA graph and required nested typedefs can be used.

one place, inside the specialization of **graph_traits**, rather than throughout your code. LEDA provides **source()** and **target()** functions, so we merely call them.

⟨ Source and target for LEDA graph 125a ⟩ ≡
```
template <typename V, typename E>
typename graph_traits< GRAPH<V,E> >::vertex_descriptor
source (typename graph_traits< GRAPH<V,E> >::edge_descriptor e,
        const GRAPH<V,E>& g)
{
  return source (e);
}
// same for target ...
```

The next function from IncidenceGraph that we need to implement is **out_edges()**. This function returns a pair of out-edge iterators. Since LEDA does not use STL-style iterators they need to be implemented. Implementing iterators that are compliant with the C++ standard can be a difficult and tedious process. Fortunately, there is a convenient Boost utility for implementing iterators, called **iterator_adaptor**. The **iterator_adaptor** class allows the user to create standard-conforming interators simply by providing policy classes. The following code is the policy class for our out-edge iterator. In LEDA, the edge object itself is used like an iterator. It has functions **Succ_Adj_Edge()** and **Pred_Adj_Edge()** to move to the next and previous (successor and predecessor) edge.

⟨ Out-edge iterator policies 125b ⟩ ≡
```
struct leda_out_edge_iterator_policies
{
  template <typename Iter>
  static void increment(Iter& i) { i.base() = Succ_Adj_Edge(i.base(), 0); }
  template <typename Iter>
  static void decrement(Iter& i) { i.base() = Pred_Adj_Edge(i.base(), 0); }
  template <typename Iter>
  static typename Iter::reference dereference(const Iter& i) { return i.base(); }
  template <typename Iter>
  static bool equal(const Iter& x, const Iter& y) { return x.base() == y.base(); }
};
```

The **iterator_adaptor** is now used to fill in the **out_edge_iterator** type. The first two template parameters for **iterator_adaptor** are the adapted type and the policy class. The following parameters specify the associated types of the iterator such as the value type and reference type.

⟨ Out-edge iterator type 125c ⟩ ≡
```
typedef iterator_adaptor<edge, leda_out_edge_iterator_policies,
  edge, const edge&, const edge*, std::forward_iterator_tag, std::ptrdiff_t
> out_edge_iterator;
```

With the *out_edge_iterator* defined in *graph_traits*, we are ready to define the *out_edges()* function. In the following definition, the return type should be a pair of out-edge iterators, so
we use *std::pair* and then *graph_traits* to access the out-edge iterator types. In the body of
the function we construct the out-edge iterators by passing in the first adjacent edge for the
begin iterator, and 0 for the end iterator (which is used in LEDA as the end sentinel). The 0
argument to *First_Adj_Edge* tells LEDA we want out-edges (and not in-edges).

⟨ Out-edges function for LEDA 126a ⟩ ≡

```
template <typename V, typename E>
std::pair<typename graph_traits< GRAPH<V,E> >::out_edge_iterator,
        typename graph_traits< GRAPH<V,E> >::out_edge_iterator>
out_edges (typename graph_traits< GRAPH<V,E> >::vertex_descriptor u,
        const GRAPH<V,E>& g)
{
  typedef typename graph_traits< GRAPH<V,E> >::out_edge_iterator Iter;
  return std::make_pair( Iter(First_Adj_Edge(u, 0)), Iter(0) );
}
```

The rest of the iterator types and interface functions are constructed using the same techniques. The complete code for the LEDA wrapper interface is in *boost/graph/leda_graph.hpp*.
In the following code we use the BGL concept checks to make sure that we have correctly
implemented the BGL interface. These checks do not test the run-time behavior of the implementation; that is tested in *test/graph.cpp*.

⟨ *leda-concept-check.cpp* 126b ⟩ ≡

```
#include <boost/graph/graph_concepts.hpp>
#include <boost/graph/leda_graph.hpp>

int main()
{
  typedef GRAPH<int,int> Graph;
  function_requires< VertexListGraphConcept<Graph> >();
  function_requires< BidirectionalGraphConcept<Graph> >();
  function_requires< VertexMutableGraphConcept<Graph> >();
  function_requires< EdgeMutableGraphConcept<Graph> >();
  return EXIT_SUCCESS;
}
```

Chapter 11

Performance Guidelines

In this chapter, we discuss the performance impact of various choices of the BGL graph family *adjacency_list*. The purpose is to give BGL users some basic guidelines for which graph types might be most efficient in different situations. We present a set of experiments that shows the performance of different basic operations on several variations of the BGL *adjacency_list*. Sparse and dense graphs are investigated, as well as the use of two different compilers (Microsoft Visual C++ and GNU C++).

As a primary BGL graph component, *adjacency_list* allows users to control the actual data structures used for internal graph data structures. Its first two template parameters, *EdgeList* and *VertexList*, are used to select actual containers to represent the sequence of out-edges and the sequence of vertices, respectively. Users can use *vecS*, *listS*, or *setS* for *EdgeList* to choose either *std::vector*, *std::list*, or *std::set*. Users can specify *vecS* or *listS* to choose *std::vector* or *std::list*, respectively, for the backbone.

11.1   Graph Class Comparisons

The experiments compare the performance of several variations of the *adjacency_list*. The experiments cover most of the basic graph operations: inserting and removing vertices and edges and traversing the graph along the vertices, edges, and the out-edges of each vertex. The experiments were performed with sparse and dense graphs with small size (100 vertices), medium size (1,000 vertices), and large size (10,000 vertices). For a sparse graph, the number of edges is ten times the number of vertices. For a dense graph, the total number of edge is the square of the number of vertices.

The timing runs were performed on a Dell dual 733MHz CPU machine, with 512 MB memory. The experiments were duplicated for two compilers: Microsoft Visual C++ 6.0 and GNU C++ 2.95.3 under cygwin. The optimization flags were set for maximal speed for Visual C++. The *-O3* and *-funroll-loops* optimization flags were used with GNU C++. Note that the *adjacency_list* implementation uses components from the STL, which are typically provided by the compiler.

The timer used was the portable POSIX *clock()* function, which is rather low resolution. Several of the tests would normally complete in less time than the minimum resolution. Therefore, the experiments were executed in a loop until the elapsed time exceeded at least 100 times the minimum resolution. Each of these looped experiments was repeated three times and the minimum time of the three was reported. We noticed a standard deviation of approximately 10% in the timings.

The following gives the full graph type used for the experiments, along with the abbreviated graph names used in the results charts.

- vec

adjacency_list<vecS, vecS, directedS, property<vertex_distance_t, int>,
> *property<edge_weight_t, int> >*

- list

adjacency_list<listS, vecS, directedS, property<vertex_distance_t, int>,
> *property<edge_weight_t, int> >*

- set

adjacency_list<setS, vecS, directedS, property<vertex_distance_t, int>,
> *property<edge_weight_t, int> >*

- listlist

adjacency_list<listS, listS, directedS, property<vertex_distance_t, int>,
> *property<edge_weight_t, int> >*

11.1.1   The Results and Discussion

Adding Edges and Vertices   For the first experiment, we make alternate calls to *add_vertex()* and *add_edge()* until the graph has $|E|$ edges and $|V|$ vertices. The results of this experiment are shown in Figure 11.1. The winner here is one of the *adjacency_list* classes with *VertexList=listS* selector.

Adding Edges   For this experiment, we add $|E|$ edges to a graph that already has $|V|$ vertices. The results are shown in Figure 11.2. The clear winner using Visual C++ is *adjacency_list* with *VertexList=vecS* selector, regardless of graph size and sparsity. Using GNU C++, *adjacency_list* class with *EdgeList=listS* wins when graphs are sparse.

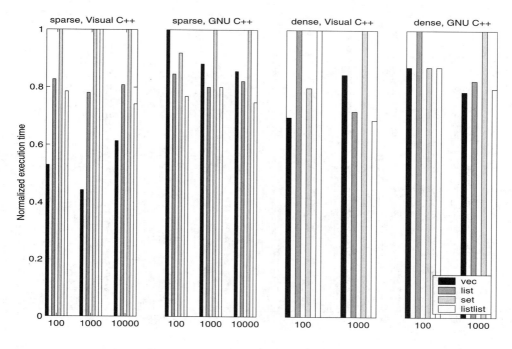

Figure 11.1 The timing results of the experiment adding edges and vertices.

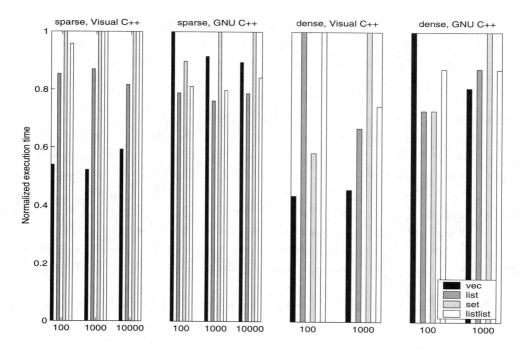

Figure 11.2 The timing results of the experiment adding edges.

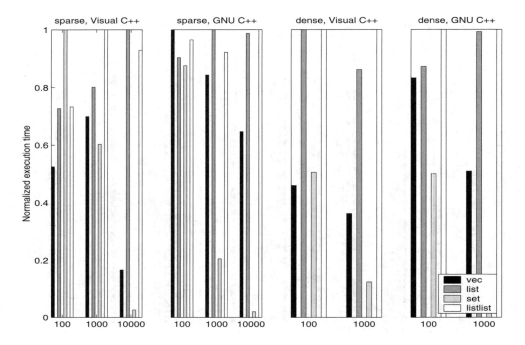

Figure 11.3 The timing results of the experiment removing edges.

Removing Edges   This experiment adds and removes $|E|$ edges to graph with $|V|$ vertices. The results are shown in Figure 11.3. The result here was not clear for graphs with small number of vertices. However, it is clear that *adjacency_list* with *VertexList=setS* selector is the winner for large graphs.

Removing Vertices   This experiment adds $|V|$ vertices and $|E|$ edges to a graph, and then removes all the vertices. The results are shown in Figure 11.4. The clear winner here is *listlist*, which was designed with this operation in mind. Other variations of *adjacency_list* perform horribly on this operation because its implementation is not of constant time complexity.

Clearing Vertices   This experiment adds $|V|$ vertices and $|E|$ edges to a graph, and then clears and removes all the vertices. The *clear_vertex()* operation traverses the graph, removing any edges the refer the vertex. The results are shown in Figure 11.5. As the graph size gets larger and larger, it is getting clearer that *adjacency_list* with *VertexList=vecS* is the winner.

Vertex Set Traversal   This experiment traverses through all the vertices in the graph, reading an internal property value from each vertex. The results are shown in Figure 11.6. There was no clear winner here in the first three graph types. Vertex traversal was fast for those graph classes because they have the same *VertexList=vecS*. Vertex traversal was slower for large graphs for *listlist* because it uses *VertexList=listS*.

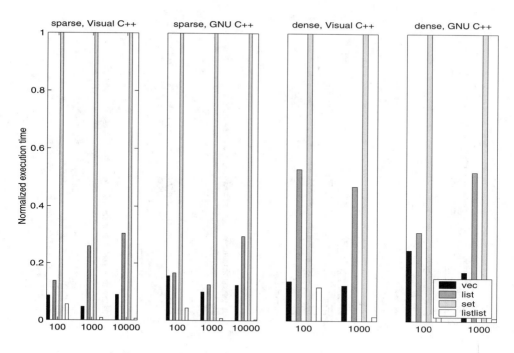

Figure 11.4 The timing results of the experiment removing vertices.

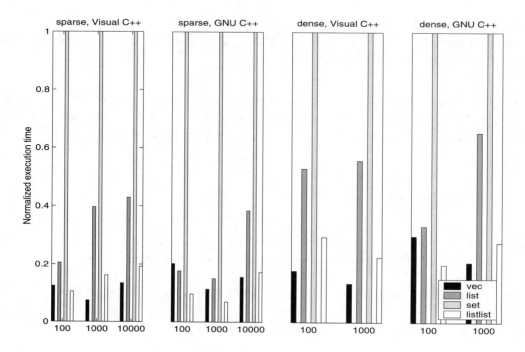

Figure 11.5 The timing results of the experiment clearing vertices.

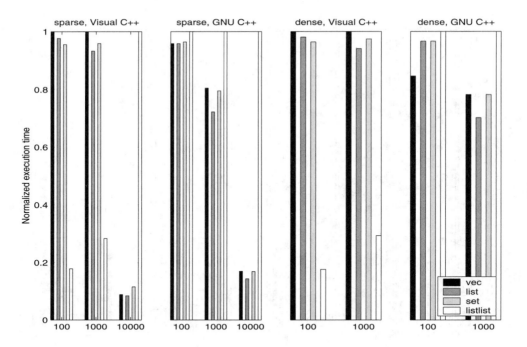

Figure 11.6 The timing results of the experiment traversing the vertex set.

Edge Set Traversal   This experiment traverses through all the edges in the graph, reading an internal property value from each edge. The results are shown in Figure 11.7. The clear winner here is *adjacency_list* with *EdgeList=vecS*.

Out-Edge Traversal   This experiment traverses through the out-edges of every vertex in the graph, reading an internal property from each vertex and from each out-edge. The results are shown in Figure 11.8. The clear winner here is *adjacency_list* with *EdgeList=vecS*.

11.2   Conclusion

Different combinations of choices have different tradeoffs between traversal speed and insertion/removal speed. The following summarizes the results of our experiments.

- Using *vecS* for *EdgeList* generally provides efficient out-edge traversal.

- Using *vecS* for *VertexList* generally provides efficent vertex set traversal.

- Efficient removal of edges is supported by *setS* for *EdgeList*. In particular, *std::set* should be used for the sequence of out-edges.

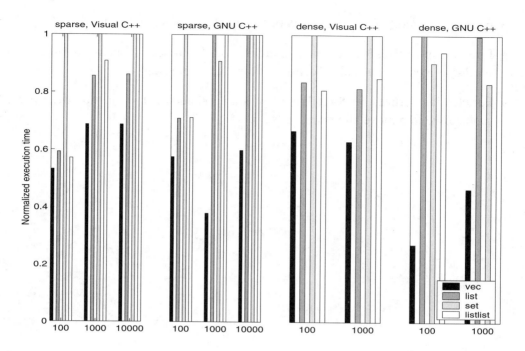

Figure 11.7 The timing results of the experiment traversing the edge set.

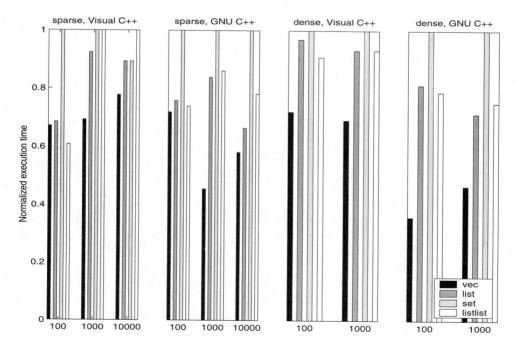

Figure 11.8 The timing results of the experiment traversing out-edges.

- For efficient addition of edges, *vecS* or *listS* for **EdgeList** should be used.

- If removing vertices is a common operation, *listS* for **VertexList** should be used because *std::list* as a backbone enables constant-time vertex removal.

- For clearing vertices, *vecS* for **VertexList** is a good choice (the function **clear_vertex ( )** can be used to remove all incident edges).

Part II

Reference Manual

Chapter 12

BGL Concepts

This chapter describes the fundamental interfaces (the fundamental concepts) for graphs in the BGL. These concepts are organized into three categories: those providing mechanisms for traversing a graph, those providing mechanisms for modifying a graph, and visitors for accessing properties attached to vertices and edges.

Notation

The notation used in the requirements for all of the graph concepts is collected here.

G	is a graph type
g	is an object of type *G*
e	is an object of type *graph_traits<G>::edge_descriptor*
eiter	is an object of type *graph_traits<G>::out_edge_iterator*
u,v	are objects of type *graph_traits<G>::vertex_descriptor*
ep	is an object of type *edge_property<G>::type*
vp	is an object of type *vertex_property<G>::type*
PropertyTag	is a type used to specify a vertex or edge property
ptag	is an object of type *PropertyTag*
X	is either the vertex or edge descriptor type for *G*
x	is a vertex or edge descriptor
PMap	is a type that models one of the property map concepts
pmap	is an object of type *PMap*

12.1 Graph Traversal Concepts

The core of the Boost Graph Library is the interfaces, as represented by concepts, that define how a graph can be examined and manipulated in a data structure neutral fashion. In fact, as shown in Chapter 9, the BGL graph interface need not even be implemented using an

137

explicit data structure. For some problems it is more natural or more efficient to define a graph implicitly based on certain functions.

The BGL graph interface does not appear as a single concept. Instead, it is factored into smaller, distinct pieces. The purpose of a concept is to encapsulate the interface requirements for algorithms. To maximize the reusability of an algorithm, it is important not to include operations in its interface that are not actually required for correct operation of the algorithm. By factoring the graph interface into smaller distinct concepts, we provide the graph algorithm writer with a good selection from which to choose the minimal concept that provides the functionality needed by the algorithm.

Figure 12.1 shows the refinement relations between the graph traversal concepts. Table 12.1 gives a summary of the valid expressions and associated types for the graph traversal concepts.

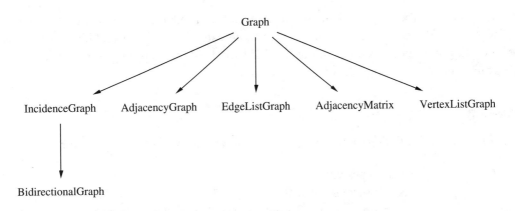

Figure 12.1 The graph concepts and refinement relationships.

12.1.1 Undirected Graphs

The interface that the BGL provides for accessing and manipulating undirected graphs is the same as the interface for directed graphs. The interface is the same because of a certain equivalence between undirected and directed graphs. That is, any undirected graph can be represented as a directed graph where each undirected edge (u, v) is replaced by two directed edges: (u, v) and (v, u). Such a directed graph is called the *directed version* of the undirected graph. Figure 12.2 shows an undirected graph and the directed version of it. Note that for every edge in the undirected graph, the directed graph has two edges. Thus, the BGL uses the *out_edges()* function (or *in_edges()*) to access the incident edges in an undirected graph. Similarly, the BGL uses *source()* and *target()* to access vertices. This may seem counterintuitive at first. However, by recognizing the equivalence between undirected and directed graphs, the BGL allows many algorithms to be applied to both directed and undirected graphs.

Expression	Return Type or Description
Graph	
graph_traits<G>::vertex_descriptor	The type of object used to identify vertices.
graph_traits<G>::directed_category	Directed or undirected edges?
graph_traits<G>::traversal_category	What kind of iterator traversal is supported?
graph_traits<G>::edge_parallel_category	Allow insertion of parallel edges?
IncidenceGraph refines Graph	
graph_traits<G>::edge_descriptor	The type of object used to identify edges.
graph_traits<G>::out_edge_iterator	Iterate through the out-edges.
graph_traits<G>::degree_size_type	The integer type for vertex degee.
out_edges(v, g)	*std::pair<out_edge_iterator, out_edge_iterator>*
source(e, g)	*vertex_descriptor*
target(e, g)	*vertex_descriptor*
out_degree(v, g)	*degree_size_type*
BidirectionalGraph refines IncidenceGraph	
graph_traits<G>::in_edge_iterator	Iterate through the in-edges.
in_edges(v, g)	*std::pair<in_edge_iterator, in_edge_iterator>*
in_degree(v, g)	*degree_size_type*
degree(e, g)	*degree_size_type*
AdjacencyGraph refines Graph	
graph_traits<G>::adjacency_iterator	Iterate through adjacent vertices.
adjacent_vertices(v, g)	*std::pair<adjacency_iterator,*
	adjacency_iterator>
VertexListGraph refines Graph	
graph_traits<G>::vertex_iterator	Iterate through the graph's vertex set.
graph_traits<G>::vertices_size_type	The unsigned integer type for representing the number of vertices.
num_vertices(g)	*vertices_size_type*
vertices(g)	*std::pair<vertex_iterator, vertex_iterator>*
EdgeListGraph refines Graph	
graph_traits<G>::edge_descriptor	The type of object used to identify edges.
graph_traits<G>::edge_iterator	Iterate through the graph's edge set.
graph_traits<G>::edges_size_type	The unsigned integer type for representing the number of edges.
num_edges(g)	*edges_size_type*
edges(g)	*std::pair<edge_iterator, edge_iterator>*
source(e, g)	*vertex_descriptor*
target(e, g)	*vertex_descriptor*
AdjacencyMatrix refines Graph	
edge(u, v, g)	*std::pair<edge_descriptor, bool>*

Table 12.1 Summary of the graph traversal concepts.

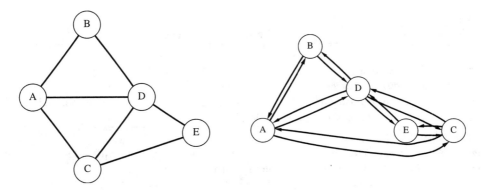

Figure 12.2 An undirected graph and its directed equivalent.

The following example demonstrates using the *out_edges* (), *source* (), and *target* () with an undirected graph. Even though edge directionality typically does not matter for undirected graphs, when applying the *out_edges* () function with a vertex u, the source vertex for the edge descriptors is always u and the target vertex is a vertex adjacent to u. The converse is true for the *in_edges* () function.

```
template  <typename UndirectedGraph>  void  undirected_graph_demo1 ()  {
    const int  V = 3;
    UndirectedGraph  undigraph (V);
    typename  graph_traits<UndirectedGraph>::vertex_descriptor zero,  one,  two;
    typename  graph_traits<UndirectedGraph>::out_edge_iterator out,  out_end;
    typename  graph_traits<UndirectedGraph>::in_edge_iterator in,  in_end;

    zero = vertex (0,  undigraph);
    one = vertex (1,  undigraph);
    two = vertex (2,  undigraph);
    add_edge (zero,  one,  undigraph);
    add_edge (zero,  two,  undigraph);
    add_edge (one,  two,  undigraph);

    std::cout << "out`edges(0): ";
    for (tie (out, out_end) = out_edges (zero, undigraph); out != out_end; ++out)
        std::cout << *out;
    std::cout << std::endl << "in`edges(0): ";
    for (tie (in, in_end) = in_edges (zero, undigraph); in != in_end; ++in)
        std::cout << *in;
    std::cout << std::endl;
}
```

The output is

```
out_edges (0):  (0,1)  (0,2)
in_edges (0):  (1,0)  (2,0)
```

Even though the interface is the same for undirected graphs, there are some behavioral differences because edge equality is defined differently. In a directed graph, edge (u, v) is never equal to edge (v, u), but in an undirected graph they may be equal. In an undirected graph that does not allow parallel edges (it is not a multigraph), (u, v) is the same edge as (v, u). However, in a multigraph the two edges may be different (because two edges (u, v) may also be different).

In the following examples the edge equality test for $(u, v) = (v, u)$ will return false for the directed graph and true for the undirected graph. The difference also affects the meaning of **add_edge ()**. In the directed graph example both edges (u, v) and (v, u) are added, whereas in the undirected graph example only one edge (u, v) is added. If (v, u) had also been added to the undirected graph, we would have been adding a parallel edge between u and v (provided the graph type allows parallel edges). The difference in edge equality also affects the attached edge properties. In the directed graph, the edges (u, v) and (v, u) can have distinct weight values, whereas in the undirected graph the weight of (u, v) is the same as the weight of (v, u) because they are the same edge.

First is the example code for the directed graph:

```
template <typename DirectedGraph> void directed_graph_demo() {
  const int V = 2;
  DirectedGraph digraph(V);
  typename graph_traits<DirectedGraph>::vertex_descriptor u, v;
  typedef typename DirectedGraph::edge_property_type Weight;
  typename property_map<DirectedGraph, edge_weight_t>::type
    weight = get(edge_weight, digraph);
  typename graph_traits<DirectedGraph>::edge_descriptor e1, e2;
  bool found;

  u = vertex(0, digraph);
  v = vertex(1, digraph);
  add_edge(u, v, Weight(1.2), digraph);
  add_edge(v, u, Weight(2.4), digraph);
  tie(e1, found) = edge(u, v, digraph);
  tie(e2, found) = edge(v, u, digraph);
  std::cout << "in a directed graph is ";
  std::cout << "(u,v) == (v,u) ? "
            << std::boolalpha << (e1 == e2) << std::endl;
  std::cout << "weight[(u,v)] = " << get(weight, e1) << std::endl;
  std::cout << "weight[(v,u)] = " << get(weight, e2) << std::endl;
}
```

The output is

```
in a directed graph is (u,v) == (v,u) ? false
weight[(u,v)] = 1.2
weight[(v,u)] = 2.4
```

Next is the example code for the undirected graph:

```
template <typename UndirectedGraph> void undirected_graph_demo2()
{
  const int V = 2;
  UndirectedGraph undigraph(V);
  typename graph_traits<UndirectedGraph>::vertex_descriptor u, v;
  typedef typename UndirectedGraph::edge_property_type Weight;
  typename property_map<UndirectedGraph, edge_weight_t>::type
    weight = get(edge_weight, undigraph);
  typename graph_traits<UndirectedGraph>::edge_descriptor e1, e2;
  bool found;

  u = vertex(0, undigraph);
  v = vertex(1, undigraph);
  add_edge(u, v, Weight(3.1), undigraph);
  tie(e1, found) = edge(u, v, undigraph);
  tie(e2, found) = edge(v, u, undigraph);
  std::cout << "in an undirected graph is ";
  std::cout << "(u,v) == (v,u) ? "
            << std::boolalpha << (e1 == e2) << std::endl;
  std::cout << "weight[(u,v)] = " << get(weight, e1) << std::endl;
  std::cout << "weight[(v,u)] = " << get(weight, e2) << std::endl;
}
```

The output is

```
in an undirected graph is (u,v) == (v,u) ? true
weight[(u,v)] = 3.1
weight[(v,u)] = 3.1
```

12.1.2 Graph

The Graph concept defines the associated types that are common to all of the graph concepts. These associated types are auxiliary types that play a part in many graph operations. Similar to the iterators of the STL, the associated types are accessed with a traits class—in this case, the *graph_traits* class. The use of the traits class mechanism is one of the reasons BGL algorithms are so flexible. For example, there is great variety in how graph data structures identify vertices. An adjacency-list style implementation might use integers to represent vertices, using the integer to offset to the appropriate out-edge list. An object-oriented graph implementation might use pointers to heap allocated vertex objects. With the *graph_traits* class, these differences are hidden by the *vertex_descriptor* associated type. Whatever the underlying type may be (integer, pointer, etc.), the graph algorithm can use *graph_traits* to obtain the type and create objects.

The Graph concept itself does not include any functions (valid expressions). The requirements for various graph operations have been factored into a family of concepts, IncidenceGraph, VertexListGraph, and so on.

One should note that a model of Graph is not required to be a model of Assignable or CopyConstructible, so algorithms with a Graph interface should pass graph objects by reference or explicitly add the Assignable and CopyConstructible requirements.

Associated Types

graph_traits<G>::vertex_descriptor
A vertex descriptor corresponds to a unique vertex in an abstract graph instance. A vertex descriptor must be DefaultConstructible, Assignable, and EqualityComparable.

graph_traits<G>::directed_category
The tags for this category are *directed_tag* and *undirected_tag*.

graph_traits<G>::edge_parallel_category
This describes whether the graph class allows the insertion of parallel edges (edges with the same source and target). The two tags are *allow_parallel_edge_tag* and *disallow_parallel_edge_tag*.

graph_traits<G>::traversal_category
This describes what kinds of iterator traversal the graph supports. The following traversal tag classes are defined:

```
struct incidence_graph_tag { };
struct adjacency_graph_tag { };
struct bidirectional_graph_tag : public virtual incidence_graph_tag { };
struct vertex_list_graph_tag { };
struct edge_list_graph_tag { };
struct adjacency_matrix_tag { };
```

12.1.3 IncidenceGraph

The IncidenceGraph concept provides an interface for efficient access to the out-edges of each vertex in the graph. The out-edges are accessed via out-edge iterators. The *out_edges(v,g)* function, given some vertex descriptor *v* and graph *g*, returns a pair of out-edge iterators. The first iterator points to the first out-edge of vertex *v*, and the second iterator points past the end of the sequence of out-edges. Dereferencing an out-edge iterator returns an edge descriptor. Incrementing an out-edge iterator moves to the next out-edge of the vertex. The order in which the out-edges appear in the iteration is not specified (although particular graph implementations may have a specified ordering).

Refinement of

Graph

Associated Types

graph_traits<G>::edge_descriptor
  An edge descriptor corresponds to a unique edge in the graph. An edge descriptor must
  be DefaultConstructible, Assignable, and EqualityComparable.

graph_traits<G>::out_edge_iterator
  An out-edge iterator for a vertex v provides access to the out-edges of v. As such, the
  value type of an out-edge iterator is the edge descriptor type of its graph. An out-edge
  iterator must meet the requirements of MultiPassInputIterator.

graph_traits<G>::degree_size_type
  This is the unsigned integral type used to represent the number out-edges or incident
  edges of a vertex.

Valid Expressions

source(e, g)
Return Type:	*vertex_descriptor*
Semantics:	Returns the vertex descriptor for u of the edge (u, v) represented by *e*.
Preconditions:	*e* is a valid edge descriptor of graph *g*.

target(e, g)
Return Type:	*vertex_descriptor*
Semantics:	Returns the vertex descriptor for v of the edge (u, v) represented by *e*.
Preconditions:	*e* is a valid edge descriptor of graph *g*.

out_edges(v, g)
Return Type:	*std::pair<out_edge_iterator, out_edge_iterator>*
Semantics:	Returns an iterator range providing access to the out-edges (for directed graphs) or incident edges (for undirected graphs) of vertex v. The vertex v shows up as the source vertex in each of the out-edges. The vertices to which v is adjacent are the target vertices for the out-edges (regardless of whether the graph is directed or undirected).
Preconditions:	*v* is a valid vertex descriptor of graph *g*.

out_degree(v, g)
Return Type:	*degree_size_type*
Semantics:	Returns the number of out-edges (for directed graphs) or the number of incident edges (for undirected graphs) of vertex v.
Preconditions:	*v* is a valid vertex descriptor of graph *g*.

Complexity Guarantees

The *source()*, *target()*, and *out_edges()* functions are required to be constant time. The *out_degree()* function must be linear in the number of out-edges for the vertex.

12.1.4   BidirectionalGraph

The BidirectionalGraph concept refines IncidenceGraph and adds the requirement for efficient access to the in-edges of each vertex. This concept is separated from IncidenceGraph because providing efficient access to in-edges of a directed graph typically requires more storage space, and many algorithms do not require access to in-edges. For undirected graphs this is not an issue because no extra space is needed to provide access to in-edges.

Refinement of

IncidenceGraph

Associated Types

graph_traits<G>::in_edge_iterator
   An in-edge iterator for a vertex v provides access to the in-edges of v. As such, the value type of an in-edge iterator is the edge descriptor type of its graph. An in-edge iterator must meet the requirements of MultiPassInputIterator.

Valid Expressions

in_edges(v, g)
   Return Type: *std::pair<in_edge_iterator, in_edge_iterator>*
   Semantics: Returns an iterator range providing access to the in-edges (for directed
                               graphs) or incident edges (for undirected graphs) of vertex v. The ver-
                               tex v shows up as the target vertex in each of the in-edges. The ver-
                               tices adjacent to v are the source vertices for the in-edges (regardless of
                               whether the graph is directed or undirected).
   Preconditions: *v* is a valid vertex descriptor of graph *g*.

in_degree(v, g)
   Return Type: *degree_size_type*
   Semantics: Returns the number of in-edges (for directed graphs) or the number of
                               incident edges (for undirected graphs) of vertex v.
   Preconditions: *v* is a valid vertex descriptor of graph *g*.

degree(v, g)

    Return Type: *degree_size_type*

    Semantics: Returns the number of in-edges plus out-edges (for directed graphs) or the number of incident edges (for undirected graphs) of vertex v.

    Preconditions: *v* is a valid vertex descriptor of graph *g*.

Complexity Guarantees

The *in_edges* **( )** function is required to be constant time. The *in_degree* **( )** function is required to be linear in the number of in-edges.

12.1.5   AdjacencyGraph

The AdjacencyGraph concept defines the interface for accessing adjacent vertices. Adjacent vertices can also be accessed as the target vertex of an out-edge; however, for some algorithms the out-edges are not needed, and it is more convenient to directly access the adjacent vertices.

Refinement of

Graph

Associated Types

graph_traits<G>::adjacency_iterator

    An adjacency iterator for a vertex v provides access to the vertices adjacent to v. As such, the value type of an adjacency iterator is the vertex descriptor type of its graph. An adjacency iterator must meet the requirements of MultiPassInputIterator.

Valid Expressions

adjacent_vertices(v, g)

    Return Type: *std::pair<adjacency_iterator, adjacency_iterator>*

    Semantics: Returns an iterator range providing access to the vertices adjacent to vertex v. More specifically, this range is equivalent to taking the target vertex for every out-edge of vertex v.

    Preconditions: *v* is a valid vertex descriptor of graph *g*.

Complexity Guarantees

The *adjacent_vertices* ( ) function must return in constant time.

12.1.6 VertexListGraph

The VertexListGraph concept defines the requirements for efficient traversal of all the vertices in the graph.

Refinement of

Graph

Associated Types

graph_traits<G>::vertex_iterator
   A vertex iterator (obtained via *vertices(g)*) provides access to all of the vertices in a graph. A vertex iterator type must meet the requirements of MultiPassInputIterator. The value type of the vertex iterator must be the vertex descriptor of the graph.

graph_traits<G>::vertices_size_type
   The unsigned integer type used to represent the number of vertices in the graph.

Valid Expressions

vertices(g)
   Return Type: *std::pair<vertex_iterator, vertex_iterator>*
   Semantics: Returns an iterator range providing access to all the vertices in graph *g*.

num_vertices(g)
   Return Type: *vertices_size_type*
   Semantics: Returns the number of vertices in the graph *g*.

Complexity Guarantees

The *vertices* ( ) function must return in constant time. The *num_vertices* ( ) function must return in time linear to the number of vertices.

12.1.7 EdgeListGraph

The EdgeListGraph concept refines the Graph concept and adds the requirement for efficient access to all the edges in the graph.

Refinement of

Graph

Associated Types

graph_traits<G>::edge_descriptor

An edge descriptor corresponds to a unique edge in the graph. An edge descriptor must be DefaultConstructible, Assignable, and EqualityComparable.

graph_traits<G>::edge_iterator

An edge iterator (obtained via *edges(g)*) provides access to all of the edges in a graph. An edge iterator type must meet the requirements of an InputIterator. The value type of the edge iterator must be the same as the edge descriptor of the graph.

graph_traits<G>::edges_size_type

This is the unsigned integer type used to represent the number of edges in the graph.

Valid Expressions

edges(g)

Return Type:	*std::pair<edge_iterator, edge_iterator>*
Semantics:	Returns an iterator range providing access to all the edges in graph *g*.

source(e, g)

Return Type:	*vertex_descriptor*
Semantics:	Returns the vertex descriptor for u of the edge (u, v) represented by *e*.
Preconditions:	*e* is a valid edge descriptor of graph *g*.

target(e, g)
    Return Type: *vertex_descriptor*
    Semantics: Returns the vertex descriptor for v of the edge (u, v) represented by *e*.
    Preconditions: *e* is a valid edge descriptor of graph *g*.

num_edges(g)
    Return Type: *edges_size_type*
    Semantics: Returns the number of edges in graph *g*.

Complexity Guarantees

The *edges()*, *source()*, and *target()* functions must return in constant time. The *num_edges()* function must be in linear time to the number of edges in the graph.

12.1.8 AdjacencyMatrix

The AdjacencyMatrix concept refines Graph concept and adds the requirement for efficient access to any edge in the graph given the source and target vertices.

Refinement of

Graph

Valid Expresions

edge(u, v, g)
    Return type: *std::pair<edge_descriptor, bool>*
    Semantics: Returns a pair consisting of a flag saying whether there exists an edge between *u* and *v* in graph *g*, and consisting of the edge descriptor if the edge was found.
    Preconditions: *u, v* are valid vertex descriptors of graph *g*.

Complexity Guarantees

The *edge()* function must return in constant time.

Expression	Return Type or Description
VertexMutableGraph refines Graph	
add_vertex(g)	*vertex_descriptor*
remove_vertex(v, g)	*void*
EdgeMutableGraph refines Graph	
clear_vertex(v, g)	*void*
add_edge(u, v, g)	*std::pair<edge_descriptor, bool>*
remove_edge(u, v, g)	*void*
remove_edge(e, g)	*void*
MutableIncidenceGraph refines IncidenceGraph and EdgeMutableGraph	
remove_edge(eiter, g)	*void*
remove_out_edge_if(u, p, g)	*void*
MutableBidirectionalGraph refines MutableIncidenceGraph and BidirectionalGraph	
remove_edge(eiter, g)	*void*
remove_out_edge_if(u, p, g)	*void*
MutableEdgeListGraph refines EdgeMutableGraph and EdgeListGraph	
remove_edge_if(p, g)	*void*
PropertyGraph refines Graph	
property_map<G, PropertyTag>::type	Type for mutable vertex property map.
property_map<G, PropertyTag>::const_type	Type for nonmutable property map.
get(ptag, g)	Function to get a vertex property map object.
get(ptag, g, x)	Get the property value for vertex or edge *x*.
put(ptag, g, x, v)	Set the property value for vertex or edge *x*.
VertexMutablePropertyGraph refines VertexMutableGraph and PropertyGraph	
add_vertex(vp, g)	*vertex_descriptor*
EdgeMutablePropertyGraph refines EdgeMutableGraph and PropertyGraph	
add_edge(u, v, ep, g)	*std::pair<edge_descriptor, bool>*

Table 12.2 Summary of the graph modifying and property access concepts.

12.2   Graph Modification Concepts

This section describes the BGL interface for modifying a graph—that is, adding and removing vertices and edges and changing the value of properties attached to vertices and edges in the graph. Like the graph-traversal concepts, the graph-modification concepts are factored into many small concepts to provide algorithm writers with a good selection of concepts with which to describe their requirements. Table 12.2 summarizes the valid expressions and associated types for each of concepts and Figure 12.3 shows the refinement relations between the graph-modification concepts. Some of the concepts from Figure 12.1 also play a role in Figure 12.3, but all of the refinement relationships from Figure 12.1 have been omitted.

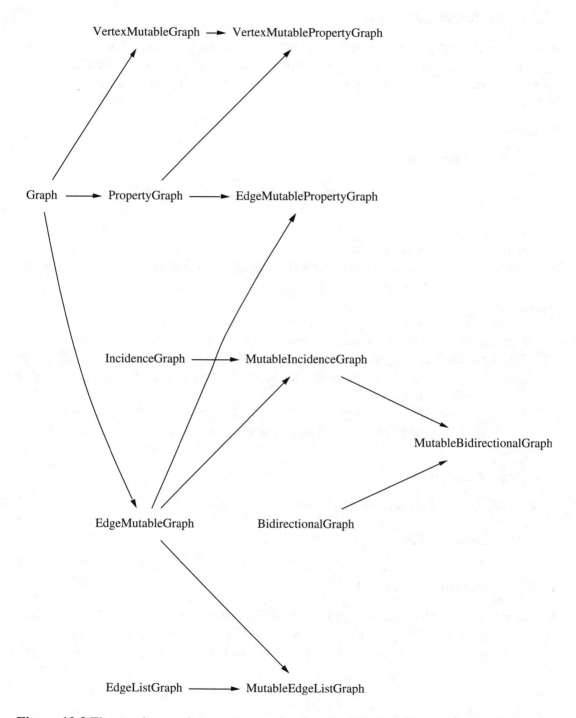

Figure 12.3 The graph-mutating concepts and refinement relationships.

12.2.1 VertexMutableGraph

A vertex mutable graph can be changed by adding or removing vertices. The memory management is the responsibility of the graph implementation. The graph user need only make calls to *add_vertex()* and *remove_vertex()* and the graph implementation does the rest.

Refinement of

Graph, DefaultConstructible

Valid Expressions

add_vertex(g)
     Return Type: *vertex_descriptor*
     Semantics: Add a new vertex to the graph. The *vertex_descriptor* for the new vertex is returned.

remove_vertex(u, g)
     Return Type: *void*
     Semantics: Remove u from the vertex set of the graph.
     Preconditions: *u* is a valid vertex descriptor of graph *g* and there are no edges incident to vertex u. The function *clear_vertex()* can be used to remove all incident edges.
     Postconditions: *num_vertices(g)* is one less; *u* no longer appears in the vertex set of the graph and it is no longer a valid vertex descriptor.

Complexity Guarantees

- Vertex insertion is guaranteed to be amortized constant time.

- Vertex removal is at most $O(|E| + |V|)$.

12.2.2 EdgeMutableGraph

An EdgeMutableGraph can be changed via the addition or removal of edges. Memory management is the responsibility of the graph implementation. The user of the graph need only make calls to *add_edge()*, *remove_edge()*, and so on, and the graph implementation does the rest.

Refinement of

Graph

Valid Expressions

add_edge(u, v, g)

Return Type:	*std::pair<edge_descriptor, bool>*
Semantics:	Attempt to insert the edge (u, v) into the graph, returning the inserted edge or a parallel edge and a flag that specifies whether an edge was inserted. This operation must not invalidate vertex descriptors or vertex iterators of the graph, though it may invalidate edge descriptors or edge iterators. The order in which the new edge appears via the graph's edge iterators is not specified.
Preconditions:	u and v are vertices in the graph.
Postconditions:	(u, v) is in the edge set of the graph. The returned edge descriptor will have u in the source position and v in the target position. If the graph allows parallel edges, then the returned flag is always true. If the graph does not allow parallel edges and if (u, v) was already in the graph then the returned flag is false. If (u, v) was not in the graph then the returned flag is true.

remove_edge(u, v, g)

Return Type:	*void*
Semantics:	Remove the edge (u, v) from the graph. If the graph allows parallel edges this removes all occurrences of (u, v).
Precondition:	(u, v) is in the edge set of the graph.
Postcondition:	(u, v) is no longer in the edge set of the graph.

remove_edge(e, g)

Return Type:	*void*
Semantics:	Remove the edge e from the graph.
Precondition:	e is an edge in the graph.
Postcondition:	e is no longer in the edge set for *g*.

clear_vertex(u, g)

Return Type:	*void*
Semantics:	Remove all edges to and from vertex u from the graph.
Precondition:	u is a valid vertex descriptor of *g*.
Postconditions:	u does not appear as a source or target of any edge in *g*.

Complexity Guarantees

- Edge insertion must be either amortized constant time or it can be $O(\log \frac{|E|}{|V|})$ if the insertion also checks to prevent the addition of parallel edges.

- Edge removal is guaranteed to be $O(|E|)$.

- Clearing a vertex is at most $O(|E| + |V|)$.

12.2.3 MutableIncidenceGraph

This concept provides the ability to remove edges from the out-edge list of a vertex.

Refinement of

IncidenceGraph and EdgeMutableGraph

Valid Expressions

remove_edge(eiter, g)
    Return type: *void*
    Semantics: Remove the edge pointed to by *eiter* from the graph, where *eiter* is an out-edge iterator for the graph.
    Precondition: *eiter* is an edge in the graph.
    Postcondition: *eiter* is no longer in the edge set for *g*.

remove_out_edge_if(u, p, g)
    Return type: *void*
    Semantics: Remove all the out-edges of vertex *u* for which the predicate *p* returns true. This expression is only required when the graph also models IncidenceGraph.
    Preconditions: *u* is a valid vertex descriptor of graph *g*.
    Postcondition: *p* returns false for all out-edges of u and all the out-edges of u for which *p* was originally false are still in the graph.

Complexity Guarantees

- The *remove_edge()* function is required to return in constant time.

- The *remove_out_edge_if()* is required to return in time linear to the number of out-edges for the vertex.

12.2.4 MutableBidirectionalGraph

The MutableBidirectionalGraph concept defines the interface for removing edges from the in-edge list of a vertex.

Refinement of

BidirectionalGraph and MutableIncidenceGraph

Valid Expressions

remove_in_edge_if(v, p, g)

    Return type: *void*

    Semantics: Remove all the in-edges of vertex *v* for which *p* returns true.

    Preconditions: *v* is a valid vertex descriptor of graph *g*.

    Postcondition: *p* returns false for all in-edges of v and all the in-edges of v for which *p* was originally false are still in the graph.

Complexity Guarantees

- The *remove_in_edge_if()* function is linear time in the number of in-edges for the vertex.

12.2.5 MutableEdgeListGraph

The MutableEdgeListGraph concept provides the ability to remove edges from the edge list of a graph.

Refinement of

EdgeMutableGraph

Valid Expressions

remove_edge_if(p, g)

    Return type: *void*

    Semantics: Remove all the edges from graph *g* for which *p* returns true.

    Postcondition: *p* returns false for all edges in the graph and the graph still contains all edges for which *p* was originally false.

Complexity Guarantees

- The *remove_edge_if()* function is required to be linear time in the number of edges in the graph.

12.2.6 PropertyGraph

A PropertyGraph is a graph that has some property associated with each of the vertices or edges in the graph. As a given graph may have several properties associated with each vertex or edge, a tag is used to identity which property is being accessed. In the following requirements description, *PropertyTag* is the type of the tag, and *tag* is an object of type *PropertyTag*. The graph provides a function that returns a property map object.

Refinement of

Graph

Associated Types

property_map<G, PropertyTag>::type
> The type of the property map for the property specified by *PropertyTag*. This type must be a mutable LvaluePropertyMap with a key type the same as the graph's vertex or edge descriptor type.

property_map<G, PropertyTag>::const_type
> The type of the const property map for the property specified by *PropertyTag*. This type must be an immutable LvaluePropertyMap with a key type the same as the graph's vertex or edge descriptor type.

Valid Expressions

get(ptag, g)
> Return type: *property_map<G, PropertyTag>::type*
> if *g* is mutable and *property_map<G, PropertyTag>::const_type*
> otherwise.
>
> Semantics: Returns the property map for the property specified by the *PropertyTag* type. The object *ptag* is only used to carry the type.

get(ptag, g, x)
> Return type: *property_traits<PMap>::value_type*
> Semantics: Returns the property value (specified by the *PropertyTag* type) associated with object *x* (a vertex or edge). The object *ptag* is only used to carry the type. This function is equivalent to: *get(get(ptag, g), x)*

Complexity Guarantees

The *get()* functions is required to return in constant time.

12.2.7   VertexMutablePropertyGraph

A VertexMutablePropertyGraph is a VertexMutableGraph and a PropertyGraph with addition functions for specifying property values when adding vertices to the graph.

Refinement of

VertexMutableGraph and PropertyGraph

Associated Types

vertex_property<G>::type
    The type of the vertex property object attached to each vertex.

Valid Expressions

add_vertex(vp, g)
Return type:	***vertex_descriptor***
Semantics:	Add a new vertex to the graph and copy ***vp*** into the property object for the new vertex. The ***vertex_descriptor*** for the new vertex is returned.

Complexity Guarantees

- ***add_vertex()*** is guaranteed to be amortized constant time.

12.2.8 EdgeMutablePropertyGraph

An EdgeMutablePropertyGraph is an EdgeMutableGraph and a PropertyGraph with addition functions for specifying property values when adding edges to the graph.

Refinement of

EdgeMutableGraph and PropertyGraph

Associated Types

edge_property<G>::type
    The type of the edge property object attached to each edge.

Valid Expressions

add_edge(u, v, ep, g)
Return type:	***std::pair<edge_descriptor, bool>***
Semantics:	Inserts the edge (u, v) into the graph, and copies object ***ep*** into the property plugin for that edge.
Preconditions:	***u, v*** are valid vertex descriptors of graph ***g***.

Complexity Guarantees

- Edge insertion must be either amortized constant time or it can be $O(\log \frac{|E|}{|V|})$ if the insertion also checks to prevent the addition of parallel edges.

12.3   Visitor Concepts

The visitor concepts play a similar role in BGL as functors play in the STL. Functors provide a mechanism for extending an algorithm—for customizing what is done at each step of the algorithm. Visitors allow users to insert their own operations at various steps within a graph algorithm. Unlike the STL algorithms, graph algorithms typically have multiple event points where the user may want to insert a callback via a functor. Therefore, visitors do not have a single *operator* ( ) method like a functor, but instead have several methods that correspond to the various event points. Each algorithm has a different set of event points. In this section we define visitor concepts for the main BGL algorithms.

Like function objects in the STL, visitors are passed by value in the BGL algorithms. This means that some care must be taken when storing state in visitor objects.

Notation

The notation used through this section is collected here.

V	is a type that is a model of the visitor concept
vis	is an object of type *V*
G	is a type that is a model of Graph
g	is an object of type *G*
e	is an object of type *graph_traits<G>::edge_descriptor*
s, u	are objects of type *graph_traits<G>::vertex_descriptor*

12.3.1 BFSVisitor

This concept defines the visitor interface for *breadth_first_search* ( ). Users can define a class with the BFSVisitor interface and pass an object of the class to *breadth_first_search* ( ), thereby augmenting the actions taken during the graph search.

Refinement of

CopyConstructible

Valid Expressions

vis.initialize_vertex(u, g)
      Return type: *void*
      Semantics: This is invoked on every vertex of the graph before the start of the graph
                        search.

vis.discover_vertex(u, g)

Return type: *void*

Semantics: This function is invoked the first time the algorithm encounters vertex u. All other vertices closer to the source vertex have been discovered, and vertices further from the source have not yet been discovered.

vis.examine_edge(e, g)

Return type: *void*

Semantics: This is invoked on every out-edge of each vertex after it is discovered.

vis.tree_edge(e, g)

Return type: *void*

Semantics: If the edge being examined is a member of the search tree, then this function is invoked. A call to this function is always preceded by a call to the *examine_edge*() function.

vis.non_tree_edge(e, g)

Return type: *void*

Semantics: If the edge being examined is not a member of the search tree, then this function is invoked. A call to this function is always preceded by a call to the *examine_edge*() function. For directed graphs, such an edge must be either a back or cross edge. For undirected graphs, such an edge is a cross edge.

vis.gray_target(e, g)

Return type: *void*

Semantics: This function is called if the edge being examined is a cycle edge, and if the target vertex is colored gray at the time of examination. A call to this function is always preceded by a call to the *cycle_edge*() function. The color gray indicates that the vertex is currently in the queue.

vis.black_target(e, g)

Return type: *void*

Semantics: This function is called if the edge being examined is a cycle edge, and if the target vertex is colored black at the time of examination. The call to this function is always preceded by a call to the *cycle_edge*() function. The color black indicates that the vertex has already been removed from the queue.

vis.finish_vertex(u, g)

Return type: *void*

Semantics: This is invoked on a vertex after all of its out-edges have been added to the search tree and all of the adjacent vertices have been discovered (but before their out-edges have been examined).

12.3.2 DFSVisitor

This concept defines the visitor interface for *depth_first_search()*. Users can define a class with the DFSVisitor interface and pass an object of the class to *depth_first_search()*, thereby augmenting the actions taken during the graph search.

Refinement of

CopyConstructible

Valid Expressions

vis.initialize_vertex(s, g)
> Return type: *void*
> Semantics: This is invoked on every vertex before the start of the search.

vis.start_vertex(s, g)
> Return type: *void*
> Semantics: This is invoked on the source vertex once before the start of the search.

vis.discover_vertex(u, g)
> Return type: *void*
> Semantics: This is invoked when a vertex is encountered for the first time.

vis.examine_edge(e, g)
> Return type: *void*
> Semantics: This is invoked on every out-edge of each vertex after it is discovered.

vis.tree_edge(e, g)
> Return type: *void*
> Semantics: This is invoked on each edge as it becomes a member of the edges that form the search tree.

vis.back_edge(e, g)
> Return type: *void*
> Semantics: This is invoked on the back edges in the graph. For an undirected graph there is some ambiguity between tree edges and back edges since the edges (u, v) and (v, u) are the same edge, but both the *tree_edge()* and *back_edge()* functions are invoked. One way to resolve this ambiguity is to record the tree edges, and then disregard the back edges that are already marked as tree edges. An easy way to record tree edges is to record predecessors in the *tree_edge()* function.

vis.forward_or_cross_edge(e, g)
> Return type: *void*
> Semantics: This is invoked on forward or cross edges in the graph. In an undirected graph this method is never called.

vis.finish_vertex(u, g)
>   Return type: ***void***
>   Semantics: This is invoked on a vertex after all of its out-edges have been added to the search tree and all of the adjacent vertices have been discovered (but before their out-edges have been examined).

12.3.3   DijkstraVisitor

This concept defines the visitor interface for ***dijkstra_shortest_paths*** **( )** and related algorithms. The user can create a class that matches this interface, and then pass objects of the class into ***dijkstra_shortest_paths*** **( )** to augment the actions taken during the search.

Refinement of

CopyConstructible

Valid Expressions

vis.discover_vertex(u, g)
>   Return type: ***void***
>   Semantics: This is invoked when a vertex is encountered for the first time.

vis.examine_edge(e, g)
>   Return type: ***void***
>   Semantics: This is invoked on every out-edge of each vertex after it is discovered.

vis.edge_relaxed(e, g)
>   Return type: ***void***
>   Semantics: Let (u, v) be the edge e, d be the distance map, and w the weight map. Upon examination, if $d[u] + w(u, v) < d[v]$, then the edge is relaxed (its distance is reduced), and this method is invoked.

vis.edge_not_relaxed(e, g)
>   Return type: ***void***
>   Semantics: Upon examination, if the edge is not relaxed (see above), then this method is invoked.

vis.finish_vertex(u, g)
>   Return type: ***void***
>   Semantics: This is invoked on a vertex after all of its out-edges have been added to the search tree and all of the adjacent vertices have been discovered (but before their out-edges have been examined).

12.3.4   BellmanFordVisitor

This concept defines the visitor interface for ***bellman_ford_shortest_paths*** **()**. Users can define a visitor class with the BellmanFordVisitor interface and pass an object of the visitor class to the ***visitor*()** parameter of ***bellman_ford_shortest_paths*** **()**, thereby augmenting the actions taken during the graph search.

Refinement of

CopyConstructible

Valid Expressions

vis.initialize_vertex(s, g)

> Return type: ***void***
>
> Semantics: This is invoked on every vertex before the start of the search.

vis.examine_edge(e, g)

> Return type: ***void***
>
> Semantics: This is invoked on every edge in the graph ***num_vertices(g)*** times.

vis.edge_relaxed(e, g)

> Return type: ***void***
>
> Semantics: Let (u, v) be the edge e, d be the distance map, and w the weight map. If $d[u] + w(u, v) < d[v]$, then the edge is relaxed (its distance is reduced), and this method is invoked.

edge_not_relaxed(e, g)

> Return type: ***void***
>
> Semantics: Upon examination, if the edge is not relaxed (see above), then this method is invoked.

vis.edge_minimized(e, g)

> Return type: ***void***
>
> Semantics: After the ***num_vertices(g)*** iterations through the edge set of the graph is complete, one last iteration is made to test whether each edge was minimized. If the edge is minimized then this function is invoked. An edge (u, v) is minimized if $d[u] + w(u, v) \geq d[v]$.

edge_not_minimized(e, g)

> Return type: ***void***
>
> Semantics: If the edge is not minimized, this function is invoked. This happens when there is a negative cycle in the graph.

Chapter 13

BGL Algorithms

13.1   Overview

This chapter provides in-depth information about how to use all of the graph algorithms in the Boost Graph Library.

The BGL generic algorithms are divided into the following categories:

1. Basic search algorithms

2. Shortest paths

3. Minimum spanning tree

4. Connected components

5. Maximum flow

6. Vertex ordering

All of the algorithms are implemented as function templates where the graph type is a template parameter. This allows the function to be used with any graph type that models the required concepts. The documentation for each algorithm lists the required graph concepts, and the documentation for each graph class lists the concepts that the graph models. By cross-referencing through the concepts one can determine which graph types can be used with which algorithm.

In addition, the algorithms are sometimes parameterized with property maps, such as the distance map for the shortest-path algorithms. The parameterized property maps give the user control over how properties are stored and retrieved. The algorithms are also parameterized on a visitor type, which allows the user to specify call-backs that will be invoked at certain event points in the algorithm.

Prototypes

The reference section for each algorithm starts with the function prototype. The template parameter names are suggestive of the purpose of the parameter, and sometimes of the concepts required of the parameters. However, the precise requirements for each template parameter are given in the parameters section.

The last parameter for many of the functions is *bgl_named_params*. This is to support the named parameter technique described in §2.7 and also discussed here. If = *all defaults* appears after *params*, then there are defaults for all of the named parameters and they can all be omitted.

Description

In the description of the function we define the problem that the function solves, explaining any graph terminology or ideas that are necessary to understand the problem. We then describe the semantics of the function in terms of its effects on the parameters.

Where Defined

In this section we list the header file that must be included to use the function.

Parameters

Here we list all of the normal parameters (named parameters come in the next section) of the function. The normal parameters are *required* (i.e., there are no defaults for these parameters).

Each parameter is categorized into one or more of the following categories:

IN parameters are read by the function; used to obtain information. The function does not change or modify these parameters in any way.

OUT parameters are written to by the function. The results of the function are stored into OUT parameters.

UTIL parameters are required by the algorithm to accomplish its task, however, the contents of the objects used as UTIL parameters are typically not of interest to the user. UTIL parameters are often read and written.

Named Parameters

As described in §2.7, the BGL uses a special technique to make it more convenient to deal with functions that have large numbers of parameters, and where many of the parameters have defaults. This section lists all of the named parameters for the function, using the same categorization as for the normal parameters. In addition, the default is listed for each named parameter.

Preconditions

In this section we describe any preconditions for the function. Often this includes requirements on the state of the property map parameters.

Complexity

The time complexity for each algorithm is given in "big-O" notation. The space complexity is never more than $O(|V|)$ unless otherwise specified.

Example

A simple example is shown to demonstrate how each algorithm is used.

13.2   Basic Algorithms

13.2.1   *breadth_first_search*

```
template <typename Graph, typename P, typename T, typename R>
void breadth_first_search (Graph& g,
        typename graph_traits<Graph>::vertex_descriptor s,
        const bgl_named_params<P, T, R>& params)
```

The *breadth_first_search*() function performs a breadth-first traversal [31] of a directed or undirected graph. A breadth-first traversal visits vertices that are closer to the source before visiting vertices that are farther away. In this context, distance is defined as the number of edges in the shortest path from the source vertex. The *breadth_first_search*() function can be used to compute the shortest path from the source to all reachable vertices and the resulting shortest-path distances. For more definitions related to BFS and a detailed example, see §4.1.

BFS uses two data structures to implement the traversal: a color marker for each vertex and a queue. White vertices are undiscovered, whereas gray vertices are discovered but are adjacent to white vertices. Black vertices are discovered and are adjacent to only other black or gray vertices. The algorithm proceeds by removing a vertex u from the queue and examining each out-edge (u, v). If an adjacent vertex v is not already discovered, it is colored gray and placed in the queue. After all of the out-edges are examined, vertex u is colored black and the process is repeated. Pseudocode for the BFS algorithm is listed as follows. In the pseudocode we show the algorithm computing predecessors π, discover time d, and finish time t. By default, the *breadth_first_search*() function does not compute these properties; however, there are predefined visitors that can be used to do this.

BFS(G, s)
    for each vertex $u \in V[G]$ ▷ initialize vertex u
       $color[u] \leftarrow WHITE$

$$d[u] \leftarrow \infty$$
$$\pi[u] \leftarrow u$$
$$color[s] \leftarrow GRAY$$
$$d[s] \leftarrow 0$$

ENQUEUE(Q, s)   ▷ discover vertex s
while ($Q \neq \emptyset$)
   $u \leftarrow$ DEQUEUE(Q)   ▷ examine vertex u
   for each $v \in Adj[u]$ ▷ examine edge (u, v)
     if ($color[v] = WHITE$)   ▷ (u, v) is a tree edge
      $color[v] \leftarrow GRAY$
      $d[v] \leftarrow d[u] + 1$
      $\pi[v] \leftarrow u$
      ENQUEUE(Q, v)   ▷ discover vertex v
    else   ▷ (u, v) is a non-tree edge
     if ($color[v] = GRAY$)
      ...   ▷ (u, v) has a gray target
     else
      ...   ▷ (u, v) has a black target
   $color[u] \leftarrow BLACK$ ▷ finish vertex u
return (d, π)

The *breadth_first_search*() function can be extended with user-defined actions that are called at certain event points. The actions must be provided in the form of a visitor object— that is, an object whose type meets the requirements for a BFSVisitor. In the preceding pseudocode, the event points are labeled with triangles. By default, the *breadth_first_search*() function does not carry out any actions, not even recording distances or predecessors. However, these can be easily added by defining a visitor.

Where Defined

boost/graph/breadth_first_search.hpp

Parameters

IN: *Graph& g*
> A directed or undirected graph. The graph type must be a model of VertexListGraph and IncidenceGraph.

IN: *vertex_descriptor s*
> The source vertex where the search is started.

Named Parameters

IN: *visitor(BFSVisitor vis)*

> A visitor object that is invoked inside the algorithm at the event points specified by the BFSVisitor concept.
>
> **Default:** *default_bfs_visitor*

UTIL/OUT: *color_map(ColorMap color)*

> This is used by the algorithm to keep track of its progress through the graph. The type *ColorMap* must be a model of ReadWritePropertyMap, its key type must be the graph's vertex descriptor type, and the value type of the color map must model ColorValue.
>
> **Default:** an *iterator_property_map* created from a *std::vector* of *default_color_type* of size *num_vertices(g)* and using the *i_map* for the index map.

IN: *vertex_index_map(VertexIndexMap i_map)*

> This maps each vertex to an integer in the range $[0, |V|)$. This parameter is only necessary when the default color property map is used. The type *VertexIndexMap* must be a model of ReadablePropertyMap. The value type of the map must be an integer type. The vertex descriptor type of the graph needs to be usable as the key type of the map.
>
> **Default:** *get(vertex_index, g)*

UTIL: *buffer(Buffer& Q)*

> The queue used to determine the order in which vertices will be discovered. If a FIFO queue is used, then the traversal will be according to the usual BFS ordering. Other types of queues can be used, but the traversal order will be different. For example Dijkstra's algorithm can be implemented using a priority queue. The type *Buffer* must be a model of Buffer.
>
> **Default:** *boost::queue*

Preconditions

The queue must be empty.

Complexity

The time complexity is $O(|E| + |V|)$. The worst-case space complexity is $O(|V|)$.

Example

This example demonstrates using the BGL breadth-first-search algorithm on the graph from Figure 13.1. The program records the order in which breadth-first search discovers the vertices in the graph. The source code for this example is in *example/bfs-example.cpp*.

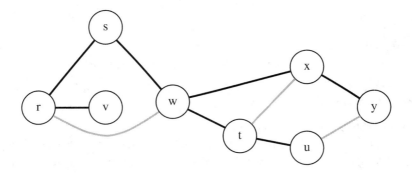

Figure 13.1 A breadth-first search of a graph. The BFS tree edges are the solid black lines.

⟨ BFS Time Visitor 168a ⟩ ≡

```
template <typename TimeMap>
class bfs_time_visitor : public default_bfs_visitor {
  typedef typename property_traits<TimeMap>::value_type T;
public:
  bfs_time_visitor(TimeMap tmap, T& t) : m_timemap(tmap), m_time(t) { }
  template <typename Vertex, typename Graph>
  void discover_vertex(Vertex u, const Graph& g) const {
    put(m_timemap, u, m_time++);
  }
  TimeMap m_timemap;
  T& m_time;
};
```

⟨ *bfs-example.cpp* 168b ⟩ ≡

```
#include <boost/graph/adjacency_list.hpp>
#include <boost/graph/breadth_first_search.hpp>
#include <boost/pending/indirect_cmp.hpp>
#include <boost/pending/integer_range.hpp>
using namespace boost;
  ⟨BFS Time Visitor 168a⟩

int main()
{
  using namespace boost;
  // Select the graph type we wish to use
  typedef adjacency_list<vecS, vecS, undirectedS> graph_t;
  // Set up the vertex IDs and names
  enum { r, s, t, u, v, w, x, y, N };
  const char* name = "rstuvwxy";
  // Specify the edges in the graph
```

```
typedef std::pair<int,int> E;
E edge_array[] = { E(r,s), E(r,v), E(s,w), E(w,r), E(w,t),
    E(w,x), E(x,t), E(t,u), E(x,y), E(u,y) };
// Create the graph object
const int n_edges = sizeof(edge_array)/sizeof(E);
graph_t g(edge_array, edge_array + n_edges, N);


// Typedefs
typedef graph_traits<graph_t>::vertex_descriptor Vertex;
typedef graph_traits<graph_t>::vertices_size_type Size;
typedef std::vector<Vertex>::iterator Piter;
typedef std::vector<Size>::iterator Iiter;


// a vector to hold the discover time property for each vertex
std::vector<Size> dtime(num_vertices(g));


Size time = 0;
bfs_time_visitor<Size*> vis(&dtime[0], time);
breadth_first_search(g, vertex(s, g), visitor(vis));


// Use std::sort to order the vertices by their discover time
std::vector<graph_traits<graph_t>::vertices_size_type> discover_order(N);
integer_range<int> range(0, N);
std::copy(range.begin(), range.end(), discover_order.begin());
std::sort(discover_order.begin(), discover_order.end(),
    indirect_cmp<Iiter, std::less<Size> >(dtime.begin()));


std::cout << "order of discovery: ";
for (int i = 0; i < N; ++i)
    std::cout << name[ discover_order[i] ] << " ";
std::cout << std::endl;
return EXIT_SUCCESS;
}
```

The output is

```
order of discovery: s r w v t x u y
```

13.2.2 breadth_first_visit

```
template <typename IncidenceGraph, typename P, typename T, typename R>
void breadth_first_visit(IncidenceGraph& g,
        typename graph_traits<IncidenceGraph>::vertex_descriptor s,
        const bgl_named_params<P, T, R>& params);
```

This function is the same as ***breadth_first_search ()*** except that the color markers are not initialized in the algorithm. The user is responsible for making sure the color for every vertex is white before calling the algorithm. With this difference, the graph type is only required to be an IncidenceGraph instead of a VertexListGraph. Also, this difference allows for more flexibility in the color property map. For example, one could use a map that only implements a partial function on the vertices, which could be more space efficient when the search only reaches a small portion of the graph.

Parameters

IN: ***IncidenceGraph& g***
> A directed or undirected graph. The graph's type must be a model of IncidenceGraph.

IN: ***vertex_descriptor s***
> The source vertex where the search is started.

Named Parameters

IN: ***visitor(BFSVisitor vis)***
> A visitor object that is invoked inside the algorithm at the event points specified by the BFSVisitor concept.
> **Default:** *bfs_visitor<null_visitor>*

IN/UTIL/OUT: ***color_map(ColorMap color)***
> This is used by the algorithm to keep track of its progress through the graph. The color of every vertex should be initialized to white before the call to ***breadth_first_visit ()***. The type ***ColorMap*** must be a model of ReadWritePropertyMap and its key type must be the graph's vertex descriptor type and the value type of the color map map must model ColorValue.
> **Default:** *get(vertex_color, g)*

UTIL: ***buffer(Buffer& Q)***
> The queue used to determine the order in which vertices will be discovered. If a FIFO queue is used, then the traversal will be according to the usual BFS ordering. Other types of queues can be used, but the traversal order will be different. For example, Dijkstra's algorithm can be implemented using a priority queue. The type ***Buffer*** must be a model of Buffer.
> **Default:** *boost::queue*

13.2.3 *depth_first_search*

> *template <typename Graph, typename P, typename T, typename R>*
> *void depth_first_search (Graph& g, const bgl_named_params<P, T, R>& params)*

The **depth_first_search()** function performs a depth-first traversal of the vertices in a directed or undirected graph. When possible, a depth-first traversal chooses a vertex adjacent to the current vertex to visit next. If all adjacent vertices have already been discovered, or there are no adjacent vertices, then the algorithm backtracks to the last vertex that had undiscovered neighbors. Once all reachable vertices have been visited, the algorithm selects from any remaining undiscovered vertices and continues the traversal. The algorithm finishes when all vertices have been visited. Depth-first search is useful for categorizing edges in a graph, and for imposing an ordering on the vertices. §4.2 describes the various properties of DFS and walks through an example.

Similar to BFS, color markers are used to keep track of which vertices have been discovered. White marks vertices that have yet to be discovered, gray marks a vertex that is discovered but still has vertices adjacent to it that are undiscovered. A black vertex is a discovered vertex that is not adjacent to any white vertices.

The **depth_first_search()** function invokes user-defined actions at certain event points within the algorithm. This provides a mechanism for adapting the generic DFS algorithm to the many situations in which it can be used. In the following pseudocode, the event points for DFS are indicated by the triangles and labels on the right. The user-defined actions must be provided in the form of a visitor object, that is, an object whose type meets the requirements for a DFSVisitor. In the pseudocode, we show the algorithm computing predecessors π, discover time d and finish time t. By default, the **depth_first_search()** function does not compute these properties; however the user can define visitors to do this.

DFS(G)
    for each vertex $u \in V$
       $color[u] \leftarrow WHITE$ ▷ initialize vertex u
       $\pi[u] = u$
    $time \leftarrow 0$
    for each vertex $u \in V$
      if $color[u] = WHITE$
        call DFS-VISIT(G, u)   ▷ start vertex u
    return (π, d, f)

DFS-VISIT(G, u)
    $color[u] \leftarrow GRAY$ ▷ discover vertex u
    $d[u] \leftarrow time \leftarrow time + 1$
    for each $v \in Adj[u]$
      if $(color[v] = WHITE)$ ▷ examine edge (u, v)
        $\pi[v] = u$
        call DFS-VISIT(G, v)   ▷ (u, v) is a tree edge
      else if $(color[v] = GRAY)$
        $\cdots$ ▷ (u, v) is a back edge

$\quad$ **else if** $(color[v] = BLACK)$

$\qquad \ldots$ $\qquad\qquad\qquad\qquad$ $\triangleright (u,v)$ is a cross or forward edge

$\quad color[u] \leftarrow BLACK$ $\qquad\qquad$ $\triangleright$ finish vertex u

$\quad f[u] \leftarrow time \leftarrow time + 1$

Where Defined

boost/graph/depth_first_search.hpp

Parameters

IN: *Graph& g*
> A directed or undirected graph. The graph's type must be a model of VertexListGraph and IncidenceGraph.

Named Parameters

IN: *visitor(DFSVisitor vis)*
> A visitor object that is invoked inside the algorithm at the event-points specified by the DFSVisitor concept.

UTIL/OUT: *color_map(ColorMap color)*
> This is used by the algorithm to keep track of its progress through the graph. The type *ColorMap* must be a model of ReadWritePropertyMap. The color property map must model ReadWritePropertyMap, its key type must be the graph's vertex descriptor type, and the value type of the color map must model ColorValue.
> **Default:** an *iterator_property_map* created from a *std::vector* of *default_color_type* of size *num_vertices(g)* and using the *i_map* for the index map.

IN: *vertex_index_map(VertexIndexMap i_map)*
> This maps each vertex to an integer in the range $[0, |V|)$. This parameter is only necessary when the default color property map is used. The type *VertexIndexMap* must be a model of ReadablePropertyMap. The value type of the map must be an integer type. The vertex descriptor type of the graph needs to be usable as the key type of the map.
> **Default:** *get(vertex_index, g)*

Complexity

The time complexity is $O(|E| + |V|)$ and the space complexity is $O(|V|)$.

Example

This example shows DFS applied to the graph in Figure 13.2. The source code for this example is in *example/dfs-example.cpp*.

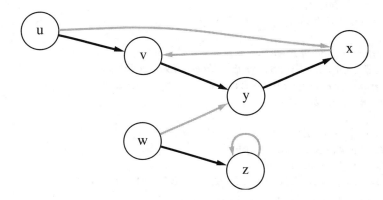

Figure 13.2 A depth-first search of a graph. The DFS forest edges are the solid black lines.

⟨ DFS Discover/Finish Time Visitor 173 ⟩ ≡

```
template <typename TimeMap>
class dfs_time_visitor : public default_dfs_visitor {
  typedef typename property_traits<TimeMap>::value_type T;
public:
  dfs_time_visitor(TimeMap dmap, TimeMap fmap, T& t)
    : m_dtimemap(dmap), m_ftimemap(fmap), m_time(t) { }
  template <typename Vertex, typename Graph>
  void discover_vertex(Vertex u, const Graph& g) const {
    put(m_dtimemap, u, m_time++);
  }
  template <typename Vertex, typename Graph>
  void finish_vertex(Vertex u, const Graph& g) const {
    put(m_ftimemap, u, m_time++);
  }
  TimeMap m_dtimemap;
  TimeMap m_ftimemap;
  T& m_time;
};
```

⟨ *dfs-example.cpp* 174 ⟩ ≡

```
#include <boost/graph/adjacency_list.hpp>
#include <boost/graph/depth_first_search.hpp>
#include <boost/pending/integer_range.hpp>
#include <boost/pending/indirect_cmp.hpp>
using namespace boost;
⟨DFS Discover/Finish Time Visitor 173⟩
int main() {
  // Select the graph type we wish to use
  typedef adjacency_list<vecS, vecS, directedS> graph_t;
  typedef graph_traits<graph_t>::vertices_size_type size_type;
  // Set up the vertex names
  enum { u, v, w, x, y, z, N };
  char name[] = { 'u', 'v', 'w', 'x', 'y', 'z' };
  // Specify the edges in the graph
  typedef std::pair<int,int> E;
  E edge_array[] = { E(u,v), E(u,x), E(x,v), E(y,x),
      E(v,y), E(w,y), E(w,z), E(z,z) };
  graph_t g(edge_array, edge_array + sizeof(edge_array)/sizeof(E), N);
  // Typedefs
  typedef boost::graph_traits<graph_t>::vertex_descriptor Vertex;
  typedef std::vector<Vertex>::iterator Piter;
  typedef std::vector<size_type>::iterator Iiter;

  // discover time and finish time properties
  std::vector<size_type> dtime(num_vertices(g));
  std::vector<size_type> ftime(num_vertices(g));
  size_type t = 0;
  dfs_time_visitor<size_type*> vis(&dtime[0], &ftime[0], t);

  depth_first_search(g, visitor(vis));

  // use std::sort to order the vertices by their discover time
  std::vector<size_type> discover_order(N);
  integer_range<size_type> r(0, N);
  std::copy(r.begin(), r.end(), discover_order.begin());
  std::sort(discover_order.begin(), discover_order.end(),
    indirect_cmp<Iiter, std::less<size_type> >(dtime.begin()));
  std::cout << "order of discovery: ";
  for (int i = 0; i < N; ++i)
    std::cout << name[ discover_order[i] ] << " ";

  std::vector<size_type> finish_order(N);
  std::copy(r.begin(), r.end(), finish_order.begin());
  std::sort(finish_order.begin(), finish_order.end(),
    indirect_cmp<Iiter, std::less<size_type> >(ftime.begin()));
```

```
std::cout << std::endl << "order of finish: ";
for (int i = 0; i < N; ++i)
  std::cout << name [ finish_order [i] ] << " ";
std::cout << std::endl;
return EXIT_SUCCESS;
}
```

The output is

> *order of discovery: u v y x w z*
> *order of finish: x y v u z w*

13.2.4 *depth_first_visit*

```
template <typename IncidenceGraph, typename DFSVisitor, typename ColorMap>
void depth_first_visit (IncidenceGraph& G,
    typename graph_traits<IncidenceGraph>::vertex_descriptor s,
    DFSVisitor vis, ColorMap color);
```

This function is the recursive part of the depth-first search. The main purpose of the function is to implement *depth_first_search()*, though sometimes it is useful on its own. See the documentation for *depth_first_search()* for more information.

Where Defined

boost/graph/depth_first_search.hpp

Parameters

IN: *IncidenceGraph& g*

> A directed or undirected graph. The graph's type must be a model of IncidenceGraph.

IN: *vertex_descriptor s*

> The source vertex from which to start the search.

IN: *DFSVisitor visitor*

> A visitor object that is invoked inside the algorithm at the event points specified by the DFSVisitor concept.

UTIL: *ColorMap color*

> This is used by the algorithm to keep track of its progress through the graph. The type *ColorMap* must be a model of ReadWritePropertyMap. The color property map must model ReadWritePropertyMap, its key type must be the graph's vertex descriptor type, and the value type of the color map must model ColorValue.

Complexity

The time complexity of this operation is $O(|E|)$. The space complexity is $O(|V|)$.

13.2.5   *topological_sort*

> *template <typename Graph, typename OutputIterator,*
> *typename P, typename T, typename R>*
> *void topological_sort (Graph& G, OutputIterator result,*
> *const bgl_named_params<P, T, R>& params = all defaults)*

The topological sort algorithm creates a linear ordering of the vertices such that if edge (u, v) appears in the graph, then u comes before v in the ordering. The graph must be a directed acyclic graph (DAG).

The reverse topological ordering is written to the *result* output iterator, so you need to somehow reverse this to obtain the topological ordering. There are several ways this can be accomplished. One is to create a *std::vector* with size $|V|$ to store the output and then use a reverse iterator from the vector for the *result* iterator. Another option is to use a *back_insert_iterator* with an empty vector, and then apply the *std::reverse()* algorithm. Yet another alternative is to use a *front_insert_iterator* with a container such as a *std::list* or *std::deque*.

The implementation consists mainly of a call to depth-first search [10]. In §1.4.1 there is an example of using topological sort to schedule tasks, and in Chapter 3 topological sort is used as an example of how to write a generic graph algorithm.

Where Defined

boost/graph/topological_sort.hpp

Parameters

IN: *Graph& g*
> A directed or undirected graph. The graph type must be a model of VertexListGraph and IncidenceGraph.

IN: *OutputIterator result*
> The vertices are output to this iterator in reverse topological order. The *OutputIterator* type must accept vertex descriptors as output, and the iterator type must be a model of OutputIterator.

Named Parameters

UTIL/OUT: *color_map(ColorMap color)*
> This is used by the algorithm to keep track of its progress through the graph. The type *ColorMap* must be a model of ReadWritePropertyMap. The color property

map must model ReadWritePropertyMap, its key type must be the graph's vertex descriptor type, and the value type of the color map must model ColorValue.
Default: an *iterator_property_map* created from a *std::vector* of *default_color_type* of size *num_vertices(g)* and using the *i_map* for the index map.

IN: *vertex_index_map(VertexIndexMap i_map)*

This maps each vertex to an integer in the range $[0, |V|)$. This parameter is only necessary when the default color property map is used. The type *VertexIndexMap* must be a model of ReadablePropertyMap. The value type of the map must be an integer type. The vertex descriptor type of the graph needs to be usable as the key type of the map.
Default: *get(vertex_index, g)*

IN: *visitor(DFSVisitor vis)*

A visitor object that is invoked inside the algorithm at the event points specified by the DFSVisitor concept.

Complexity

The time complexity is $O(|V| + |E|)$ and the space complexity is $O(|V|)$.

Example

See §1.4.1 for an example of using *toplogical_sort( )*.

13.3   Shortest-Path Algorithms

13.3.1   *dijkstra_shortest_paths*

```
template <typename Graph, typename P, typename T, typename R>
void dijkstra_shortest_paths (const Graph& g,
    typename graph_traits<Graph>::vertex_descriptor s,
    const bgl_named_params<P, T, R>& params)
```

Dijkstra's algorithm [10, 11] solves the single-source shortest-paths problem on a weighted, directed, or undirected graph for the case where all edge weights are nonnegative. Use the Bellman–Ford algorithm for the case when some edge weights are negative. Use breadth-first search instead of Dijkstra's algorithm when all edge weights are equal to one. For the definition of the shortest-path problem, see §5.1.

There are two main options for obtaining output from the *dijkstra_shortest_paths( )* function. If you provide a distance property map through the *distance_map( )* parameter, then the shortest distance from the source vertex to every other vertex in the graph will be recorded in the distance map. Also, you can record the shortest-paths tree in a predecessor map: For each vertex $u \in V$, $\pi[u]$ will be the predecessor of u in the shortest-paths tree (unless $\pi[u] = u$, in which case u is either the source or a vertex unreachable from the source). In addition to these two options, users can provide their own custom-made visitor that can take actions during any of the algorithm's event points.

Dijkstra's algorithm finds all the shortest paths from the source vertex to every other vertex by iteratively growing the set of vertices S to which it knows the shortest path. At each step of the algorithm, the next vertex added to S is determined by a priority queue. The queue contains the vertices in $V - S$ prioritized by their distance label, which is the length of the shortest path seen so far for each vertex.[1] The vertex u at the top of the priority queue is then added to S, and each of its out-edges is relaxed. If the distance to u plus the weight of the out-edge (u, v) is less than the distance label for v, then the estimated distance for vertex v is reduced. The algorithm then loops back, processing the next vertex at the top of the priority queue. The algorithm finishes when the priority queue is empty.

The algorithm uses color markers (white, gray, and black) to keep track of which set each vertex is in. Vertices colored black are in S. Vertices colored white or gray are in $V - S$. White vertices have not yet been discovered and gray vertices are in the priority queue. By default, the algorithm allocates an array to store a color marker for each vertex in the graph. You can provide your own storage and access for colors with the *color_map* ( ) named parameter.

The following is the pseudocode for Dijkstra's single-source shortest-paths algorithm. The w denotes edge weight, d the distance label, and π the predecessor of each vertex that is used to encode the shortest-paths tree. Q is a priority queue that supports the DECREASE-KEY operation. The visitor event points for the algorithm are indicated by the triangles.

DIJKSTRA (G, s, w)
   for each vertex $u \in V$ ▷ initialize vertex u
      $d[u] \leftarrow \infty$
      $\pi[u] \leftarrow u$
      $color[u] \leftarrow WHITE$
   $color[s] \leftarrow GRAY$
   $d[s] \leftarrow 0$
   INSERT(Q, s) ▷ discover vertex s
   while $(Q \neq \emptyset)$
      $u \leftarrow$ EXTRACT-MIN(Q) ▷ examine vertex u
      $S \leftarrow S \cup \{u\}$
      for each $v \in Adj[u]$ ▷ examine edge (u, v)
         if $(w(u, v) + d[u] < d[v])$
            $d[v] \leftarrow w(u, v) + d[u]$ ▷ edge (u, v) relaxed
            $\pi[v] \leftarrow u$

---

[1]The algorithm used here saves a little space by not putting all $V - S$ vertices in the priority queue at once, but instead only those vertices in $V - S$ that are discovered and therefore have a distance less than infinity.

if $(color[v] = WHITE)$
    $color[v] \leftarrow GRAY$
    INSERT(Q, v) $\triangleright$ discover vertex v
else if $(color[v] = GRAY)$
    DECREASE-KEY$(Q, v, w(u, v) + d[u])$
else
    $\ldots$ $\triangleright$ edge (u, v) not relaxed
  $color[u] \leftarrow BLACK$ $\triangleright$ finish vertex u
return (d, π)

Where Defined

boost/graph/dijkstra_shortest_paths.hpp

Parameters

IN: ***const Graph& g***
> The graph object on which the algorithm is applied. The type ***Graph*** must be a model of VertexListGraph and IncidenceGraph.

IN: ***vertex_descriptor s***
> The source vertex. All distance is calculated from this vertex, and the shortest-paths tree is rooted at this vertex.

Named Parameters

IN: ***weight_map(WeightMap w_map)***
> The weight or "length" of each edge in the graph. The type ***WeightMap*** must be a model of ReadablePropertyMap. The edge descriptor type of the graph needs to be usable as the key type for the weight map. The value type of the weight map must be the same type as the value type of the distance map.
> **Default:** *get(edge_weight, g)*

IN: ***vertex_index_map(VertexIndexMap i_map)***
> This maps each vertex to an integer in the range $[0, |V|)$. This is necessary for efficient updates of the heap data structure when an edge is relaxed. The type ***VertexIndexMap*** must be a model of ReadablePropertyMap. The value type of the map must be an integer type. The vertex descriptor type of the graph needs to be usable as the key type of the map.
> **Default:** *get(vertex_index, g)*

OUT: ***predecessor_map(PredecessorMap p_map)***
> The predecessor map records the edges in the minimum spanning tree. Upon completion of the algorithm, the edges $(\pi[u], u) \; \forall u \in V$ are in the minimum spanning

tree. If $\pi[u] = u$, then u is either the source vertex or a vertex that is not reachable from the source. The *PredecessorMap* type must be a ReadWritePropertyMap with key and vertex types the same as the vertex descriptor type of the graph.
Default: *dummy_property_map*

UTIL/OUT: *distance_map(DistanceMap d_map)*

The shortest-path weight from the source vertex *s* to each vertex in the graph *g* is recorded in this property map. The shortest-path weight is the sum of the edge weights along the shortest path. The type *DistanceMap* must be a model of Read-WritePropertyMap. The vertex descriptor type of the graph needs to be usable as the key type of the distance map. The value type of the distance map is the element type of a Monoid formed with the *combine* function object and the *zero* object for the identity element. Also the distance value type must have a StrictWeakOrdering provided by the *compare* function object.
Default: an *iterator_property_map* created from a *std::vector* of the *WeightMap*'s value type of size *num_vertices(g)* and using the *i_map* for the index map.

IN: *distance_combine(BinaryFunction combine)*

A function object that is the Monoid operation for the distance value type. This function object combines distances to form the distance of a path.
Default: *closed_plus*<D> where *D* is the value type of the distance map. *closed_plus* is defined in *boost/graph/relax.hpp*.

IN: *distance_compare(BinaryPredicate compare)*

A function object that defines a StrictWeakOrdering on the distance values. The function object is used to determine which of two paths is shorter.
Default: *std::less*<D> where *D* is the value type of the distance map.

IN: *distance_inf(D inf)*

The *inf* object must be the greatest value of any *D* object. That is, *compare(d, inf)* == *true* for any *d != inf*. The type *D* is the value type of the *DistanceMap*.
Default: *std::numeric_limits*<D>::*max* ( )

IN: *distance_zero(D zero)*

The *zero* value must be the identity element for the Monoid formed by the distance values and the *combine* function object. The type *D* is the value type of the *DistanceMap*.
Default: *D*

UTIL/OUT: *color_map(ColorMap c_map)*

This is used during the execution of the algorithm to mark the vertices. The vertices start out white and become gray when they are inserted in the queue. They then turn black when they are removed from the queue. At the end of the algorithm, vertices reachable from the source vertex will have been colored black. All other vertices will still be white. The type *ColorMap* must be a model of ReadWritePropertyMap. A vertex descriptor must be usable as the key type of the map, and the value type of the map must be a model of ColorValue.

Default: an *iterator_property_map* created from a *std::vector* of *default_color_type* of size *num_vertices(g)* and using the *i_map* for the index map.

OUT: *visitor(Vis v)*

Use this to specify actions that you would like to happen during certain event points within the algorithm. The type *Vis* must be a model of DijkstraVisitor.

Default: *default_dijkstra_visitor*

Complexity

The time complexity is $O((|V| + |E|) \log |V|)$, or just $O(|E| \log |V|)$ if all vertices are reachable from the source.

Example

The source code for this example is in *example/dijkstra-example.cpp*. The graph used for this example is shown in Figure 13.3. The edges in the shortest-paths tree use black lines.

```
typedef adjacency_list<listS, vecS, directedS,
        no_property, property<edge_weight_t, int> > graph_t;
typedef graph_traits<graph_t>::vertex_descriptor vertex_descriptor;
typedef std::pair<int,int> Edge;

const int num_nodes = 5;
enum nodes { A, B, C, D, E };
char name[] = "ABCDE";
Edge edge_array[] = { Edge(A,C), Edge(B,B), Edge(B,D), Edge(B,E),
        Edge(C,B), Edge(C,D), Edge(D,E), Edge(E,A), Edge(E,B) };
int weights[] = { 1, 2, 1, 2, 7, 3, 1, 1, 1};
int num_arcs = sizeof(edge_array)/sizeof(Edge);
graph_t g(edge_array, edge_array + num_arcs, weights, num_nodes);
std::vector<vertex_descriptor> p(num_vertices(g));
std::vector<int> d(num_vertices(g));
vertex_descriptor s = vertex(A, g);
dijkstra_shortest_paths(g, s, predecessor_map(&p[0]).distance_map(&d[0]));

std::cout << "distances and parents:" << std::endl;
graph_traits<graph_t>::vertex_iterator vi, vend;
for(tie(vi, vend) = vertices(g); vi != vend; ++vi) {
  std::cout << "distance(" << name[*vi] << ") = " << d[*vi] << ", ";
  std::cout << "parent(" << name[*vi] << ") = " << name[p[*vi]] <<std::endl;
}
std::cout << std::endl;
```

The output is

distances and parents:
distance (*A*) = **0,** *parent* (*A*) = *A*
distance (*B*) = **6,** *parent* (*B*) = *E*
distance (*C*) = **1,** *parent* (*C*) = *A*
distance (*D*) = **4,** *parent* (*D*) = *C*
distance (*E*) = **5,** *parent* (*E*) = *D*

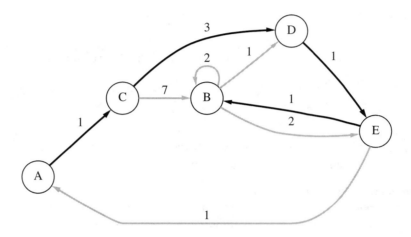

Figure 13.3 The graph used for the Dijkstra's algorithm example.

13.3.2   *bellman_ford_shortest_paths*

template <typename EdgeListGraph, typename Size,
typename P, typename T, typename R>
bool bellman_ford_shortest_paths (*EdgeListGraph& g, Size N,*
const bgl_named_params<P, T, R>& params)

The Bellman–Ford algorithm [5, 10, 13, 26] solves the single-source shortest-paths problem for a graph with both positive and negative edge weights. For the definition of the shortest-paths problem, see §5.1. If you only need to solve the shortest-paths problem for positive edge weights, Dijkstra's algorithm provides a more efficient alternative. If all the edge weights are equal to one, breadth-first search provides an even more efficient alternative.

Before calling the ***bellman_ford_shortest_paths*** () function, the user must assign the source vertex a distance of zero (or the identity element of the Monoid formed by the distance values and the ***combine*** function object) and all other vertices a distance of infinity (which must be the greatest distance value according to the ordering defined by the ***compare*** function object).

Typically *std::numeric_limits<D>::max* ( ) is the right choice for infinity, where *D* is the value type of the distance map. The Bellman–Ford algorithm proceeds by looping through all of the edges in the graph, applying the relaxation operation to each edge. In the following pseudocode, v is a vertex adjacent to u, w maps edges to their weight, and d is a distance map that records the length of the shortest path to each vertex seen so far.

RELAX(u, v, w, d)
   if $(w(u, v) + d[u] < d[v])$
      $d[v] \leftarrow w(u, v) + d[u]$

The algorithm repeats this loop $|V|$ times, after which it is guaranteed that the distances to each vertex have been reduced to the minimum possible unless there is a negative cycle in the graph. If there is a negative cycle, then there will be edges in the graph that were not properly minimized. That is, there will be edges (u, v) such that $w(u, v) + d[u] < d[v]$. The algorithm loops over the edges in the graph one final time to check if all the edges were minimized, returning true if they were and returning false otherwise.

There are two main options for obtaining output from the *bellman_ford_shortest_paths* ( ) function. If the user provides a distance property map through the *distance_map* ( ) parameter, then the shortest distance from the source vertex to every other vertex in the graph is recorded in the distance map (provided the function returns *true*). The user can also record the shortest-paths tree by providing a predecessor property map through the *predecessor_map* ( ) parameter. In addition to these two options, users can provide their own custom-made visitor that can take actions during any of the algorithm's event points (see BellmanFordVisitor). If you are only interested in some of the event points, derive your visitor from *default_bellman_visitor* to provide empty versions of the remaining event points.

Where defined

boost/graph/bellman_ford_shortest_paths.hpp

Parameters

  IN: *EdgeListGraph& g*
      A directed or undirected graph whose type must be a model of EdgeListGraph.

  IN: *Size N*
      The number of vertices in the graph. The type *Size* must be an integer type.

Named Parameters

  IN: *weight_map(WeightMap w)*
      The weight (also know as "length" or "cost") of each edge in the graph. The *WeightMap* type must be a model of ReadablePropertyMap. The key type for this

property map must be the edge descriptor of the graph. The value type for the weight map the same as the distance map's value type.

Default: *get(edge_weight, g)*

OUT: *predecessor_map(PredecessorMap p_map)* The predecessor map records the edges in the minimum spanning tree. Upon completion of the algorithm, the edges $(p[u], u)$ for all $u \in V$ are in the minimum spanning tree. If $p[u] = u$ then u is either the source vertex or a vertex that is not reachable from the source. The *PredecessorMap* type must be a ReadWritePropertyMap which key and vertex types the same as the vertex descriptor type of the graph.

Default: *dummy_property_map*

UTIL/OUT: *distance_map(DistanceMap d_map)*

The shortest-path weight from the source vertex *s* to each vertex in the graph *g* is recorded in this property map. The shortest-path weight is the sum of the edge weights along the shortest path. The type *DistanceMap* must be a model of Read-WritePropertyMap. The key type of the distance map must be the vertex descriptor type of the graph. The value type of the distance map is the element type of a Monoid formed with the *combine* function object and the *zero* object for the identity element. Also the distance value type must have a StrictWeakOrdering provided by the *compare* function object.

Default: *get(vertex_distance, g)*

IN: *visitor(BellmanFordVisitor v)*

The visitor object, whose type must be a model of BellmanFordVisitor. The *default_bellman_visitor* is a model of BellmanFordVisitor that does nothing at all of the event points.

Default: *default_bellman_visitor*

IN: *distance_combine(BinaryFunction combine)*

This function object is the Monoid operation for the distance value type. This function object combines distances to form the distance of a path.

Default: *closed_plus<D>* where *D* is the value type of the distance map. *closed_plus* is defined in *boost/graph/relax.hpp*.

IN: *distance_compare(BinaryPredicate compare)*

This function object defines an ordering on the distance values that corresponds with the summary function. That is, the summary function always returns the argument that is earlier in the ordering according to the *compare* function.

Default: *std::less<D>* where *D* is the value type of the distance map.

Complexity

The time complexity is $O(|V||E|)$.

Example

The source code for this example is in *example/bellman-example.cpp*. The graph used in the example is shown in Figure 13.4.

```
enum { u, v, x, y, z, N };
char name[] = { 'u', 'v', 'x', 'y', 'z' };
typedef std::pair<int,int> E;
const int n_edges = 10;
typedef boost::array<E,n_edges> EdgeList;
EdgeList edge_array = {{ E(u,y), E(u,x), E(u,v), E(v,u),
        E(x,y), E(x,v), E(y,v), E(y,z), E(z,u), E(z,x) }};
int weight[n_edges] = { -4, 8, 5, -2, 9, -3, 7, 2, 6, 7 };

typedef adjacency_list<vecS, vecS, directedS,
  no_property, property<edge_weight_t, int> > Graph;
Graph g(edge_array.begin(), edge_array.end(), N);
graph_traits<Graph>::edge_iterator ei, ei_end;
int i = 0;
for (tie(ei, ei_end) = edges(g); ei != ei_end; ++ei, ++i)
  get(edge_weight, g)[*ei] = weight[i];

std::vector<int> distance(N, std::numeric_limits<short>::max());
std::vector<std::size_t> parent(N);
for (i = 0; i < N; ++i)
  parent[i] = i;
distance[z] = 0;
bool r = bellman_ford_shortest_paths(g, int(N),
  weight_map(get(edge_weight, g)).distance_map(&distance[0]).
  predecessor_map(&parent[0]));

if (r)
  for (i = 0; i < N; ++i)
    std::cout << name[i] << ": " << std::setw(3) << distance[i]
      << " " << name[parent[i]] << std::endl;
    else
      std::cout << "negative cycle" << std::endl;
```

The distance and predecessor for each vertex is

```
u:    2 v
v:    4 x
x:    7 z
y:   -2 u
z:    0 z
```

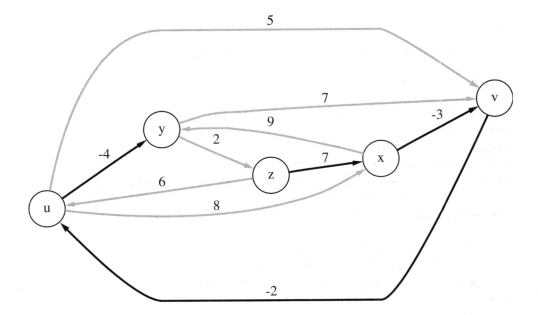

Figure 13.4 The graph used for the example of the Bellman–Ford algorithm.

13.3.3   *johnson_all_pairs_shortest_paths*

template <typename Graph, typename DistanceMatrix,
           typename P, typename T, typename R>
bool johnson_all_pairs_shortest_paths (Graph& g, DistanceMatrix& D,
    const bgl_named_params<P, T, R>& params = all defaults)

This algorithm finds the shortest distance between every pair of vertices in the graph. The algorithm returns false if there is a negative weight cycle in the graph and true otherwise. The distance between each pair of vertices is stored in the distance matrix **D**. This is one of the more time intensive graph algorithms, having a time complexity of $O(|V||E| \log |V|)$.

Where Defined

boost/graph/johnson_all_pairs_shortest_paths.hpp

Parameters

IN: *const Graph& g*
> The graph object on which the algorithm is applied. The type **Graph** must be a model of VertexListGraph, IncidenceGraph, and EdgeListGraph.

OUT: *DistanceMatrix& D*
> The shortest path length from vertex **u** to **v** is stored in *D[u][v]*.

Named Parameters

IN: *weight_map(WeightMap w_map)*

> The weight or "length" of each edge in the graph. The type **WeightMap** must be a model of ReadablePropertyMap. The edge descriptor type of the graph needs to be usable as the key type for the weight map. The value type of the weight map must be the same type as the value type of the distance map.
>
> **Default:** *get(edge_weight, g)*

UTIL: *weight_map2(WeightMap2 w_map2)*

> An auxiliary weight map. The type **WeightMap2** must be a model of ReadWritePropertyMap. The edge descriptor type of the graph needs to be usable as the key type for the weight map. The value type of the weight map must be the same type as the value type of the distance map.
>
> **Default:** *get(edge_weight2, g)*

IN: *vertex_index_map(VertexIndexMap i_map)*

> This maps each vertex to an integer in the range $[0, |V|)$. This is necessary for efficient updates of the heap data structure when an edge is relaxed. The type **VertexIndexMap** must be a model of ReadablePropertyMap. The value type of the map must be an integer type. The vertex descriptor type of the graph needs to be usable as the key type of the map.
>
> **Default:** *get(vertex_index, g)*

UTIL/OUT: *distance_map(DistanceMap d_map)*

> The shortest-path weight from the source vertex *s* to each vertex in the graph *g* is recorded in this property map. The shortest-path weight is the sum of the edge weights along the shortest path. The type **DistanceMap** must be a model of ReadWritePropertyMap. The vertex descriptor type of the graph needs to be usable as the key type of the distance map. The value type of the distance map is the element type of a Monoid formed with the addition operator and the *zero* object for the identity element. Also the distance value type must be LessThanComparable.
>
> **Default:** an *iterator_property_map* created from a *std::vector* of the **WeightMap**'s value type of size *num_vertices(g)* and using the *i_map* for the index map.

IN: *distance_zero(D zero)*

> The identity element for the Monoid formed by the distance value type and the addition operator. The type *D* must be the value type of the **DistanceMap**.
>
> **Default:** *D ( )*

Complexity

The time complexity is $O(|V||E| \log |V|)$.

Example

Johnson's algorithm for all-pairs shortest paths applied to the example graph from page 568 of the *Introduction to Algorithms* [10], also shown in Figure 13.5. The resulting distance matrix *D[u][v]* gives the shortest path from vertex *u* to *v*.

```
typedef adjacency_list<vecS, vecS, directedS, no_property,
    property<edge_weight_t, int, property<edge_weight2_t, int> > > Graph;

const int V = 6;
typedef std::pair<int,int> Edge;
Edge edge_array[] =
  { Edge(0,1), Edge(0,2), Edge(0,3), Edge(0,4), Edge(0,5),
    Edge(1,2), Edge(1,5), Edge(1,3), Edge(2,4), Edge(2,5),
    Edge(3,2), Edge(4,3), Edge(4,1), Edge(5,4) };
const int E = sizeof(edge_array)/sizeof(Edge);

Graph g(edge_array, edge_array + E, V);

property_map<Graph, edge_weight_t>::type
  w = get(edge_weight, g);
int weights[] = { 0, 0, 0, 0, 0, 3, -4, 8, 1, 7, 4, -5, 2, 6 };
int* wp = weights;

graph_traits<Graph>::edge_iterator e, e_end;
for (boost::tie(e, e_end) = edges(g); e != e_end; ++e)
  w[*e] = *wp++;

std::vector<int> d(V, std::numeric_limits<int>::max());
int D[V][V];

johnson_all_pairs_shortest_paths(g, D, distance_map(&d[0]));
```

This is the resulting distance matrix:

	0	1	2	3	4	5
0	0	0	-1	-5	0	-4
1	inf	0	1	-3	2	-4
2	inf	3	0	-4	1	-1
3	inf	7	4	0	5	3
4	inf	2	-1	-5	0	-2
5	inf	8	5	1	6	0

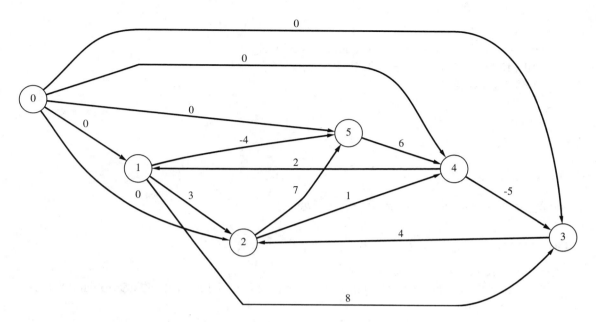

Figure 13.5 The graph used for the Johnson's algorithm example.

13.4 Minimum-Spanning-Tree Algorithms

13.4.1 *kruskal_minimum_spanning_tree*

> *template <typename Graph, typename OutputIterator,*
>   *typename P, typename T, typename R>*
> *void kruskal_minimum_spanning_tree(Graph& g, OutputIterator spanning_tree_edges,*
>   *const bgl_named_params<P, T, R>& params = all defaults)*

The *kruskal_minimum_spanning_tree()* function finds a minimum spanning tree (MST) in an undirected graph with weighted edges. An MST is a set of edges that connects all the vertices in the graph where the total weight of the edges in the tree is minimized. The *kruskal_-minimum_spanning_tree()* function outputs the edges of an MST to the *spanning_tree_edges* output iterator using Kruskal's algorithm [10, 18, 23, 44].

Kruskal's algorithm starts with each vertex in a tree by itself, and with no edges in the minimum spanning tree T. The algorithm then examines each edge in the graph in order of increasing edge weight. If an edge connects two vertices in different trees, the algorithm merges the two trees into a single tree and adds the edge to T. We use the *union by rank* and *path compression* heuristics to provide fast implementations of the disjoint set operations (MAKE-SET, FIND-SET, and UNION-SET). The algorithm is as follows:

KRUSKAL-MST(G, w)
   for each vertex $u \in V$
      MAKE-SET(S, u)

$T \leftarrow \emptyset$
for each $(u, v) \in E$ in order of nondecreasing weight
   if FIND-SET$(S, u) \neq$ FIND-SET(S, v)
    UNION-SET(S, u, v)
     $T \leftarrow T \bigcup \{(u, v)\}$
return T

Where Defined

boost/graph/kruskal_minimum_spanning_tree.hpp

Parameters

IN: *const Graph& g*
> An undirected graph. The graph type must be a model of VertexListGraph and Edge-ListGraph.

IN: *OutputIterator spanning_tree_edges*
> The edges of the minimum spanning tree are output to this OutputIterator.

Named Parameters

IN: *weight_map(WeightMap w_map)*
> The weight or "length" of each edge in the graph. The *WeightMap* type must be a model of ReadablePropertyMap and its value type must be LessThanComparable. The key type of this map needs to be the graph's edge descriptor type.
> **Default:** *get(edge_weight, g)*

UTIL: *rank_map(RankMap r_map)*
> The type *RankMap* must be a model of ReadWritePropertyMap. The vertex descriptor type of the graph needs to be usable as the key type of the rank map. The value type of the rank map must be an integer type.
> **Default:** an *iterator_property_map* created from a *std::vector* of the integers of size *num_vertices(g)* and using the *i_map* for the index map.

UTIL: *predecessor_map(PredecessorMap p_map)*
> The type *PredecessorMap* must be a model of ReadWritePropertyMap. The key type value types of the predecessor map must be the vertex descriptor type of the graph.
> **Default:** an *iterator_property_map* created from a *std::vector* of vertex descriptors of size *num_vertices(g)* and using the *i_map* for the index map.

IN: *vertex_index_map(VertexIndexMap i_map)*
> This maps each vertex to an integer in the range $[0, |V|)$. This is only necessary if the default is used for the rank or predecessor maps. The type *VertexIndexMap* must be a

model of ReadablePropertyMap. The value type of the map must be an integer type. The vertex descriptor type of the graph needs to be usable as the key type of the map. **Default:** *get(vertex_index, g)*

Complexity

The time complexity is $O(|E| \log |E|)$.

Example

The source code for this example is in *example/kruskal-example.cpp*. Figure 13.6 shows the graph used in this example.

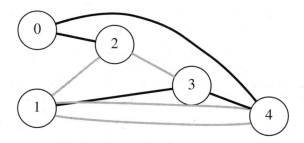

Figure 13.6 The graph used for the Kruskal's algorithm example.

```
typedef adjacency_list<vecS, vecS, undirectedS,
    no_property, property<edge_weight_t, int> > Graph;
typedef graph_traits<Graph>::edge_descriptor Edge;
typedef graph_traits<Graph>::vertex_descriptor Vertex;
typedef std::pair<int,int> E;

const int num_nodes = 5;
E edge_array[] = { E(0,2), E(1,3), E(1,4), E(2,1), E(2,3),
    E(3,4), E(4,0), E(4,1) };
int weights[] = { 1, 1, 2, 7, 3, 1, 1, 1};
int num_edges = sizeof(edge_array) / sizeof(E);
Graph g(edge_array, edge_array + num_edges, weights, num_nodes);
property_map<Graph, edge_weight_t>::type weight = get(edge_weight, g);
std::vector<Edge> spanning_tree;

kruskal_minimum_spanning_tree(g, std::back_inserter(spanning_tree));

std::cout << "Print the edges in the MST:" << std::endl;
```

```
for (std::vector<Edge>::iterator ei = spanning_tree.begin();
     ei != spanning_tree.end(); ++ei) {
  std::cout << source(*ei, g) << " ¡-¿ " << target(*ei, g)
            << " with weight of " << weight[*ei]
            << std::endl;
}
```

The output is

Print the edges in the MST:
0 <--> **2** *with weight of* **1**
3 <--> **4** *with weight of* **1**
4 <--> **0** *with weight of* **1**
1 <--> **3** *with weight of* **1**

13.4.2 *prim_minimum_spanning_tree*

```
template <typename Graph, typename PredecessorMap,
          typename P, typename T, typename R>
void prim_minimum_spanning_tree(Graph& G, PredecessorMap p_map,
   const bgl_named_params<P, T, R>& params = all defaults)
```

The *prim_minimum_spanning_tree()* function finds a minimum spanning tree (MST) in an undirected graph with weighted edges. An MST is a set of edges that connects all the vertices in the graph where the total weight of the edges in the tree is minimized. The minimum spanning tree is recorded in the predecessor map: for each vertex $v \in V$, $\pi[v]$ is the parent of v in the computed minimum spanning tree. The implementation uses Prim's algorithm to compute the MST [10, 18, 38, 44].

The way Prim's algorithm grows the minimum spanning tree, one vertex at a time, is very similar to the way Dijkstra's algorithm builds the shortest-paths tree.[2] At each step, Prim's algorithm chooses an edge to add to the minimum spanning tree. The edge is the shortest edge that connects any of the vertices already in the tree to a vertex that is not in the tree. The algorithm uses a priority queue to make this choice in an efficient manner. If vertex u is at the top of the priority queue, then edge $(\pi[u], u)$ is the next shortest edge and is added to the tree. The pseudocode for the algorithm is as follows:

PRIM-MST(G, r, w)
    for each vertex $u \in V$ ▷ initialize vertex u
        $d[u] \leftarrow \infty$
        $\pi[u] \leftarrow u$
        $color[u] \leftarrow WHITE$

---

[2]In fact, the BGL implementation of Prim's algorithm is simply a call to Dijkstra's algorithm with particular arguments for the *distance_compare()* and *distance_combine()* parameters.

$color[r] \leftarrow$ GRAY
$d[r] \leftarrow 0$
INSERT(Q, r) $\triangleright$ discover vertex r
while ($Q \neq \emptyset$)
   $u \leftarrow$ EXTRACT-MIN(Q) $\triangleright$ examine vertex u
   for each $v \in Adj[u]$ $\triangleright$ examining edge (u, v)
     if ($w(u, v) < d[v]$)
       $d[v] \leftarrow w(u, v)$ $\triangleright$ edge (u, v) relaxed
       $\pi[v] \leftarrow u$
       if ($color[v] = $ WHITE)
         $color[v] \leftarrow$ GRAY
         INSERT(Q, v) $\triangleright$ discover vertex v
       else if ($color[v] = $ GRAY)
         DECREASE-KEY(Q, v)
     else
       ... $\triangleright$ edge (u, v) is not relaxed
   $color[u] \leftarrow$ BLACK $\triangleright$ finish u
 return (π)

Where Defined

boost/graph/prim_minimum_spanning_tree.hpp

Parameters

IN: *const Graph& g*

> The graph object on which the algorithm is applied. The type *Graph* must be a model of VertexListGraph and IncidenceGraph.

OUT: *PredecessorMap p_map*

> The predecessor map records the edges in the minimum spanning tree. Upon completion of the algorithm, the edges $(\pi[u], u)$ $\forall u \in V$ are in the minimum spanning tree. If $\pi[u] = u$, then u is either the root of the tree or is a vertex that is not reachable from the root. The *PredecessorMap* type must be a ReadWritePropertyMap with key and vertex types the same as the vertex descriptor type of the graph.

Named Parameters

IN: *root_vertex(vertex_descriptor r)*

> The vertex that will be the root of the minimum spanning tree. The choice of the root vertex is arbitrary; it does not affect the ability of the algorithm to find a minimum spanning tree.
> **Default:** **vertices(g).first*

IN: *weight_map(WeightMap w_map)*

> The weight or "length" of each edge in the graph. The type *WeightMap* must be a model of ReadablePropertyMap. The edge descriptor type of the graph needs to be usable as the key type for the weight map. The value type of the weight map must be the same type as the value type of the distance map.
>
> **Default:** *get(edge_weight, g)*

IN: *vertex_index_map(VertexIndexMap i_map)*

> This maps each vertex to an integer in the range $[0, |V|)$. This is necessary for efficient updates of the heap data structure when an edge is relaxed. The type *VertexIndexMap* must be a model of ReadablePropertyMap. The value type of the map must be an integer type. The vertex descriptor type of the graph needs to be usable as the key type of the map.
>
> **Default:** *get(vertex_index, g)*

UTIL: *distance_map(DistanceMap d_map)*

> The type *DistanceMap* must be a model of ReadWritePropertyMap. The vertex descriptor type of the graph needs to be usable as the key type of the distance map. The value type of the distance map is the element type of a Monoid formed with the addition operator and a defualt-constructed distance value object for the identity element. The value type of the distance map must also be LessThanComparable.
>
> **Default:** an *iterator_property_map* created from a *std::vector* of the *WeightMap*'s value type of size *num_vertices(g)* and using the *i_map* for the index map.

UTIL/OUT: *color_map(ColorMap c_map)*

> This is used during the execution of the algorithm to mark the vertices. The vertices start out white and become gray when they are inserted in the queue. They then turn black when they are removed from the queue. At the end of the algorithm, vertices reachable from the source vertex are colored black. All other vertices are still be white. The type *ColorMap* must be a model of ReadWritePropertyMap. A vertex descriptor must be usable as the key type of the map, and the value type of the map must be a model of ColorValue.
>
> **Default:** an *iterator_property_map* created from a *std::vector* of *default_color_type* of size *num_vertices(g)* and using the *i_map* for the index map.

Complexity

The time complexity is $O(|E| \log |V|)$.

Example

The source code for this example is in ***example/prim-example.cpp***.

```
typedef adjacency_list<vecS, vecS, undirectedS,
  property<vertex_distance_t, int>, property<edge_weight_t, int> > Graph;
```

```
typedef std::pair<int,int> E;
const int num_nodes = 5;
E edges[] = { E(0,2), E(1,1), E(1,3), E(1,4), E(2,1), E(2,3),
    E(3,4), E(4,0) };
int weights[] = { 1, 2, 1, 2, 7, 3, 1, 1};
Graph g(num_nodes, edges, edges + sizeof(edges)/sizeof(E), weights);
std::vector<graph_traits<Graph>::vertex_descriptor> p(num_vertices(g));

prim_minimum_spanning_tree(g, &p[0]);

for (std::size_t i = 0; i != p.size(); ++i)
  if (p[i] != i)
    std::cout << "parent[" << i << "] = " << p[i] << std::endl;
  else
    std::cout << "parent[" << i << "] = no parent" << std::endl;
```

The output is

```
parent[0] = 0
parent[1] = 3
parent[2] = 0
parent[3] = 4
parent[4] = 0
```

13.5   Static Connected Components

13.5.1   *connected_components*

```
template <typename Graph, typename ComponentMap,
    typename P, typename T, typename R>
typename property_traits<ComponentMap>::value_type
connected_components(const Graph& g, ComponentMap c,
    const bgl_named_params<P, T, R>& params = all defaults)
```

The *connected_components*() function computes the connected components of an undirected graph using a DFS-based approach. A *connected component* of an undirected graph is a set of vertices that are all reachable from each other. If the connected components need to be maintained while a graph is growing, the disjoint-set based approach of function *incremental_components*() is faster. For static graphs this DFS-based approach is faster[10].

The output of the algorithm is recorded in the component property map *c*, which contains numbers giving the component number assigned to each vertex. The total number of components is the return value of the function.

Where Defined

boost/graph/connected_components.hpp

Parameters

IN: *const Graph& g*
>   An undirected graph. The graph type must be a model of VertexListGraph and Incidence Graph.

OUT: *ComponentMap c*
>   The algorithm computes how many connected components are in the graph, and assigns each component an integer label. The algorithm then records to which component each vertex in the graph belongs by recording the component number in the component property map. The *ComponentMap* type must be a model of WritablePropertyMap. The value type must be the *vertices_size_type* of the graph. The key type must be the graph's vertex descriptor type.

Named Parameters

UTIL: *color_map(ColorMap color)*
>   This is used by the algorithm to keep track of its progress through the graph. The type *ColorMap* must be a model of ReadWritePropertyMap and its key type must be the graph's vertex descriptor type and the value type of the color map must model ColorValue.
>   **Default:** an *iterator_property_map* created from a *std::vector* of *default_color_type* of size *num_vertices(g)* and using the *i_map* for the index map.

IN: *vertex_index_map(VertexIndexMap i_map)*
>   This maps each vertex to an integer in the range $[0, N)$ where N is the number of vertices in the graph. This parameter is only necessary when the default color property map is used. The type *VertexIndexMap* must be a model of ReadablePropertyMap. The value type of the map must be an integer type. The vertex descriptor type of the graph needs to be usable as the key type of the map.
>   **Default:** *get(vertex_index, g)*

Complexity

The time complexity for the strongly connected components algorithm is $O(|V| + |E|)$. The time complexity for the connected components algorithm is also $O(|V| + |E|)$.

Example

Calculating the connected components of an undirected graph.

⟨ *connected-components.cpp* 197 ⟩ ≡

```cpp
#include <iostream>
#include <vector>
#include <boost/graph/connected_components.hpp>
#include <boost/graph/adjacency_list.hpp>

int main()
{
  using namespace boost;
  typedef adjacency_list <vecS, vecS, undirectedS> Graph;
  typedef graph_traits<Graph>::vertex_descriptor Vertex;

  const int N = 6;
  Graph G(N);
  add_edge(0, 1, G);
  add_edge(1, 4, G);
  add_edge(4, 0, G);
  add_edge(2, 5, G);

  std::vector<int> c(num_vertices(G));
  int num = connected_components(G,
    make_iterator_property_map(c.begin(), get(vertex_index, G)));

  std::cout << std::endl;
  std::vector<int>::iterator i;
  std::cout << "Total number of components: " << num << std::endl;
  for (i = c.begin(); i != c.end(); ++i)
    std::cout << "Vertex " << i - c.begin()
          << " is in component " << *i << std::endl;
  std::cout << std::endl;
  return EXIT_SUCCESS;
}
```

The output is

Total number of components: 3
Vertex 0 *is in component* 0
Vertex 1 *is in component* 0
Vertex 2 *is in component* 1
Vertex 3 *is in component* 2
Vertex 4 *is in component* 0
Vertex 5 *is in component* 1

13.5.2   *strong_components*

> *template <class Graph, class ComponentMap, class P, class T, class R>*
> *typename property_traits<ComponentMap>::value_type*
> *strong_components (Graph& g, ComponentMap comp,*
>   *const bgl_named_params<P, T, R>& params = all defaults)*

The *strong_components ()* function computes the strongly connected components (SCC) of a directed graph using Tarjan's algorithm, which is based on depth-first search [43].

The output of the algorithm is recorded in the component property map *comp*, which contains numbers giving the component ID assigned to each vertex. The ID numbers are from zero to one less than the number of components in the graph. The number of components is the return value of the function.

Where Defined

boost/graph/strong_components.hpp

Definitions

A *strongly connected component* of a directed graph $G = (V, E)$ is a maximal set of vertices $U \subseteq V$, such that for every pair of vertices u and v in U, we have both a path from u to v and path from v to u. That is to say that u and v are reachable from each other.

The following is an informal description of Tarjan's algorithm for computing strongly connected components. It is basically a variation on depth-first search, with extra actions taken at the "discover vertex" and "finish vertex" event points. It may help to think of the actions taken at the "discover vertex" event point as occurring "on the way down" a DFS tree (from the root toward the leaves), and actions taken at the "finish vertex" event point as occurring "on the way back up."

Three things need to happen on the way down. For each vertex u visited, we record the discover time $d[u]$, push vertex u onto an auxiliary stack, and set $root[u] = u$. The root field will end up mapping each vertex to the topmost vertex in the same strongly connected component. By setting $root[u] = u$ we are starting with each vertex in a component by itself.

Now to describe what happens on the way back up. Suppose we have just finished visiting all of the vertices adjacent to some vertex u. We then scan each of the adjacent vertices again, checking the root of each for which one has the earliest discover time, which we call root a. We then compare a with vertex u and consider the following cases:

1. If $d[a] < d[u]$, then we know that a is really an ancestor of u in the DFS tree and therefore we have a cycle and u must be in an SCC with a. We then set $root[u] = a$ and continue our way back up the DFS.

2. If $a = u$, then we know that u must be the topmost vertex of a subtree that defines an SCC. All of the vertices in this subtree are farther down on the stack than vertex u, so we pop the vertices off of the stack until we reach u and mark each one as being in the same component.

3. If $d[a] > d[u]$ then the adjacent vertices are in different strongly connected components. We continue our way back up the DFS.

Parameters

IN: *const Graph& g*
> A directed graph. The graph type must be a model of VertexListGraph and Incidence-Graph.

OUT: *ComponentMap comp*
> The algorithm computes how many connected components are in the graph, and assigns each component an integer label. The algorithm then records to which component each vertex in the graph belongs by recording the component number in the component property map. The *ComponentMap* type must be a model of WritablePropertyMap. The value type shouch be an integer type, preferably the same as the *vertices_size_type* of the graph. The key type must be the graph's vertex descriptor type.

Named Parameters

UTIL: *root_map(RootMap r_map)*
> This is used by the algorithm to record the candidate root vertex for each vertex. By the end of the algorithm, there is a single root vertex for each component and *get(r_map, v)* returns the root vertex for whichever component vertex *v* is a member. The *RootMap* must be a ReadWritePropertyMap, where the key type and the value type are the vertex descriptor type of the graph.
> **Default:** an *iterator_property_map* created from a *std::vector* of vertex descriptors of size *num_vertices(g)* and using the *i_map* for the index map.

UTIL: *discover_time(TimeMap t_map)*
> This is used by the algorithm to keep track of the DFS ordering of the vertices. The *TimeMap* must be a model of ReadWritePropertyMap and its value type must be an integer type. The key type must be the vertex descriptor type of the graph.
> **Default:** an *iterator_property_map* created from a *std::vector* of integers with size *num_vertices(g)* and using the *i_map* for the index map.

UTIL: *color_map(ColorMap c_map)*
> This is used by the algorithm to keep track of its progress through the graph. The type *ColorMap* must be a model of ReadWritePropertyMap. The key type must be the graph's vertex descriptor type and the value type must model ColorValue.

Default: an *iterator_property_map* created from a *std::vector* of *default_color_type* of size *num_vertices(g)* and using the *i_map* for the index map.

IN: *vertex_index_map(VertexIndexMap i_map)*

This maps each vertex to an integer in the range $[0, N)$ where N is the number of vertices in the graph. This parameter is only necessary when a default is used for one of the other named parameters. The type *VertexIndexMap* must be a model of ReadablePropertyMap. The value type of the map must be an integer type. The vertex descriptor type of the graph needs to be usable as the key type of the map.

Default: *get(vertex_index, g)*

Complexity

The time complexity for the strongly connected components algorithm is $O(|V| + |E|)$.

See Also

connected_components ( ) and *incremental_components* ( )

Example

Calculating the strongly connected components of a directed graph.

⟨ *strong-components.cpp* 200 ⟩ ≡

```
#include <vector>
#include <iostream>
#include <boost/graph/strong_components.hpp>
#include <boost/graph/adjacency_list.hpp>

int main ()
{
  using namespace boost;
  typedef adjacency_list< vecS, vecS, directedS>    Graph;
  const int N = 6;
  Graph G(N);
  add_edge(0, 1, G);
  add_edge(1, 1, G); add_edge(1, 3, G); add_edge(1, 4, G);
  add_edge(3, 4, G); add_edge(3, 0, G);
  add_edge(4, 3, G);
  add_edge(5, 2, G);

  std::vector<int> c(N);
  int num = strong_components(G,
    make_iterator_property_map(c.begin(), get(vertex_index, G)));
```

```
std::cout << "Total number of components: " << num << std::endl;
std::vector<int>::iterator i;
for (i = c.begin(); i != c.end(); ++i)
  std::cout << "Vertex " << i - c.begin()
      << " is in component " << *i << std::endl;
  return EXIT_SUCCESS;
}
```

The output is

Total number of components: **3**
Vertex **0** *is in component* **0**
Vertex **1** *is in component* **0**
Vertex **2** *is in component* **1**
Vertex **3** *is in component* **0**
Vertex **4** *is in component* **0**
Vertex **5** *is in component* **2**

13.6 Incremental Connected Components

This section describes a family of functions and classes that calculate the connected components of an undirected graph. The algorithm used here is based on the disjoint-sets data structure [10, 44], which is the best method for situations where the graph is growing (edges are being added) and the connected components information needs to be updated repeatedly. The disjoint-sets class is described in §16.6.

The following five operations are the primary functions that you use to calculate and maintain the connected components. The objects used here are a graph *g*, a disjoint-sets object *ds*, and vertices *u* and *v*.

- *initialize_incremental_components(g,ds)*
  Basic initialization of the disjoint-sets structure. Each vertex in the graph *g* is in its own set.

- *incremental_components(g,ds)*
  The connected components are calculated based on the edges in the graph *g* and the information is embedded in *ds*.

- *ds.find_set(v)*
  Extracts the component information for vertex *v* from the disjoint-sets object.

- *ds.union_set(u,v)*
  Update the disjoint-sets object when edge (u, v) is added to the graph.

Complexity

The time complexity for the whole process is $O(|V| + |E|\alpha(|E|, |V|))$, where $|E|$ is the total number of edges in the graph (by the end of the process) and $|V|$ is the number of vertices. α is the inverse of Ackermann's function, which has explosive recursively exponential growth. Therefore, its inverse function grows *very* slowly. For all practical purposes, $\alpha(m, n) \leq 4$, which means the time complexity is only slightly larger than $O(|V| + |E|)$.

Example

Maintain the connected components of a graph while adding edges using the disjoint-sets data structure. The full source code for this example can be found in ***example/incremental-components-eg.cpp***.

```
// Create a graph
typedef adjacency_list <vecS, vecS, undirectedS> Graph;
typedef graph_traits<Graph>::vertex_descriptor Vertex;
const int N = 6;
Graph G(N);
add_edge(0, 1, G);
add_edge(1, 4, G);
// create the disjoint-sets object, which requires rank and parent vertex properties
std::vector<Vertex> rank(num_vertices(G));
std::vector<Vertex> parent(num_vertices(G));
typedef std::vector<graph_traits<Graph>::vertices_size_type>::iterator Rank;
typedef std::vector<Vertex>::iterator Parent;
disjoint_sets<Rank, Parent> ds(rank.begin(), parent.begin());

// determine the connected components, storing the results in the disjoint-sets object
initialize_incremental_components(G, ds);
incremental_components(G, ds);

// Add a couple more edges and update the disjoint-sets
graph_traits<Graph>::edge_descriptor e;
bool flag;
tie(e,flag) = add_edge(4, 0, G);
ds.union_set(4,0);
tie(e,flag) = add_edge(2, 5, G);
ds.union_set(2,5);

graph_traits<Graph>::vertex_iterator i,end;
for (tie(i,end) = vertices(G); i != end; ++i)
  std::cout << "representative[" << *i << "] = " <<
    ds.find_set(*i) << std::endl;;
std::cout << std::endl;
```

```
typedef component_index<unsigned int> Components;
Components components(parent.begin(), parent.end());
for (Components::size_type i = 0; i < components.size(); ++i) {
  std::cout << "component " << i << " contains: ";
  for (Components::value_type::iterator j = components[i].begin();
       j != components[i].end(); ++j)
    std::cout << *j << " ";
  std::cout << std::endl;
}
```

The output is

```
representative[0] = 1
representative[1] = 1
representative[2] = 5
representative[3] = 3
representative[4] = 1
representative[5] = 5

component 0 contains: 4 1 0
component 1 contains: 3
component 2 contains: 5 2
```

Where Defined

All of the functions in this section are defined in *boost/graph/incremental_components.hpp*.

13.6.1 *initialize_incremental_components*

```
template <typename VertexListGraph, typename DisjointSets>
void initialize_incremental_components(VertexListGraph& G, DisjointSets& ds)
```

This prepares the disjoint-sets data structure for the incremental connected components algorithm by making each vertex in the undirected graph a member of its own component.

Complexity

The time complexity is $O(|V|)$.

13.6.2 *incremental_components*

```
template <typename EdgeListGraph, typename DisjointSets>
void incremental_components(EdgeListGraph& g, DisjointSets& ds)
```

This function calculates the connected components of an undirected graph, embedding the results in the disjoint-sets data structure.

Complexity

The time complexity is $O(|E|)$.

13.6.3   *same_component*

template <typename Vertex, typename DisjointSets>
bool same_component(Vertex u, Vertex v, DisjointSets& ds)

This function determines whether *u* and *v* are in the same component.

Complexity

The time complexity is $O(\alpha(|E|, |V|))$.

13.6.4   *component_index*

component_index<Index>

This class provide an STL container-like view for the components of the graph. Each component is a container-like object, and the *component_index* object provides access to the component objects via *operator[]*. A *component_index* object is initialized with the parents property in the disjoint-sets calculated from the *incremental_components()* function.

Template Parameters

Index   The unsigned integer type used to count components.

Where Defined

boost/graph/incremental_components.hpp

Associated Types

component_index::value_type
    The type for a component object. The component type has the following members.

component_index::size_type
    The type used for representing the number of components.

Member Functions

template <typename ComponentsContainer>
component_index::component_index (*const ComponentsContainer& c*)
> Constructs the *component_index* using the information from the components container *c*, which was the result of executing *incremental_components*.

template <typename ParentIterator>
component_index::component_index (*ParentIterator first*, *ParentIterator last*)
> Constructs a component index from the "parents" computed by the *incremental_components* ( ) function.

value_type component_index::operator [ ] (*size_type i*) *const*
> Returns the *i*th component in the graph.

size_type component_index::size ( ) *const*
> Returns the number of components in the graph.

Associated Types of a Component

The *value_type* of the *component_index* is a component that has the following associated types.

value_type::value_type
> The value type of a component object is a vertex ID.

value_type::iterator
value_type::const_iterator
> This iterator can be used to traverse all of the vertices in the component. This iterator dereferences to give a vertex ID.

Member Functions of a Component

The *value_type* of the *component_index* is the representation of a component and has the following member functions.

iterator begin ( ) *const*
> Returns an iterator pointing to the first vertex in the component.

iterator end ( ) *const*
> Returns an iterator pointing past the end of the last vertex in the component.

13.7   Maximum-Flow Algorithms

13.7.1   *edmunds_karp_max_flow*

> *template* *<typename Graph, typename P, typename T, typename R>*
> *typename detail::edge_capacity_value<Graph, P, T, R>::type*
> *edmunds_karp_max_flow (Graph& g,*
>   *typename graph_traits<Graph>::vertex_descriptor src,*
>   *typename graph_traits<Graph>::vertex_descriptor sink,*
>   *const bgl_named_params<P, T, R>& params = all defaults)*

The *push_relabel_flow()* function calculates the maximum flow of a network (see Chapter 8). The maximum flow is the return value of the function. The function also calculates the flow values $f(u, v) \; \forall (u, v) \in E$, which are returned in the form of the residual capacity $r(u, v) = c(u, v) - f(u, v)$.

Where Defined

boost/graph/edmunds_karp_max_flow.hpp

Parameters

IN: *Graph& g*
> A directed graph. The graph's type must be a model of VertexListGraph and IncidenceGraph. For each edge (u, v) in the graph, the reverse edge (v, u) must also be in the graph.

IN: *vertex_descriptor src*
> The source vertex for the flow network graph.

IN: *vertex_descriptor sink*
> The sink vertex for the flow network graph.

Named Parameters

IN: *capacity_map(CapacityEdgeMap cap)*
> The edge-capacity property map. The type must be a model of a constant LvaluePropertyMap. The key type of the map must be the graph's edge descriptor type.
> **Default:** *get(edge_capacity, g)*

OUT: *residual_capacity_map(ResidualCapacityEdgeMap res)*
> The edge-residual-capacity property map. The type must be a model of a mutable LvaluePropertyMap. The key type of the map must be the graph's edge descriptor type.
> **Default:** *get(edge_residual_capacity, g)*

IN: *reverse_edge_map(ReverseEdgeMap rev)*

> An edge property map that maps every edge (u, v) in the graph to the reverse edge (v, u). The map must be a model of constant LvaluePropertyMap. The key type of the map must be the graph's edge descriptor type.
>
> **Default:** *get(edge_reverse, g)*

UTIL: *predecessor_map(PredecessorMap p_map)*

> The predecessor map differs from the usual predecessor map in that the value type is the *edge_descriptor* type instead of *vertex_descriptor*. The key type for this predecessor map is still *vertex_descriptor*.
>
> **Default:** an *iterator_property_map* created from a *std::vector* of *edge_descriptor* of size *num_vertices(g)* and using the *i_map* for the index map.

UTIL: *color_map(ColorMap c_map)*

> This map is used for internal bookkeeping. The type *ColorMap* must be a model of ReadWritePropertyMap. A vertex descriptor must be usable as the key type of the map, and the value type of the map must be a model of ColorValue.
>
> **Default:** an *iterator_property_map* created from a *std::vector* of *default_color_type* of size *num_vertices(g)* and using the *i_map* for the index map.

IN: *vertex_index_map(VertexIndexMap index_map)*

> This map is only needed if the default color map or default predecessor map is used. Each vertex of the graph is mapped to an integer in the range $[0, |V|)$. The map must be a model of constant LvaluePropertyMap. The key type of the map must be the graph's vertex descriptor type.
>
> **Default:** *get(vertex_index, g)*

Example

This reads in an example maximum-flow problem (a graph with edge capacities) from a file in the DIMACS file format [1].

⟨ *edmunds-karp-eg.cpp* 207 ⟩ ≡

```
#include <boost/config.hpp>
#include <iostream>
#include <string>
#include <boost/graph/edmunds_karp_max_flow.hpp>
#include <boost/graph/adjacency_list.hpp>
#include <boost/graph/read_dimacs.hpp>
#include <boost/graph/graph_utility.hpp>

int main()
{
  using namespace boost;
```

```
typedef adjacency_list_traits<vecS, vecS, directedS> Traits;
typedef adjacency_list<listS, vecS, directedS,
  property<vertex_name_t, std::string>,
  property<edge_capacity_t, long,
    property<edge_residual_capacity_t, long,
      property<edge_reverse_t, Traits::edge_descriptor> > >
> Graph;

Graph g;

property_map<Graph, edge_capacity_t>::type
  capacity = get(edge_capacity, g);
property_map<Graph, edge_reverse_t>::type
  rev = get(edge_reverse, g);
property_map<Graph, edge_residual_capacity_t>::type
  residual_capacity = get(edge_residual_capacity, g);

Traits::vertex_descriptor s, t;
read_dimacs_max_flow(g, capacity, rev, s, t);

long flow = edmunds_karp_max_flow(g, s, t);

std::cout << "c   The total flow:" << std::endl;
std::cout << "s " << flow << std::endl << std::endl;

std::cout << "c flow values:" << std::endl;
graph_traits<Graph>::vertex_iterator u_iter, u_end;
graph_traits<Graph>::out_edge_iterator ei, e_end;
for (tie(u_iter, u_end) = vertices(g); u_iter != u_end; ++u_iter)
  for (tie(ei, e_end) = out_edges(*u_iter, g); ei != e_end; ++ei)
    if (capacity[*ei] > 0)
      std::cout << "f " << *u_iter << " " << target(*ei, g) << " "
                << (capacity[*ei] - residual_capacity[*ei]) << std::endl;

return EXIT_SUCCESS;
}
```

The output is

```
c   The total flow:
s 13

c flow values:
f 0 6 3
f 0 1 6
f 0 2 4
f 1 5 1
```

```
f 1 0 0
f 1 3 5
f 2 4 4
f 2 3 0
f 2 0 0
f 3 7 5
f 3 2 0
f 3 1 0
f 4 5 4
f 4 6 0
f 5 4 0
f 5 7 5
f 6 7 3
f 6 4 0
f 7 6 0
f 7 5 0
```

13.7.2   *push_relabel_max_flow*

template <typename Graph, typename P, typename T, typename R>
typename detail::edge_capacity_value<Graph, P, T, R>::type
push_relabel_max_flow (Graph& g,
   typename graph_traits<Graph>::vertex_descriptor src,
   typename graph_traits<Graph>::vertex_descriptor sink,
   const bgl_named_params<P, T, R>& params)

The *push_relabel_flow()* function calculates the maximum flow of a network (see Chapter 8). The maximum flow is the return value of the function. The function also calculates the flow values $f(u, v)$ $\forall (u, v) \in E$, which are returned in the form of the residual capacity $r(u, v) = c(u, v) - f(u, v)$. Figure 13.7 shows a network with edges labeled with flow and capacity values.

There are several special requirements on the input graph and property map parameters for this algorithm. First, the directed graph $G = (V, E)$ that represents the network must be augmented to include the reverse edge for every edge in E. That is, the input graph should be $G_{in} = (V, \{E \bigcup E^T\})$. The *ReverseEdgeMap* argument *rev* must map each edge in the original graph to its reverse edge, that is $(u, v) \rightarrow (v, u)$ $\forall (u, v) \in E$. The *CapacityEdgeMap* argument *cap* must map each edge in E to a positive number, and each edge in E^T to 0. In other words, the capacity map should satisfy these constraints: $c(u, v) > 0$ and $c(v, u) = 0$ for each $(u, v) \in E$.

Where Defined

boost/graph/push_relabel_max_flow.hpp

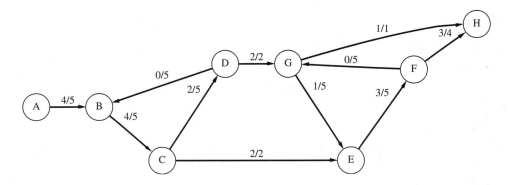

Figure 13.7 A flow network that has edges labeled with flow and capacity values.

Parameters

IN: *Graph& g*

A directed graph. The graph's type must be a model of VertexListGraph and IncidenceGraph. For each edge (u, v) in the graph, the reverse edge (v, u) must also be in the graph.

IN: *vertex_descriptor src*

The source vertex for the flow network graph.

IN: *vertex_descriptor sink*

The sink vertex for the flow network graph.

Named Parameters

IN: *capacity_map(CapacityEdgeMap cap)*

The edge capacity property map. The type must be a model of a constant LvaluePropertyMap. The key type of the map must be the graph's edge descriptor type.
Default: *get(edge_capacity, g)*

OUT: *residual_capacity_map(ResidualCapacityEdgeMap res)*

The edge residual capacity property map. The type must be a model of a mutable LvaluePropertyMap. The key type of the map must be the graph's edge descriptor type.
Default: *get(edge_residual_capacity, g)*

IN: *reverse_edge_map(ReverseEdgeMap rev)*

An edge property map that maps every edge (u, v) in the graph to the reverse edge (v, u). The map must be a model of constant LvaluePropertyMap. The key type of the map must be the graph's edge descriptor type.
Default: *get(edge_reverse, g)*

IN: *vertex_index_map(VertexIndexMap index_map)*
> This maps each vertex to an integer in the range $[0, N)$ where N is the number of vertices in the graph. The map must be a model of constant LvaluePropertyMap. The key type of the map must be the graph's vertex descriptor type.
> **Default:** *get(vertex_index, g)*

Example

This reads in an example maximum-flow problem (a graph with edge capacities) from a file in the DIMACS file format [1].

⟨ *push-relabel-eg.cpp* 211 ⟩ ≡

```
#include <iostream>
#include <string>
#include <boost/graph/push_relabel_max_flow.hpp>
#include <boost/graph/adjacency_list.hpp>
#include <boost/graph/read_dimacs.hpp>
int main()
{
  using namespace boost;
  typedef adjacency_list_traits<vecS, vecS, directedS> Traits;
  typedef adjacency_list<vecS, vecS, directedS,
    property<vertex_name_t, std::string>,
    property<edge_capacity_t, long,
      property<edge_residual_capacity_t, long,
        property<edge_reverse_t, Traits::edge_descriptor> > >
  > Graph;
  Graph g;

  property_map<Graph, edge_capacity_t>::type
    capacity = get(edge_capacity, g);
  property_map<Graph, edge_residual_capacity_t>::type
    residual_capacity = get(edge_residual_capacity, g);
  property_map<Graph, edge_reverse_t>::type
    rev = get(edge_reverse, g);
  Traits::vertex_descriptor s, t;
  read_dimacs_max_flow(g, capacity, rev, s, t);

  long flow = push_relabel_max_flow(g, s, t);

  std::cout << "c  The total flow:" << std::endl;
  std::cout << "s " << flow << std::endl << std::endl;
  std::cout << "c flow values:" << std::endl;
  graph_traits<Graph>::vertex_iterator u_iter, u_end;
  graph_traits<Graph>::out_edge_iterator ei, e_end;
```

```
for (tie(u_iter, u_end) = vertices(g); u_iter != u_end; ++u_iter)
  for (tie(ei, e_end) = out_edges(*u_iter, g); ei != e_end; ++ei)
    if (capacity[*ei] > 0)
      std::cout << "f " << *u_iter << " " << target(*ei, g) << " "
                << (capacity[*ei] - residual_capacity[*ei]) << std::endl;
return EXIT_SUCCESS;
}
```

The output is

```
c  The total flow:
s 13

c flow values:
f 0 6 3
f 0 1 0
f 0 2 10
f 1 5 1
f 1 0 0
f 1 3 0
f 2 4 4
f 2 3 6
f 2 0 0
f 3 7 5
f 3 2 0
f 3 1 1
f 4 5 4
f 4 6 0
f 5 4 0
f 5 7 5
f 6 7 3
f 6 4 0
f 7 6 0
f 7 5 0
```

Chapter 14

BGL Classes

14.1 Graph Classes

14.1.1 *adjacency_list*

> *adjacency_list<EdgeList, VertexList, Directed,*
> *VertexProperties, EdgeProperties, GraphProperties>*

The *adjacency_list* class implements the BGL graph interface using several different variations on the traditional adjacency-list graph structure.

An adjacency-list reprepresentation of a graph stores an out-edge sequence for each vertex. For sparse graphs this saves space compared to an adjacency matrix because only $O(|V| + |E|)$ memory is required, compared to $O(|V|^2)$. In addition, the out-edges for each vertex can be accessed efficiently. Figure 14.1 shows an adjacency-list representation of a directed graph.

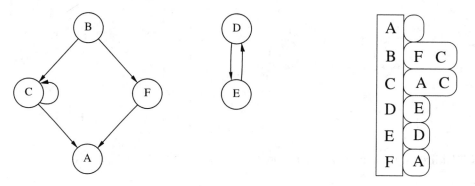

Figure 14.1 Adjacency-list representation of a directed graph.

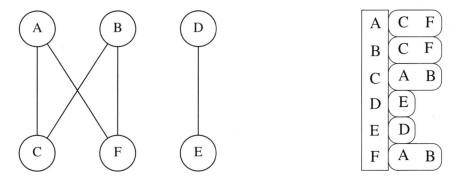

Figure 14.2 Adjacency-list representation of an undirected graph.

The template parameters of the ***adjacency_list*** class provide many configuration options so that you can pick a version of the class that best meets your needs. The ***VertexList*** template parameter of the ***adjacency_list*** class controls what kind of container is used to represent the sequence of vertices (the rectangle in Figure 14.1). The ***EdgeList*** template parameter controls what kind of container is used to represent the sequence of out-edges for each vertex (the ovals in Figure 14.1). The choices for ***EdgeList*** and ***VertexList*** affect the memory consumption of the graph and determine the efficiency for various graph operations. The possible choices and tradeoffs are discussed later in this section.

The ***Directed*** template parameter controls whether the graph is directed, undirected, or directed with access to both the in-edges and out-edges (which we call bidirectional). The bidirectional graph takes up twice the space (per edge) of a directed graph because each edge will appear in both an out-edge and in-edge list. Figure 14.2 shows an adjacency-list representation of an undirected graph, and Figure 14.3 shows a bidirectional representation of a directed graph.

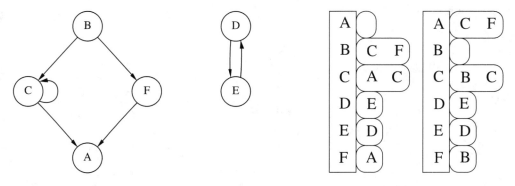

Figure 14.3 Bidirectional adjacency-list representation of a directed graph.

Example

The graph in the following example is used to represent a family tree.

⟨ *family-tree-eg.cpp* 215 ⟩ ≡

```
#include <iostream>
#include <vector>
#include <string>
#include <boost/graph/adjacency_list.hpp>
#include <boost/tuple/tuple.hpp>
enum family { Jeanie, Debbie, Rick, John, Amanda, Margaret, Benjamin, N };
int main()
{
  using namespace boost;
  const char* name[] = { "Jeanie", "Debbie", "Rick", "John", "Amanda",
    "Margaret", "Benjamin" };

  adjacency_list<>   g(N);
  add_edge(Jeanie, Debbie, g);
  add_edge(Jeanie, Rick, g);
  add_edge(Jeanie, John, g);
  add_edge(Debbie, Amanda, g);
  add_edge(Rick, Margaret, g);
  add_edge(John, Benjamin, g);

  graph_traits<adjacency_list<> >::vertex_iterator i, end;
  graph_traits<adjacency_list<> >::adjacency_iterator ai, a_end;
  property_map<adjacency_list<>, vertex_index_t>::type
    index_map = get(vertex_index, g);

  for(tie(i, end) = vertices(g); i != end; ++i) {
    std::cout << name[get(index_map, *i)];
    tie(ai, a_end) = adjacent_vertices(*i, g);
    if (ai == a_end)
      std::cout << " has no children";
    else
      std::cout << " is the parent of ";
    for (; ai != a_end; ++ai) {
      std::cout << name[get(index_map, *ai)];
      if (boost::next(ai) != a_end)
        std::cout << ", ";
    }
    std::cout << std::endl;
  }
  return EXIT_SUCCESS;
}
```

The output is

> *Jeanie is the parent of Debbie, Rick, John*
> *Debbie is the parent of Amanda*
> *Rick is the parent of Margaret*
> *John is the parent of Benjamin*
> *Amanda has no children*
> *Margaret has no children*
> *Benjamin has no children*

Template Parameters

EdgeList	The selector for the container that represents the edge-list for each vertex. **Default:** *vecS*
VertexList	The selector for the container that represents the vertex set of the graph. **Default:** *vecS*
Directed	A selector to choose whether the graph is directed, undirected, or directed with bidirectional edge access (access to both out-edges and in-edges). The options are ***directedS***, ***undirectedS***, and ***bidirectionalS***. **Default:** *directedS*
VertexProperties	Specify internal vertex property storage. **Default:** *no_property*
EdgeProperties	Specify internal edge property storage. **Default:** *no_property*
GraphProperties	Specify property graph property storage. **Default:** *no_property*

Model Of

DefaultConstructible, CopyConstructible, Assignable, VertexListGraph, EdgeListGraph, IncidenceGraph, AdjacencyGraph, VertexMutableGraph, andEdgeMutableGraph. Also, ***adjacency_list*** models BidirectionalGraph when ***Directed=bidirectionalS*** or ***Directed=undirectedS***, and it models VertexMutablePropertyGraph and EdgeMutablePropertyGraph when the appropriate internal properties have been added.

Where Defined

boost/graph/adjacency_list.hpp

Associated Types

graph_traits<adjacency_list>::vertex_descriptor
    The type for the vertex descriptors associated with the ***adjacency_list***.
    (Required by Graph.)

graph_traits<adjacency_list>::edge_descriptor
    The type for the edge descriptors associated with the *adjacency_list*.
    (Required by Graph.)

graph_traits<adjacency_list>::vertex_iterator
    The type for the iterators returned by *vertices()*.
    (Required by VertexListGraph.)

graph_traits<adjacency_list>::edge_iterator
    The type for the iterators returned by *edges()*.
    (Required by EdgeListGraph.)

graph_traits<adjacency_list>::out_edge_iterator
    The type for the iterators returned by *out_edges()*.
    (Required by IncidenceGraph.)

graph_traits<adjacency_list>::in_edge_iterator
    This type is available for undirected and bidirectional adjacency lists, but not for directed.
    The *in_edge_iterator* is the iterator type returned by the *in_edges()* function.
    (Required by BidirectionalGraph.)

graph_traits<adjacency_list>::adjacency_iterator
    The type for the iterators returned by *adjacent_vertices()*.
    (Required by AdjacencyGraph.)

graph_traits<adjacency_list>::directed_category
    Provides information about whether the graph is directed (*directed_tag*) or undirected
    (*undirected_tag*).
    (Required by Graph.)

graph_traits<adjacency_list>::edge_parallel_category
    This describes whether the graph class allows the insertion of parallel edges (edges with
    the same source and target). The two tags are *allow_parallel_edge_tag* and *disallow_parallel-*
    _edge_tag. The *setS* and *hash_setS* variants disallow parallel edges whereas the others allow
    parallel edges.
    (Required by Graph.)

graph_traits<adjacency_list>::traversal_category
    The traversal category reflects which kinds of iterators are supported by the graph class.
    For adjacency list, this includes vertex, edge, out-edge, and adjacency iterators. The
    in-edge iterator is also available for undirected and bidirectional but not for directed
    adjacency lists.

graph_traits<adjacency_list>::vertices_size_type
    The type used for dealing with the number of vertices in the graph.
    (Required by VertexListGraph.)

graph_traits<adjacency_list>::edges_size_type
> The type used for dealing with the number of edges in the graph.
> (Required by EdgeListGraph.)

graph_traits<adjacency_list>::degree_size_type
> The type used for dealing with the number of out-edges of a vertex.
> (Required by IncidenceGraph.)

property_map<adjacency_list, PropertyTag>::type
property_map<adjacency_list, PropertyTag>::const_type
> The map type for vertex or edge properties in the graph. The property is specified by
> the *PropertyTag* template argument, and must match one of the properties specified in the
> *VertexProperties* or *EdgeProperties* for the graph.
> (Required by PropertyGraph.)

Member Functions

adjacency_list (const GraphProperties& p = GraphProperties ( ))
> Default constructor. It creates an empty graph object with zero vertices and zero edges.
> (Required by DefaultConstructible.)

adjacency_list (vertices_size_type n, const GraphProperties& p = GraphProperties ( ))
> Creates a graph object with *n* vertices and zero edges.

template <typename EdgeIterator>
adjacency_list (EdgeIterator first, EdgeIterator last,
>   *vertices_size_type n, edges_size_type m = 0,*
>   *const GraphProperties& p = GraphProperties ( ))*
> Creates a graph object with n vertices and m edges, with the edges specified in the edge
> list given by the range $[first, last)$. If n or m is zero, then the number of vertices or
> edges is deduced from the edge list. The value type of the *EdgeIterator* must be a *std::pair*,
> where the type in the pair is an integer type. The integers correspond to vertices, and they
> must all fall in the range of $[0, n)$.

template <typename EdgeIterator, typename EdgePropertiesIterator>
adjacency_list (EdgeIterator first, EdgeIterator last, EdgePropertiesIterator ep_iter,
>   *vertices_size_type n, edges_size_type m = 0,*
>   *const GraphProperties& p = GraphProperties ( ))*
> Creates a graph object with n vertices and m edges, with the edges specified in the edge
> list given by the range $[first, last)$. If n or m is zero, then the number of vertices or
> edges is deduced from the edge list. The value type of the *EdgeIterator* must be a *std::pair*,
> where the type in the pair is an integer type. The integers correspond to vertices, and
> they must all fall in the range of $[0, n)$. The *value_type* of the *ep_iter* should match the
> *EdgeProperties* template parameter.

Nonmember Functions

std::pair<vertex_iterator, vertex_iterator>
vertices (const adjacency_list& g)
    Returns an iterator range providing access to the vertex set of graph g.
    (Required by VertexListGraph.)

std::pair<edge_iterator, edge_iterator>
edges (const adjacency_list& g)
    Returns an iterator range providing access to the edge set of graph g.
    (Required by EdgeListGraph.)

std::pair<adjacency_iterator, adjacency_iterator>
adjacent_vertices (vertex_descriptor v, const adjacency_list& g)
    Returns an iterator range providing access to the vertices adjacent to vertex v in graph g.
    (Required by AdjacencyGraph.)

std::pair<out_edge_iterator, out_edge_iterator>
out_edges (vertex_descriptor v, const adjacency_list& g)
    Returns an iterator range providing access to the out-edges of vertex v in graph g. If the
    graph is undirected, this iterator range provides access to all edges incident on vertex v.
    (Required by IncidenceGraph.)

std::pair<in_edge_iterator, in_edge_iterator>
in_edges (vertex_descriptor v, const adjacency_list& g)
    Returns an iterator range providing access to the in-edges of vertex v in graph g. This
    operation is not available if *directedS* is specified for the **Directed** template parameter. It is
    available for **undirectedS** and **bidirectionalS**.
    (Required by BidirectionalGraph.)

vertex_descriptor source (edge_descriptor e, const adjacency_list& g)
    Returns the source vertex of edge e.
    (Required by IncidenceGraph.)

vertex_descriptor target (edge_descriptor e, const adjacency_list& g)
    Returns the target vertex of edge e.
    (Required by IncidenceGraph.)

degree_size_type out_degree (vertex_descriptor u, const adjacency_list& g)
    Returns the number of edges leaving vertex u.
    (Required by IncidenceGraph.)

degree_size_type in_degree (vertex_descriptor u, const adjacency_list& g)
    Returns the number of edges entering vertex u. This operation is only available if **bidirec-
    tionalS** is specified for the **Directed** template parameter.
    (Required by BidirectionalGraph.)

vertices_size_type num_vertices (*const adjacency_list& g*)
  Returns the number of vertices in the graph g.
  (Required by VertexListGraph.)

edges_size_type num_edges (*const adjacency_list& g*)
  Returns the number of edges in the graph g.
  (Required by EdgeListGraph.)

vertex_descriptor vertex (*vertices_size_type n, const adjacency_list& g*)
  Returns the nth vertex in the graph's vertex list.

std::pair<edge_descriptor, bool>
edge (*vertex_descriptor u, vertex_descriptor v, const adjacency_list& g*)
  Returns the edge connecting vertex u to vertex v in graph g.
  (Required by AdjacencyMatrix.)

std::pair<out_edge_iterator, out_edge_iterator>
edge_range (*vertex_descriptor u, vertex_descriptor v, const adjacency_list& g*)
  Returns a pair of out-edge iterators that give the range for all the parallel edges from
  u to *v*. This function only works when the *EdgeList* for the *adjacency_list* is a container
  that sorts the out-edges according to the target vertex, and allows for parallel edges. The
  multisetS selector chooses such a container.

std::pair<edge_descriptor, bool>
add_edge (*vertex_descriptor u, vertex_descriptor v, adjacency_list& g*)
  Adds edge (u, v) to the graph and returns the edge descriptor for the new edge. For
  graphs that do not allow parallel edges, if the edge is already in the graph, then a duplicate
  will not be added and the *bool* flag will be false. Also, if u and v are descriptors for the
  same vertex (creating a self loop) and the graph is undirected, then the edge will not be
  added and the flag will be false. When the flag is false, the edge descriptor is invalid
  and any use of it is undefined. The placement of the new edge in the out-edge list is in
  general unspecified, though ordering of the out-edge list can be accomplished through the
  choice of *EdgeList*. If the *VertexList* selector is *vecS*, and if either vertex descriptor *u* or *v*
  (which are integers) has a value greater than the current number of vertices in the graph,
  the graph is enlarged so that the number of vertices is *std::max(u,v) + 1*. If the *EdgeList*
  selector is *vecS*, then this operation invalidates any *out_edge_iterator* for vertex u. This
  also applies if the *EdgeList* is a user-defined container that invalidates its iterators when
  push(container, x) is invoked. If the graph is also bidirectional, then any *in_edge_iterator*
  for v is also invalidated. If instead the graph is undirected, then any *out_edge_iterator* for v
  is also invalidated. If instead the graph is directed, then *add_edge* () also invalidates any
  edge_iterator.
  (Required by EdgeMutableGraph.)

std::pair<edge_descriptor, bool>
add_edge (*vertex_descriptor u, vertex_descriptor v, const EdgeProperties& p,*
  adjacency_list& g)

Adds edge (u, v) to the graph and attaches *p* as the value of the edge's internal property storage. Also see the previous *add_edge* ( ) member function for more details.
(Required by EdgeMutablePropertyGraph.)

void remove_edge (*vertex_descriptor u, vertex_descriptor v, adjacency_list& g*)

Removes the edge (u, v) from the graph. This operation causes any outstanding edge descriptors or iterators that point to edge (u, v) to become invalid. In addition, if the *EdgeList* selector is *vecS*, then this operation invalidates any iterators that point into the edge-list for vertex u and also for vertex v in the undirected and bidirectional case. Also, for directed graphs this invalidates any *edge_iterator*.
(Required by EdgeMutableGraph.)

void remove_edge (*edge_descriptor e, adjacency_list& g*)

Removes the edge *e* from the graph. This differs from the *remove_edge(u, v, g)* function in the case of a multigraph. This *remove_edge(e, g)* function removes a single edge, whereas the *remove_edge(u, v, g)* function removes all edges (u, v). This operation invalidates any outstanding edge descriptors and iterators for the same edge pointed to by descriptor *e*. In addition, this operation invalidates any iterators that point into the edge-list for the *target(e, g)*. Also, for directed graphs this invalidates any *edge_iterator* for the graph.
(Required by EdgeMutableGraph.)

void remove_edge (*out_edge_iterator iter, adjacency_list& g*)

This has the same effect as *remove_edge(*iter, g)*. The difference is that this function has constant time complexity in the case of directed graphs, whereas *remove_edge(e, g)* has time complexity $O(|E|/|V|)$.
(Required by MutableIncidenceGraph.)

template <typename Predicate>
void remove_out_edge_if (*vertex_descriptor u, Predicate predicate, adjacency_list& g*)

Removes all out-edges of vertex u from the graph that satisfy the *predicate*. That is, if the predicate returns true when applied to an edge descriptor, then the edge is removed. The effect on descriptor and iterator stability is the same as that of invoking *remove_edge* ( ) on each of the removed edges.
(Required by MutableIncidenceGraph.)

template <typename Predicate>
void remove_in_edge_if (*vertex_descriptor v, Predicate predicate, adjacency_list& g*)

Removes all in-edges of vertex v from the graph that satisfy the *predicate*. That is, if the predicate returns true when applied to an edge descriptor, then the edge is removed.

The effect on descriptor and iterator stability is the same as that of invoking *remove_edge* **( )** on each of the removed edges.
(Required by MutableBidirectionalGraph.)

template <typename Predicate>
void remove_edge_if **(** *Predicate predicate* **,** *adjacency_list&* *g* **)**
  Removes all edges from the graph that satisfy the *predicate*. That is, if the predicate returns true when applied to an edge descriptor, then the edge is removed. The effect on descriptor and iterator stability is the same as that of invoking *remove_edge* **( )** on each of the removed edges.
  (Required by MutableEdgeListGraph.)

vertex_descriptor add_vertex **(** *adjacency_list&* *g* **)**
  Adds a vertex to the graph and returns the vertex descriptor for the new vertex.
  (Required by VertexMutableGraph.)

vertex_descriptor add_vertex **(** *const VertexProperties&* *p* **,** *adjacency_list&* *g* **)**
  Adds a vertex to the graph and returns the vertex descriptor for the new vertex.
  (Required by VertexMutablePropertyGraph.)

void clear_vertex **(** *vertex_descriptor u* **,** *adjacency_list&* *g* **)**
  Removes all edges to and from vertex u. The vertex still appears in the vertex set of the graph. The effect on descriptor and iterator stability is the same as that of invoking *remove_edge* **( )** for all of the edges that have u as the source or target.
  (Required by EdgeMutableGraph.)

void clear_out_edges **(** *vertex_descriptor u* **,** *adjacency_list&* *g* **)**
  Removes all edges from vertex u. The vertex still appears in the vertex set of the graph. The effect on descriptor and iterator stability is the same as that of invoking *remove_-edge* **( )** for all of the edges that have *u* as the source. This operation is not applicable to undirected graphs (use *clear_vertex()* instead).

void clear_in_edges **(** *vertex_descriptor u* **,** *adjacency_list&* *g* **)**
  Removes all edges to and from vertex u. The vertex still appears in the vertex set of the graph. The effect on descriptor and iterator stability is the same as that of invoking *remove_edge* **( )** for all of the edges that have u as the source or target. This operation is only applicable to bidirectional graphs.

void remove_vertex **(** *vertex_descriptor u* **,** *adjacency_list&* *g* **)**
  Remove vertex u from the vertex set of the graph. It is assumed that there are no edges to or from vertex u when it is removed. One way to make sure of this is to invoke *clear_vertex* **( )** beforehand. If the *VertexList* template parameter of the *adjacency_list* is *vecS*, then all vertex descriptors, edge descriptors, and iterators for the graph are invalidated by this operation. The built-in *vertex_index_t* property for each vertex is

renumbered so that after the operation the vertex indices still form a contiguous range $[0, |V|)$. If you are using external property storage based on the built-in vertex index, then the external storage needs to be adjusted. Another option is to not use the built-in vertex index, and instead use a property to add your own vertex index property. If you need to make frequent use of the *remove_vertex()* function, the *listS* selector is a much better choice for the *VertexList* template parameter.

(Required by VertexMutableGraph.)

template <*typename PropertyTag*>
property_map<*adjacency_list, PropertyTag*>*::type*
get (*PropertyTag, adjacency_list& g*)

Returns a mutable property map object for the vertex property specified by *PropertyTag*. The *PropertyTag* must match one of the properties specified in the graph's *VertexProperties* template argument.

(Required by PropertyGraph.)

template <*typename PropertyTag*>
property_map<*adjacency_list, PropertyTag*>*::const_type*
get (*PropertyTag, const adjacency_list& g*)

Returns a constant property map object for the vertex property specified by *PropertyTag*. The *PropertyTag* must match one of the properties specified in the graph's *VertexProperties* template argument.

(Required by PropertyGraph.)

template <*typename PropertyTag, typename X*>
typename property_traits<
  typename property_map<*adjacency_list, PropertyTag*>*::const_type*
>*::value_type*
get (*PropertyTag, const adjacency_list& g, X x*)

This returns the property value for *x*, which is either a vertex or an edge descriptor.

(Required by PropertyGraph.)

template <*typename PropertyTag, typename X, typename Value*>
void put (*PropertyTag, const adjacency_list& g, X x, const Value& value*)

This sets the property value for *x* to *value*. *x* is either a vertex or an edge descriptor. *Value* must be convertible to *typename property_traits*<*property_map*<*adjacency_list, PropertyTag*>*::type*>*::value_type*

(Required by PropertyGraph.)

template <*typename GraphProperties, typename GraphProperties*>
typename property_value<*GraphProperties, GraphProperties*>*::type&*
get_property (*adjacency_list& g, GraphProperties*);

Returns the property specified by *GraphProperties* that is attached to the graph object *g*. The *property_value* traits class is defined in *boost/pending/property.hpp*.

template <*typename GraphProperties*, *typename GraphProperties*>
const typename property_value<*GraphProperties*, *GraphProperties*>*::type&*
get_property (*const adjacency_list& g*, *GraphProperties*);
    Returns the property specified by *GraphProperties* that is attached to the graph object *g*.
The *property_value* traits class is defined in *boost/pending/property.hpp*.

Choosing the *Edgelist* and *VertexList*

This section focuses on how to decide which version of the *adjacency_list* class to use in different situations. The *adjacency_list* is like a Swiss Army knife in that it can be configured in many ways. The parameters that we focus on in this section are *EdgeList* and *VertexList*, which control the underlying data structures used to represent the graph. The choice of *EdgeList* and *VertexList* affects the time complexity of many of the graph operations and the space complexity of the graph object.

    BGL uses containers from the STL such as *std::vector*, *std::list*, and *std::set* to represent the set of vertices and the adjacency structure (out-edges and in-edges) of the graph. Several selector types are used to specify the choice of container for *EdgeList* and *VertexList*:

- *vecS* selects *std::vector*.

- *listS* selects *std::list*.

- *slistS* selects *std::slist*.[1]

- *setS* selects *std::set*.

- *hash_setS* selects *std::hash_set*.[2]

Choosing the *VertexList* type

The *VertexList* parameter determines what kind of container will be used to represent the vertex set, or two-dimensional structure of the graph. The container must model Sequence or RandomAccessContainer. In general, *listS* is a good choice if you need to add and remove vertices quickly. The price for this is extra space overhead compared to choosing *vecS*.

Space Complexity   The *std::list* has a higher per-vertex space overhead than the *std::vector*, storing two more pointers per vertex.

---

[1] Provided the implementation of STL that you use implements *std::slist*.
[2] Provided that the implementation of STL that you use implements *std::hash_set*. The SGI STL is an example of an implementation that does.

Time Complexity   The choice of *VertexList* affects the time complexity of the following operations.

add_vertex ( )

This operation is amortized constant time for both *vecS* and *listS* (implemented with *push_back* ( )). However, when the *VertexList* type is *vecS*, the time for this operation is occasionally large because the vector is reallocated and the whole graph is copied.

remove_vertex ( )

This operation is constant time for *listS* and $O(|V| + |E|)$ for *vecS*. The large time complexity for *vecS* is because the vertex descriptors (which in this case are indices that correspond to the vertices' place in the vertex list) must be adjusted in the out-edges for the whole graph.

vertex ( )

This operation is constant time for *vecS* and $O(|V|)$ for *listS*.

Choosing the *EdgeList* type

The *EdgeList* parameter determines what kind of container is used to store the out-edges (and possibly in-edges) for each vertex in the graph. The containers used for edge lists must satisfy the requirements for either Sequence or AssociativeContainer.

One of the first things to consider when choosing the *EdgeList* is whether you want *adjacency_list* to enforce the absence of parallel edges in the graph (that is, enforce that the graph does not become a multigraph). If you want this enforced, then use the *setS* or *hash_setS* selectors. If you want to represent a multigraph, or know that you will not be inserting parallel edges into the graph, then choose one of the Sequence types: *vecS*, *listS*, or *slistS*. In addition, you will want to take into account the differences in time and space complexity for the various graph operations. We use $|V|$ for the total number of vertices in the graph and $|E|$ for the total number of edges. Operations not discussed here are constant time.

Space Complexity   The selection of the *EdgeList* affects the amount of space overhead per edge in the graph object. In the order of least space to most space, the selectors are *vecS*, *slistS*, *listS*, *hash_setS*, and *setS*.

Time Complexity   In the following description of the time complexity for various operations, we use $\frac{|E|}{|V|}$ inside of the "big-O" notation to express the length of an out-edge list. Strictly speaking, this is not accurate because $\frac{|E|}{|V|}$ merely gives the average number of edges per vertex in a graph. The worst-case number of out-edges for a vertex is $|V|$ (unless it is a multigraph). For sparse graphs, $\frac{|E|}{|V|}$ is typically much smaller than $|V|$ and can be considered a constant.

add_edge ( )

When the *EdgeList* is a UniqueAssociativeContainer like *std::set*, the absence of parallel edges is enforced when an edge is added. The extra lookup involved has time complexity $O(\log \frac{|E|}{|V|})$. The *EdgeList* types that model Sequence do not perform this check, and therefore, *add_edge ( )* is amortized constant time. This means that if you do not care whether the graph has parallel edges, or know that the input to the graph does not contain them, then it is better to use the sequence-based *EdgeList*. The *add_edge ( )* for the sequence-based *EdgeList* is implemented with *push_front ( )* or *push_back ( )*. However, for *std::list* and *std::slist*, this operation is typically faster than with *std::vector*, which occasionally reallocates and copies all elements.

remove_edge ( )

For sequence-based *EdgeList* types, this operation is implemented with *std::remove_if ( )*, which means the average time is $\frac{|E|}{|V|}$. For set-based *EdgeList* types this is implemented with the *erase ( )* member function, which has average time $\log \frac{E}{V}$.

edge ( )

The time complexity for this operation is $O(\frac{|E|}{|V|})$ when the *EdgeList* type is a Sequence and it is $O(\log(\frac{|E|}{|V|}))$ when the *EdgeList* type is an AssociativeContainer.

clear_vertex ( )

For directed graphs with sequence-based *EdgeList* types the time complexity is $O(|V| + |E|)$, whereas for associative-container-based *EdgeList* types the operation is faster, with time complexity $O(|V| \log \frac{|E|}{|V|})$. For undirected graphs this operation is $O(\frac{|E|^2}{|V|^2})$ or $O(\frac{|E|}{|V|} \log(\frac{|E|}{|V|}))$.

remove_vertex ( )

The time complexity for this operation is $O(|V| + |E|)$ regardless of the *EdgeList* type.

out_edge_iterator::operator++ ( )

This operation is constant time for all the *EdgeList* types. However, there is a significant constant-factor time difference between the various types, which is important because this operation is the workhorse of most graph algorithms. The speed of this operation in order of fastest to slowest is *vecS, slistS, listS, setS, hash_setS*.

in_edge_iterator::operator++ ( )

This operation is constant time and exhibits a similar speed ordering as the *out_edge_iterator* with respect to the *EdgeList* selection.

vertex_iterator::operator++ ( )

This operation is constant time and fast (same speed as incrementing a pointer). The selection of *OneD* does not affect the speed of this operation.

edge_iterator::operator++ ( )

This operation is constant time and exhibits a similar speed ordering as the *out_edge_iterator* with respect to the *EdgeList* selection. Traversing through the whole edge set is $O(|V| + |E|)$.

adjacency_iterator::operator++ ( )

This operation is constant time and exhibits a similar speed ordering as the *out_edge_iterator* with respect to the *EdgeList* selection.

Iterator and Descriptor Stability/Invalidation

Some care must be taken when changing the structure of a graph (via adding or removing edges). Depending on the type of *adjacency_list* and on the operation, some of the iterator or descriptor objects that point into the graph may become invalid. For example, the following code results in undefined (bad) behavior:

```
// VertexList=vecS
typedef adjacency_list<listS, vecS> Graph;
Graph G(N);

// Fill in the graph...

// Attempt to remove all the vertices. Wrong!
graph_traits<Graph>::vertex_iterator vi, vi_end;
for (tie(vi, vi_end) = vertices(G); vi != vi_end; ++vi)
  remove_vertex(*vi, G);

// Another attempt to remove all the vertices. This is still wrong!
graph_traits<Graph>::vertex_iterator vi, vi_end, next;
tie(vi, vi_end) = vertices(G);
for (next = vi; vi != vi_end; vi = next) {
  ++next;
  remove_vertex(*vi, G);
}
```

The reason this is a problem is that we are invoking *remove_vertex()*, which when used with an *adjacency_list* where *VertexList=vecS*, invalidates all iterators and descriptors for the graph (such as *vi* and *vi_end*), thereby causing trouble in subsequent iterations of the loop.

If we use a different kind of *adjacency_list*, where *VertexList=listS*, then the iterators are not invalidated by calling *remove_vertex* unless the iterator is pointing to the actual vertex that was removed. The code on the following page demonstrates this.

```
// VertexList=listS
typedef adjacency_list<listS, listS> Graph;
Graph G(N);
// Fill in the graph...

// Attempt to remove all the vertices. Wrong!
graph_traits<Graph>::vertex_iterator vi, vi_end;
for (tie(vi, vi_end) = vertices(G); vi != vi_end; ++vi)
  remove_vertex(*vi, G);

// Remove all the vertices. This is OK.
graph_traits<Graph>::vertex_iterator vi, vi_end, next;
tie(vi, vi_end) = vertices(G);
for (next = vi; vi != vi_end; vi = next) {
  ++next;
  remove_vertex(*vi, G);
}
```

The safest and most efficient way to remove multiple edges from an *adjacency_list* is to use the *remove_edge_if()* function.

The stability issue also affects vertex and edge descriptors. For example, suppose you use vector of vertex descriptors to keep track of the parents (or predecessors) of vertices in a shortest-paths tree (see *example/dijkstra-example.cpp*). You create the parent vector with a call to *dijkstra_shortest_paths()*, and then remove a vertex from the graph. Subsequently you try to use the parent vector, but since all vertex descriptors have become invalid, the result is incorrect.

```
std::vector<Vertex> parent(num_vertices(G));
std::vector<Vertex> distance(num_vertices(G));
dijkstra_shortest_paths(G, s, distance_map(&distance[0]).
  predecessor_map(&parent[0]));
// The following is a bad idea! It invalidates vertex descriptors
// in the parent vector.
remove_vertex(s, G);
// The following will produce incorrect results
for(tie(vi, vend) = vertices(G); vi != vend; ++vi)
  std::cout << p[*vi] << " is the parent of " << *vi << std::endl;
```

Note that in this discussion iterator and descriptor invalidation is concerned with the invalidation of iterators and descriptors that are *not directly affected* by the operation. For example, performing *remove_edge(u,v,g)* always invalidates any edge descriptor for (u, v) or edge iterator pointing to (u, v), regardless of the kind of *adjacency_list*. In this discussion of iterator and descriptor invalidation, we are only concerned with the effect of *remove_edge(u,v,g)* on edge descriptors and iterators that point to other edges (not (u, v)).

In general, if you want your vertex and edge descriptors to be stable (never invalidated) then use *listS* or *setS* for the *VertexList* and *EdgeList* template parameters of *adjacency_list*. If you are not as concerned about descriptor and iterator stability, and are more concerned about memory consumption and graph traversal speed, use *vecS* for the *VertexList* and/or *EdgeList* template parameters.

Directed and Undirected Adjacency Lists

The *adjacency_list* class can be used to represent both directed and undirected graphs, depending on the argument passed to the *Directed* template parameter. Selecting *directedS* or *bidirectionalS* chooses a directed graph, whereas *undirectedS* selects the representation for an undirected graph. See §12.1.1 for a description of the difference between directed and undirected graphs in BGL. The *bidirectealS* selector specifies that the graph will provide the *in_edges()* function as well as the *out_edges()* function. This imposes twice as much space overhead per edge, which is why *in_edges()* is optional.

Internal Properties

Properties can be attached to the vertices or edges of an *adjacency_list* graph via the property interface. The template parameters *VertexProperties* and *EdgeProperties* of the *adjacency_list* class are meant to be filled by the property class, which is declared as follows.

> *template <typename PropertyTag, typename T, typename NextProperty = no_property>*
> *struct property;*

The *PropertyTag* is a type that simply identifies or gives a unique name to the property. There are several predefined tags (see §15.2.3), and it is easy to add more. For convenience, BGL also provides predefined objects of the tag types (in this case, enum values) for use as arguments to functions that expect property tag objects (such as *adjacency_list*'s *get()* property map functions.

The *T* parameter of *property* specifies the type of the property values. The *NextProperty* parameter allows *property* types to be nested, so that an arbitrary number of properties can be attached to the same graph.

The following code shows how a vertex and edge property type can be assembled and used to create a graph type. We have attached a distance property with values of type *float* and a name property with values of type *std::string* to the vertices of the graph. We have attached a weight property with values of type *float* to the edges of the graph.

> *typedef property<distance_t, float,*
>   *property<name_t, std::string> > VertexProperties;*
> *typedef property<weight_t, float> EdgeProperties;*
> *typedef adjacency_list<mapS, vecS, undirectedS,*
>   *VertexProperties, EdgeProperties> Graph;*
> *Graph g(num_vertices); // construct a graph object*

The property values can then be read from and written to using property maps. See § 3.6 for a description of how to obtain property maps from a graph, and read all of Chapter 15 for how to use property maps.

Vertex Index Property

If the *VertexList* of the graph is *vecS*, then the graph has a built-in vertex index property accessed via the *vertex_index_t* property. The indices fall in the range $[0, |V|)$ and are contiguous. When a vertex is removed, the indices are adjusted so that they retain these properties. Some care must be taken when using these indices to access external property storage, since the user must remember to update the external storage to match the new vertex indices.

Custom Edge Properties

Creating your own property types and properties is easy; just define a tag class for your new property. Here we define a tag class for capacity and flow properties, which we attach to the edges on the graph.

```
enum edge_capacity_t { edge_capacity };
enum edge_flow_t { edge_flow };

namespace boost {
  BOOST_INSTALL_PROPERTY (edge, flow);
  BOOST_INSTALL_PROPERTY (edge, capacity);
}
```

Now you can use your new property tag in the definition of properties just as you would one of the built-in tags.

```
typedef property<capacity_t, int> Cap;
typedef property<flow_t, int, Cap> EdgeProperties;
typedef adjacency_list<vecS, vecS, no_property, EdgeProperties> Graph;
```

Just as before, the property maps for these properties can be obtained from the graph via the *get()* function.

```
property_map<Graph, edge_capacity_t>::type
  capacity = get (edge_capacity, G);

property_map<Graph, edge_flow_t>::type
  flow = get (edge_flow, G);
```

The file *edge_property.cpp* shows the complete source code for this example.

Custom Vertex Properties

Attaching your own properties to vertices is just as easy as attaching properties to edges. Here we want to attach people's first names to the vertices in the graph.

```
enum vertex_first_name_t { vertex_first_name };
namespace boost {
    BOOST_INSTALL_PROPERTY (vertex, first_name);
}
```

Now we can use the new tag in the *property* class, in the assembly of a graph type. The following code shows creating the graph type, and then creating the graph object. We fill in the edges and also assign names to the vertices. The edges represent "who owes whom."

```
typedef property<vertex_first_name_t, std::string> FirstNameProperty;
typedef adjacency_list<vecS, vecS, directedS,
    FirstNameProperty> MyGraphType;

typedef pair<int,int> Pair;
Pair edge_array[11] = { Pair(0,1), Pair(0,2), Pair(0,3),
    Pair(0,4), Pair(2,0), Pair(3,0),
    Pair(2,4), Pair(3,1), Pair(3,4),
    Pair(4,0), Pair(4,1) };

MyGraphType G(5);
for (int i = 0; i < 11; ++i)
    add_edge(G, edge_array[i].first, edge_array[i].second);

property_map<MyGraphType, vertex_first_name_t>::type
    name = get(vertex_first_name, G);

put(name, 0, "Jeremy");
put(name, 1, "Rich");
put(name, 2, "Andrew");
put(name, 3, "Jeff");
name[4] = "Kinis"; // you can use operator[] too

who_owes_who(edges(G).first, edges(G).second, G);
```

The *who_owes_who()* function written for this example was implemented in a generic style. The input is templated so we do not know the actual graph type. To find out the type of the property map for our first name property, we need to use the *vertex_property_map* traits class. The *const_type* is used because the graph parameter is const. Once we have the property map type, we can deduce the value type of the property using the *property_traits* class. In this example, we know that the property's value type is *std::string*, but written in this generic fashion the *who_owes_who()* function could work with other property value types.

```
template <typename EdgeIter, typename Graph>
void who_owes_who(EdgeIter first, EdgeIter last, const Graph& G)
{
  // Access the propety acessor type for this graph
  typedef typename vertex_property_map<Graph,
    first_name_t>::const_type NamePA;
  NamePA name = get_vertex_property_map(G, first_name_t());
  typedef typename property_traits<NamePA>::value_type NameType;
  NameType src_name, targ_name;

  while (first != last) {
    src_name = get(name, source(*first, G));
    targ_name = get(name, target(*first, G));
    cout << src_name << " owes "
   << targ_name << " some money" << endl;
    ++first;
  }
}
```

The output is

Jeremy owes Rich some money
Jeremy owes Andrew some money
Jeremy owes Jeff some money
Jeremy owes Kinis some money
Andrew owes Jeremy some money
Andrew owes Kinis some money
Jeff owes Jeremy some money
Jeff owes Rich some money
Jeff owes Kinis some money
Kinis owes Jeremy some money
Kinis owes Rich some money

The complete source code to this example is in the file *interior_property_map.cpp*.

Customizing the Adjacency List Storage

The *adjacency_list* class is implemented using two kinds of containers. One type of container holds all the vertices in the graph, and another type holds the out-edge list (and potentially in-edge list) for each vertex. BGL provides selector classes that allow the user to choose among several of the containers from the STL. It is also possible to use your own container types. When customizing the *VertexList*, you need to define a container generator. When customizing the *EdgeList* you need to define a container generator and the parallel edge traits. The file *container_gen.cpp* has an example of how to use custom storage types.

Container Generator

The *adjacency_list* class uses a traits class called *container_gen* to map the *EdgeList* and *VertexList* selectors to the actual container types used for the graph storage. The default version of the traits class follows, along with an example of how the class is specialized for the *listS* selector.

```
namespace boost {
  template <typename Selector, typename ValueType>
  struct container_gen { };
  template <typename ValueType>
  struct container_gen<listS, ValueType> {
    typedef std::list<ValueType> type;
  };
}
```

To use some other container of your choice, define a selector class and then specialize the *container_gen* for your selector.

```
struct custom_containerS { }; // your selector
namespace boost {
  // the specialization for your selector
  template <typename ValueType>
  struct container_gen<custom_containerS, ValueType> {
    typedef custom_container<ValueType> type;
  };
}
```

There may also be situations when you want to use a container that has more template parameters than just *ValueType*. For instance, you may want to supply the allocator type. One way to do this is to hard-code in the extra parameters within the specialization of *container_gen*. However, if you want more flexibility, then you can add a template parameter to the selector class. In the following code we show how to create a selector that lets you specify the allocator to be used with the *std::list*.

```
template <typename Allocator> struct list_with_allocatorS {};
namespace boost {
  template <typename Alloc, typename ValueType>
  struct container_gen<list_with_allocatorS<Alloc>, ValueType>
  {
    typedef typename Alloc::template rebind<ValueType>::other Allocator;
    typedef std::list<ValueType, Allocator> type;
  };
}
// now you can define a graph using std::list and a specific allocator
typedef adjacency_list< list_with_allocatorS< std::allocator<int> >,
  vecS, directedS> MyGraph;
```

Parallel Edge Traits

In addition to specializing the *container_gen* class, one must also specialize the *parallel_edge_traits* class to specify whether the container type allows parallel edges (and is a Sequence) or if the container does not allow parallel edges (and is an AssociativeContainer).

```
template <typename StorageSelector>
struct parallel_edge_traits { };
template <> struct parallel_edge_traits<vecS> {
  typedef allow_parallel_edge_tag type;
};
template <> struct parallel_edge_traits<setS> {
  typedef disallow_parallel_edge_tag type;
};
//...
```

Push and Erase for the Edge-List Container

One must also tell the *adjacency_list* how edges can be efficiently added and removed from the edge-list container. This is accomplished by overloading the *push()* and *erase()* functions for the custom container type. The *push()* function must return an iterator pointing to the newly inserted edge and a Boolean flag saying whether the edge was inserted. If you specified *allow_parallel_edge_tag* for the *parallel_edge_traits* then *push()* should always insert the edge and return *true*. If you specified *disallow_parallel_edge_tag* for the *parallel_edge_traits* then *push()* must return false and not insert the edge if the same edge is already in the container, and the iterator returned should point to the already existing edge.

The following default *push()* and *erase()* functions are already supplied for all STL container types. The family of *push_dispatch()* and *erase_dispatch()* function overloads handles the various ways that inserting and erasing can be done with standard containers.

```
template <typename Container, typename T>
std::pair<typename Container::iterator, bool>
push (Container& c, const T& v)
{
  return push_dispatch (c, v, container_category (c));
}

template <typename Container, typename T>
void erase (Container& c, const T& x)
{
  erase_dispatch (c, x, container_category (c));
}
```

14.1.2 *adjacency_matrix*

adjacency_matrix<Directed, VertexProperty, EdgeProperty, GraphProperty>

The *adjacency_matrix* class implements the BGL graph interface using the traditional adjacency matrix storage format. For a graph with $|V|$ vertices, a $|V| \times |V|$ matrix is used, where each element a_{ij} is a boolean flag that says whether there is an edge from vertex i to vertex j. Figure 14.4 shows the adjacency-matrix representation of a graph.

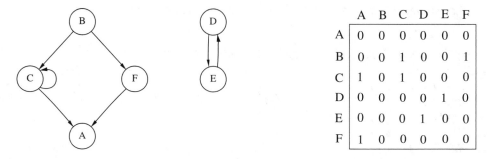

	A	B	C	D	E	F
A	0	0	0	0	0	0
B	0	0	1	0	0	1
C	1	0	1	0	0	0
D	0	0	0	0	1	0
E	0	0	0	1	0	0
F	1	0	0	0	0	0

Figure 14.4 Adjacency-matrix representation of a directed graph.

The advantage of this matrix format over the adjacency list is that edge insertion and removal is constant time. There are several disadvantages. The first is that the amount of memory used is $O(|V|^2)$ instead of $O(|V| + |E|)$ (where $|E|$ is the number of edges). The second is that operations that traverse all the out-edges of each vertex (such as breadth-first search) run in $O(|V| \times |V|)$ time instead of $O(|V| + |E|)$ time for the adjacency list. In short, it is better to use the *adjacency_matrix* for dense graphs (where $|E| \approx |V|^2$) and it is better to use the *adjacency_list* for sparse graphs (where $|E|$ is much smaller than $|V|^2$).

The *adjacency_matrix* class extends the traditional data structure by allowing objects to be attached to vertices and edges via the the property template parameters. See §3.6 for an explanation of how to use internal properties.

In the case of an undirected graph, the *adjacency_matrix* class does not use a full $|V| \times |V|$ matrix but instead uses a lower triangle (the diagonal and below) since the matrix for an undirected graph is symmetric. This reduces the storage to $(|V| \times |V|)/2$. Figure 14.5 shows an adjacency-matrix representation of an undirected graph.

Example

Creating the graph of Figure 14.4.

```
enum { A, B, C, D, E, F, N };
const char* name = "ABCDEF";
```

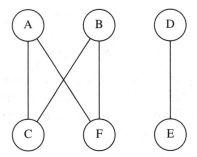
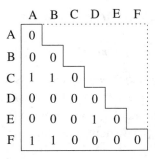

Figure 14.5 Adjacency-matrix representation of an undirected graph.

```
typedef  boost::adjacency_matrix<boost::directedS>  Graph;
Graph  g(N);
add_edge(B,  C,  g);
add_edge(B,  F,  g);
add_edge(C,  A,  g);
add_edge(C,  C,  g);
add_edge(D,  E,  g);
add_edge(E,  D,  g);
add_edge(F,  A,  g);

std::cout  <<  "vertex set:  ";
boost::print_vertices(g,  name);
std::cout  <<  std::endl;

std::cout  <<  "edge set:  ";
boost::print_edges(g,  name);
std::cout  <<  std::endl;

std::cout  <<  "out-edges:  "  <<  std::endl;
boost::print_graph(g,  name);
std::cout  <<  std::endl;
```

The output is

```
vertex set: A  B  C  D  E  F

edge set:  (B,C)  (B,F)  (C,A)  (C,C)  (D,E)  (E,D)  (F,A)

out-edges:
A  -->
B  -->  C  F
C  -->  A  C
D  -->  E
E  -->  D
F  -->  A
```

Creating the graph of Figure 14.5.

```
enum { A, B, C, D, E, F, N };
const char* name = "ABCDEF";

typedef boost::adjacency_matrix<boost::undirectedS> UGraph;
UGraph ug(N);
add_edge(B, C, ug);
add_edge(B, F, ug);
add_edge(C, A, ug);
add_edge(D, E, ug);
add_edge(F, A, ug);

std::cout << "vertex set: ";
boost::print_vertices(ug, name);
std::cout << std::endl;

std::cout << "edge set: ";
boost::print_edges(ug, name);
std::cout << std::endl;

std::cout << "incident edges: " << std::endl;
boost::print_graph(ug, name);
std::cout << std::endl;
```

The output is

```
vertex set: A B C D E F

edge set: (C,A) (C,B) (E,D) (F,A) (F,B)

incident edges:
A <--> C F
B <--> C F
C <--> A B
D <--> E
E <--> D
F <--> A B
```

Where Defined

boost/graph/adjacency_matrix.hpp

Template Parameters

Directed	A selector to choose whether the graph is directed or undirected. The options are *directedS* and *undirectedS*.
	Default: *directedS*
VertexProperty	specifies internal vertex property storage.
	Default: *no_property*
EdgeProperty	specifies internal edge property storage.
	Default: *no_property*
GraphProperty	specifies property storage for the graph object.
	Default: *no_property*

Model Of

VertexListGraph, EdgeListGraph, IncidenceGraph, AdjacencyGraph, AdjacencyMatrix, VertexMutablePropertyGraph, and EdgeMutablePropertyGraph

Type Requirements

Property value types must be DefaultConstructible and CopyConstructible.

Associated Types

graph_traits<adjacency_matrix>::vertex_descriptor
   The type for the vertex descriptors associated with the *adjacency_matrix*.
   (Required by Graph.)

graph_traits<adjacency_matrix>::edge_descriptor
   The type for the edge descriptors associated with the *adjacency_matrix*.
   (Required by Graph.)

graph_traits<adjacency_matrix>::vertex_iterator
   The type for the iterators returned by *vertices()*.
   (Required by VertexListGraph.)

graph_traits<adjacency_matrix>::edge_iterator
   The type for the iterators returned by *edges()*.
   (Required by EdgeListGraph.)

graph_traits<adjacency_matrix>::out_edge_iterator
   The type for the iterators returned by *out_edges()*.
   (Required by IncidenceGraph.)

graph_traits<adjacency_matrix>::adjacency_iterator
   The type for the iterators returned by *adjacent_vertices()*.
   (Required by AdjacencyGraph.)

graph_traits<adjacency_matrix>::directed_category
Provides information about whether the graph is directed (*directed_tag*) or undirected (*undirected_tag*).
(Required by Graph.)

graph_traits<adjacency_matrix>::edge_parallel_category
An adjacency matrix does not allow the insertion of parallel edges, so this type is always *disallow_parallel_edge_tag*.
(Required by Graph.)

graph_traits<adjacency_matrix>::vertices_size_type
The type used for dealing with the number of vertices in the graph.
(Required by VertexListGraph.)

graph_traits<adjacency_matrix>::edges_size_type
The type used for dealing with the number of edges in the graph.
(Required by EdgeListGraph.)

graph_traits<adjacency_matrix>::degree_size_type
The type used for dealing with the number of out-edges of a vertex.
(Required by IncidenceGraph.)

property_map<adjacency_matrix, PropertyTag>::type
property_map<adjacency_matrix, PropertyTag>::const_type
The map type for vertex or edge properties in the graph. The property is specified by the *PropertyTag* template argument, and must match one of the properties specified in the *VertexProperty* or *EdgeProperty* for the graph.
(Required by PropertyGraph.)

Member Functions

adjacency_matrix (*vertices_size_type n, const GraphProperty& p = GraphProperty()*)
Creates a graph object with *n* vertices and zero edges.

template <typename EdgeIterator>
adjacency_matrix (*EdgeIterator first, EdgeIterator last, vertices_size_type n,*
    const GraphProperty& p = GraphProperty())
Creates a graph object with *n* vertices with the edges specified in the edge list given by the range $[first, last)$. The value type of the *EdgeIterator* must be a *std::pair*, where the type in the pair is an integer type. The integers correspond to vertices, and they must all fall in the range of $[0, n)$.

template <typename EdgeIterator, typename EdgePropertyIterator>
adjacency_matrix (*EdgeIterator first, EdgeIterator last, EdgePropertyIterator ep_iter,*
    vertices_size_type n, const GraphProperty& p = GraphProperty())
Creates a graph object with *n* vertices, with the edges specified in the edge list given by the range $[first, last)$ and with edge properties specified in the edge property list

specified by *ep_iter*. The value type of the *EdgeIterator* must be a *std::pair*, where the type in the pair is an integer type. The integers correspond to vertices, and they must all fall in the range of $[0, n)$. The *value_type* of the *ep_iter* should be *EdgeProperty*.

Nonmember Functions

std::pair<vertex_iterator, vertex_iterator> vertices (const adjacency_matrix& g)
    Returns an iterator range providing access to the vertex set of graph g.
    (Required by VertexListGraph.)

std::pair<edge_iterator, edge_iterator> edges (const adjacency_matrix& g)
    Returns an iterator range providing access to the edge set of graph g.
    (Required by EdgeListGraph.)

std::pair<adjacency_iterator, adjacency_iterator>
adjacent_vertices (vertex_descriptor v, const adjacency_matrix& g)
    Returns an iterator range providing access to the vertices adjacent to vertex v in graph g.
    (Required by AdjacencyGraph.)

std::pair<out_edge_iterator, out_edge_iterator>
out_edges (vertex_descriptor v, const adjacency_matrix& g)
    Returns an iterator range providing access to the out-edges of vertex v in graph g. If the graph is undirected, this iterator range provides access to all edge incident on vertex v.
    (Required by IncidenceGraph.)

vertex_descriptor source (edge_descriptor e, const adjacency_matrix& g)
    Returns the source vertex of edge e.
    (Required by IncidenceGraph.)

vertex_descriptor target (edge_descriptor e, const adjacency_matrix& g)
    Returns the target vertex of edge e.
    (Required by IncidenceGraph.)

degree_size_type out_degree (vertex_descriptor u, const adjacency_matrix& g)
    Returns the number of edges leaving vertex u.
    (Required by IncidenceGraph.)

vertices_size_type num_vertices (const adjacency_matrix& g)
    Returns the number of vertices in the graph g.
    (Required by VertexListGraph.)

edges_size_type num_edges (const adjacency_matrix& g)
    Returns the number of edges in the graph g.
    (Required by EdgeListGraph.)

vertex_descriptor vertex (vertices_size_type n, const adjacency_matrix& g)

Returns the nth vertex in the graph's vertex list.

std::pair<edge_descriptor, bool>
edge (vertex_descriptor u, vertex_descriptor v, const adjacency_matrix& g)

Returns the edge connecting vertex u to vertex v in graph g.

(Required by AdjacencyMatrix.)

std::pair<edge_descriptor, bool>
add_edge (vertex_descriptor u, vertex_descriptor v, adjacency_matrix& g)

Adds edge (u, v) to the graph and returns the edge descriptor for the new edge. If the edge is already in the graph then a duplicate will not be added and the Boolean flag will be false. This operation does not invalidate any of the graph's iterators or descriptors.

(Required by EdgeMutableGraph.)

std::pair<edge_descriptor, bool>
add_edge (vertex_descriptor u, vertex_descriptor v, const EdgeProperty& p,
    adjacency_matrix& g)

Adds edge (u, v) to the graph and attaches *p* as the value of the edge's internal property storage. See the previous *add_edge ( )* member function for more details.

void remove_edge (vertex_descriptor u, vertex_descriptor v, adjacency_matrix& g)

Removes the edge (u, v) from the graph.

(Required by EdgeMutableGraph.)

void remove_edge (edge_descriptor e, adjacency_matrix& g)

Removes the edge *e* from the graph.

(Required by EdgeMutableGraph.)

void clear_vertex (vertex_descriptor u, adjacency_matrix& g)

Removes all edges to and from vertex u. The vertex still appears in the vertex set of the graph. The effect on descriptor and iterator stability is the same as that of invoking *remove_edge ( )* for all of the edges that have *u* as the source or target.

(Required by EdgeMutableGraph.)

template <typename Property>
property_map<adjacency_matrix, Property>::type
get (Property, adjacency_matrix& g)

template <typename Property>
property_map<adjacency_matrix, Property>::const_type
get (Property, const adjacency_matrix& g)

Returns the property map object specified by *Property*. The *Property* must match one of the properties specified in the graph's *VertexProperty* template argument.

(Required by PropertyGraph.)

```
template <typename Property, typename X>
typename property_traits<
  typenamae property_map<adjacency_matrix, Property>::const_type
>::value_type
get(Property, const adjacency_matrix& g, X x)
```
This returns the property value for *x*, which is either a vertex or edge descriptor.
(Required by PropertyGraph.)

```
template <typename Property, typename X, typename Value>
void put(Property, const adjacency_matrix& g, X x, const Value& value)
```
This sets the property value for *x* to *value*. *x* is either a vertex or edge descriptor. *Value* must be convertible to the value type of the property map specified by the *Property* tag.
(Required by PropertyGraph.)

```
template <typename GraphProperties, typename GraphProperty>
typename property_value<GraphProperties, GraphProperty>::type&
get_property(adjacency_matrix& g, GraphProperty);
```
Returns the property specified by *GraphProperty* that is attached to the graph object *g*. The *property_value* traits class is defined in *boost/pending/property.hpp*.

```
template <typename GraphProperties, typename GraphProperty>
const typename property_value<GraphProperties, GraphProperty>::type&
get_property(const adjacency_matrix& g, GraphProperty);
```
Returns the property specified by *GraphProperty* that is attached to the graph object *g*. The *property_value* traits class is defined in *boost/pending/property.hpp*.

14.2   Auxiliary Classes

14.2.1   *graph_traits*

graph_traits<Graph>

The *graph_traits* class provides the mechanism for accessing the *associated types* of a graph type, as defined by the various BGL graph concepts (see §12.1). When you wish to use one of the associated types of a graph, instantiate the *graph_traits* template with the graph type and access the appropriate typedef. For example, to obtain the *vertex_descriptor* type for some graph, do the following:

```
template <typename Graph> void my_graph_algorithm(Graph& g)
{
  // Instantiate graph_traits with the graph type.
  typedef boost::graph_traits<Graph> Traits;
  // Access the associated type.
  typedef typename Traits::vertex_descriptor Vertex;
  // ...
}
```

The unspecialized (default) version of the ***graph_traits*** class template assumes that the graph type provides nested typedefs for all of the associated types. This version is defined here.

```
namespace boost {
  template <typename G>
  struct graph_traits {
    typedef typename G::vertex_descriptor           vertex_descriptor;
    typedef typename G::edge_descriptor             edge_descriptor;
    typedef typename G::adjacency_iterator          adjacency_iterator;
    typedef typename G::out_edge_iterator           out_edge_iterator;
    typedef typename G::in_edge_iterator            in_edge_iterator;
    typedef typename G::vertex_iterator             vertex_iterator;
    typedef typename G::edge_iterator               edge_iterator;

    typedef typename G::directed_category           directed_category;
    typedef typename G::edge_parallel_category edge_parallel_category;
    typedef typename G::traversal_category          traversal_category;

    typedef typename G::vertices_size_type          vertices_size_type;
    typedef typename G::edges_size_type             edges_size_type;
    typedef typename G::degree_size_type            degree_size_type;
  };
} // namespace boost
```

Alternatively, ***graph_traits*** can be specialized on the graph type. For example, the following code specializes ***graph_traits*** for the Stanford GraphBase ***Graph*** struct. The complete BGL wrapper interface for SGB graph is in ***boost/graph/stanford_graph.hpp***.

```
namespace boost {
  template <>
  struct graph_traits<Graph*> {
    // ...
  };
}
```

If the graph type is a class template, then the ***graph_traits*** class can be partially specialized. This means there are still "free" template parameters. The following is the partial specialization of ***graph_traits*** for the parameterized LEDA ***GRAPH*** type. The complete BGL wrapper interface for the LEDA ***GRAPH*** is in ***boost/graph/leda_graph.hpp***.

```
namespace boost {
  template <typename vtype, typename etype>
  struct graph_traits< GRAPH<vtype,etype> > {
    // ...
  };
}
```

Any particular graph concept does not require that all of the associated types be defined. When implementing a graph class that fullfils one or more graph concepts, for associated types that are not required by the concepts, it is all right to use *void* as the type (when using nested typedefs inside the graph class), or to leave the typedef out of the *graph_traits* specialization for the graph class.

Category Tags

The *directed_category* should be a typedef for one of the following two types.

```
namespace boost {
  struct directed_tag { };
  struct undirected_tag { };
}
```

The *edge_parallel_category* should be a typedef for one of the following two types.

```
namespace boost {
  struct allow_parallel_edge_tag {};
  struct disallow_parallel_edge_tag {};
}
```

The *traversal_category* should be a typedef for one of the following classes, or a type that inherits from one of these classes.

```
namespace boost {
  struct incidence_graph_tag { };
  struct adjacency_graph_tag { };
  struct bidirectional_graph_tag :
    public virtual incidence_graph_tag { };
  struct vertex_list_graph_tag :
    public virtual incidence_graph_tag,
    public virtual adjacency_graph_tag { };
  struct edge_list_graph_tag { };
  struct vertex_and_edge_list_graph_tag :
    public virtual edge_list_graph_tag,
    public virtual vertex_list_graph_tag { };
  struct adjacency_matrix_tag { };
}
```

Template Parameters

   Graph   The graph type, a model of Graph.

Where Defined

boost/graph/graph_traits.hpp

Members

graph_traits::vertex_descriptor
  The type for the vertex descriptors associated with the **Graph**.

graph_traits::edge_descriptor
  The type for the edge descriptors associated with the **Graph**.

graph_traits::vertex_iterator
  The type for the iterators returned by *vertices()*.

graph_traits::edge_iterator
  The type for the iterators returned by *edges()*.

graph_traits::out_edge_iterator
  The type for the iterators returned by *out_edges()*.

graph_traits::adjacency_iterator
  The type for the iterators returned by *adjacent_vertices()*.

graph_traits::directed_category
  Reports whether the graph is directed or undirected.

graph_traits::edge_parallel_category
  Reports whether the graph allows parallel edges to be inserted.

graph_traits::traversal_category
  Reports what kind of traversal patterns are provided by the graph.

graph_traits::vertices_size_type
  The unsigned integer type used for dealing with the number of vertices in the graph.

graph_traits::edges_size_type
  The unsigned integer type used for dealing with the number of edges in the graph.

graph_traits::degree_size_type
  The unsigned integer type used for dealing with the number out edges for each vertex.

14.2.2 *adjacency_list_traits*

adjacency_list_traits<EdgeList, VertexList, Directed>

This class provides an alternate method for accessing some of the associated types of the *adjacency_list* class. The main reason for this class is that sometimes one would like to create graph properties whose values are vertex or edge descriptors. If you try to use **graph_traits** for this you will run into a problem with mutually recursive types. To get around this problem, the *adjacency_list_traits* class is provided, which gives the user access to the vertex and edge descriptor types without requiring the user to provide the property types for the graph.

```
template <typename EdgeList, typename VertexList, typename Directed>
  struct adjacency_list_traits {
    typedef . . . vertex_descriptor;
    typedef . . . edge_descriptor;
    typedef . . . directed_category;
    typedef . . . edge_parallel_category;
  };
```

Where Defined

boost/graph/adjacency_list.hpp

Template Parameters

EdgeList	The selector type for the edge container implementation. **Default:** *vecS*
VertexList	The selector type for the vertex container implementation. **Default:** *vecS*
Directed	The selector type whether the graph is directed or undirected. **Default:** *directedS*

Model Of

DefaultConstructible and Assignable

Members

adjacency_list_traits::vertex_descriptor
   The type for the objects used to identify vertices in the graph.

adjacency_list_traits::edge_descriptor
   The type for the objects used to identify edges in the graph.

adjacency_list_traits::directed_category
   This says whether the graph is undirected (*undirected_tag*) or directed (*directed_tag*).

adjacency_list_traits::edge_parallel_category
   This says whether the graph allows parallel edges to be inserted (*allow_parallel_edge_tag*) or if it automatically removes parallel edges (*disallow_parallel_edge_tag*).

See Also

adjacency_list

14.2.3 *adjacency_matrix_traits*

adjacency_matrix_traits<Directed>

This class provides an alternate method for accessing some of the associated types of the *adjacency_matrix* class. The main reason for this class is that sometimes you would like to create graph properties whose values are vertex or edge descriptors. If you try to use *graph_traits* for this, you will run into a problem with mutually recursive types. To get around this problem, the *adjacency_matrix_traits* class is provided, which gives the user access to the vertex and edge descriptor types without requiring the user to provide the property types for the graph.

```
template <typename Directed>
  struct adjacency_matrix_traits {
    typedef ... vertex_descriptor;
    typedef ... edge_descriptor;
    typedef ... directed_category;
    typedef ... edge_parallel_category;
  };
```

Where Defined

boost/graph/adjacency_matrix.hpp

Template Parameters

Directed   Specifies whether the graph is directed or undirected.
                  Default: *directedS*

Model Of

DefaultConstructible and Assignable

Members

adjacency_matrix_traits::vertex_descriptor
  The type for the objects used to identify vertices in the graph.

adjacency_matrix_traits::edge_descriptor
  The type for the objects used to identify edges in the graph.

adjacency_matrix_traits::directed_category
  This says whether the graph is undirected (*undirected_tag*) or directed (*directed_tag*).

adjacency_matrix_traits::edge_parallel_category

An adjacency matrix does not allow the insertion of parallel edges, so this type is **disallow_parallel_edge_tag**.

See Also

adjacency_matrix

14.2.4 *property_map*

property_map<Graph, PropertyTag>

A traits class for accessing the type of an internal property map for a graph. A specialization of this traits class is required of types that model the PropertyGraph concept.

Example

The following example creates a graph with an internal property for vertex names, and then accesses the vertex name property map type using the **property_map** traits class. The property map object is obtained from the graph using the **get()** function.

⟨ *property-map-traits-eg.cpp* 248 ⟩ ≡

```
#include <string>
#include <boost/graph/adjacency_list.hpp>
int main()
{
  using namespace boost;
  typedef adjacency_list<listS, listS, directedS,
    property<vertex_name_t, std::string> > graph_t;
  graph_t g;
  graph_traits<graph_t>::vertex_descriptor u = add_vertex(g);
  property_map<graph_t, vertex_name_t>::type
    name_map = get(vertex_name, g);
  name_map[u] = "Joe";
  std::cout << name_map[u] << std::endl;
  return EXIT_SUCCESS;
}
```

The output is

Joe

Where Defined

boost/graph/properties.hpp

Template Parameters

Graph	The graph type, which must be a model of PropertyGraph.
PropertyTag	The tag class to specify which property.

Model Of

None.

Public Base Classes

None.

Associated Types

property_map<Graph, PropertyTag>::type
  The type for a mutable property map that accessing the internal property specified by the *PropertyTag*.

property_map<Graph, PropertyTag>::const_type
  The type for a constant property map that accessing the internal property specified by the *PropertyTag*.

Member Functions

None.

Nonmember Functions

None.

14.2.5 *property*

property<PropertyTag, T, NextProperty>

This class can be used with the *adjacency_list* and the *adjacency_matrix* classes to specify what kind of properties should be attached to the vertices and edges of the graph, and to the graph object itself.

Template Parameters

PropertyTag A type to identify (give a unique name to) the property. There are several predefined tags, and it is easy to add more. For convenience, BGL also provides predefined objects of the tag types (in this case enum values) for use as arguments to functions that expect property tag objects (such as *adjacency_list*'s *get()* property map functions).

T   This type specifies the type of the property values.

NextProperty This parameter allows *property* types to be nested, so that an arbitrary number of properties can be attached to the same graph.
       Default: *no_property*

Where Defined

boost/pending/property.hpp

Property Tags

The following property tags are defined in *boost/graph/properties.hpp*.

```
namespace boost {
    enum edge_name_t { edge_name };
    enum edge_weight_t { edge_weight };
    enum edge_index_t { edge_index };
    enum edge_capacity_t { edge_capacity };
    enum edge_residual_capacity_t { edge_residual_capacity };
    enum edge_reverse_t { edge_reverse };
    enum vertex_name_t { vertex_name };
    enum vertex_distance_t { vertex_distance };
    enum vertex_index_t { vertex_index };
    enum vertex_color_t { vertex_color };
    enum vertex_degree_t { vertex_degree };
    enum vertex_out_degree_t { vertex_out_degree };
    enum vertex_in_degree_t { vertex_in_degree };
    enum vertex_discover_time_t { vertex_discover_time };
    enum vertex_finish_time_t { vertex_finish_time };
    enum graph_name_t { graph_name };

    BOOST_INSTALL_PROPERTY(vertex, index);
    BOOST_INSTALL_PROPERTY(edge, index);
    // ...
}
```

14.3 Graph Adaptors

14.3.1 *edge_list*

edge_list<EdgeIterator, ValueType, DiffType>

The *edge_list* class is an adaptor that turns a pair of edge iterators into a class that models EdgeListGraph. The *value_type* of the edge iterator must be a *std::pair* (or at least have *first* and *second* members). The *first_type* and *second_type* of the pair must be the same and they are used for the graph's *vertex_descriptor*. The *ValueType* and *DiffType* template parameters are only needed if your compiler does not support partial specialization. Otherwise they default to the correct types.

Example

See §5.3 for an example of using *edge_list*.

Template Parameters

EdgeIterator	a model of InputIterator whose *value_type* must be a pair of vertex descriptors.
ValueType	is the *value_type* of the *EdgeIterator*.
	Default: *std::iterator_traits<EdgeIterator>::value_type*
DiffType	is the *difference_type* of the *EdgeIterator*.
	Default: *std::iterator_traits<EdgeIterator>::difference_type*

Model Of

EdgeListGraph

Where Defined

boost/graph/edge_list.hpp

Associated Types

graph_traits<edge_list>::vertex_descriptor
This is the type for vertex descriptors associated with the *edge_list*. This is the same type as the *first_type* of the *std::pair* that is the value type of the *EdgeIterator*.

graph_traits<edge_list>::edge_descriptor
The type for the edge descriptors associated with the *edge_list*.

graph_traits<edge_list>::edge_iterator
   The type for the iterators returned by *edges( )*. The iterator category of the *edge_iterator* is the same as that of the *EdgeIterator*.

Member Functions

edge_list (EdgeIterator first, EdgeIterator last)
   Creates a graph object with n vertices and with the edges specified in the edge list given by the range $[first, last)$.

Nonmember Functions

std::pair<edge_iterator, edge_iterator> edges (const edge_list& g)
   Returns an iterator range providing access to the edge set of graph *g*.

vertex_descriptor source (edge_descriptor e, const edge_list& g)
   Returns the source vertex of edge *e*.

vertex_descriptor target (edge_descriptor e, const edge_list& g)
   Returns the target vertex of edge *e*.

14.3.2   *reverse_graph*

reverse_graph<BidirectionalGraph>

The *reverse_graph* adaptor flips the in-edges and out-edges of a BidirectionalGraph, effectively transposing the graph. The construction of the *reverse_graph* is constant time, providing a highly efficient way to obtain a transposed-view of a graph.

Example

The example is from *examples/reverse_graph.cpp*.

```
typedef adjacency_list<vecS, vecS, bidirectionalS> Graph;
Graph G(5);

add_edge(0, 2, G);
add_edge(1, 1, G);
add_edge(1, 3, G);
add_edge(1, 4, G);
add_edge(2, 1, G);
add_edge(2, 3, G);
add_edge(2, 4, G);
add_edge(3, 1, G);
```

```
add_edge(3, 4, G);
add_edge(4, 0, G);
add_edge(4, 1, G);

std::cout << "original graph:" << std::endl;
print_graph(G, get(vertex_index, G));

std::cout << std::endl << "reversed graph:" << std::endl;
print_graph(make_reverse_graph(G), get(vertex_index, G));
```

The output is

```
original graph:
0 --> 2
1 --> 1 3 4
2 --> 1 3 4
3 --> 1 4
4 --> 0 1

reversed graph:
0 --> 4
1 --> 1 2 3 4
2 --> 0
3 --> 1 2
4 --> 1 2 3
```

Template Parameters

BidirGraph   The graph type to be adapted.

Model Of

BidirectionalGraph and optionally VertexListGraph and PropertyGraph

Where Defined

boost/graph/reverse_graph.hpp

Associated Types

graph_traits<reverse_graph>::vertex_descriptor
   The type for the vertex descriptors associated with the *reverse_graph*.
   (Required by Graph.)

graph_traits<reverse_graph>::edge_descriptor
>   The type for the edge descriptors associated with the ***reverse_graph***.
>   (Required by Graph.)

graph_traits<reverse_graph>::vertex_iterator
>   The type for the iterators returned by ***vertices()***.
>   (Required by VertexListGraph.)

graph_traits<reverse_graph>::edge_iterator
>   The type for the iterators returned by ***edges()***.
>   (Required by EdgeListGraph.)

graph_traits<reverse_graph>::out_edge_iterator
>   The type for the iterators returned by ***out_edges()***.
>   (Required by IncidenceGraph.)

graph_traits<reverse_graph>::adjacency_iterator
>   The type for the iterators returned by ***adjacent_vertices()***.
>   (Required by BidirectionalGraph.)

graph_traits<reverse_graph>::directed_category
>   Provides information about whether the graph is directed or undirected.
>   (Required by Graph.)

graph_traits<reverse_graph>::edge_parallel_category
>   This describes whether the graph class allows the insertion of parallel edges (edges with the same source and target). The two tags are ***allow_parallel_edge_tag*** and ***disallow_parallel_edge_tag***. The *setS* and ***hash_setS*** variants disallow parallel edges whereas the others allow parallel edges.
>   (Required by Graph.)

graph_traits<reverse_graph>::traversal_category
>   The traversal category reflects which kinds of iterators are supported by the graph class. For a ***reverse_graph*** this will be the same type as the underlying graph's ***traversal_category***.
>   (Required by Graph.)

graph_traits<reverse_graph>::vertices_size_type
>   The type used for dealing with the number of vertices in the graph.
>   (Required by VertexListGraph.)

graph_traits<reverse_graph>::edge_size_type
>   The type used for dealing with the number of edges in the graph.
>   (Required by EdgeListGraph.)

graph_traits<reverse_graph>::degree_size_type
>   The type used for dealing with the number of edges incident to a vertex in the graph.
>   (Required by IncidenceGraph.)

property_map<reverse_graph, Property>::type
property_map<reverse_graph, Property>::const_type

 The property map type for vertex or edge properties in the graph. The specific property is specified by the **Property** template argument, and must match one of the properties specified in the **VertexProperty** or **EdgeProperty** for the graph.
 (Required by PropertyGraph.)

Member Functions

reverse_graph (BidirectionalGraph& g)

 Constructor. Creates a reversed (transposed) view of the graph **g**.

Nonmember Functions

template <class BidirectionalGraph>
reverse_graph<BidirectionalGraph>
make_reverse_graph (BidirectionalGraph& g)

 Helper function for creating a **reverse_graph**.

std::pair<vertex_iterator, vertex_iterator>
vertices (const reverse_graph& g)

 Returns an iterator range providing access to the vertex set of graph **g**.
 (Required by VertexListGraph.)

std::pair<out_edge_iterator, out_edge_iterator>
out_edges (vertex_descriptor v, const reverse_graph& g)

 Returns an iterator range providing access to the out-edges of vertex *v* in graph **g**. These out-edges correspond to the in-edges of the adapted graph.
 (Required by IncidenceGraph.)

std::pair<in_edge_iterator, in_edge_iterator>
in_edges (vertex_descriptor v, const reverse_graph& g)

 Returns an iterator range providing access to the in-edges of vertex *v* in graph **g**. These in-edges correspond to the out-edges of the adapted graph.
 (Required by BidirectionalGraph.)

std::pair<adjacency_iterator, adjacency_iterator>
adjacent_vertices (vertex_descriptor v, const reverse_graph& g)

 Returns an iterator range providing access to the adjacent vertices of vertex *v* in graph **g**.
 (Required by AdjacencyGraph.).

vertex_descriptor source (edge_descriptor e, const reverse_graph& g)

 Returns the source vertex of edge *e*.
 (Required by IncidenceGraph.)

vertex_descriptor target (edge_descriptor e, const reverse_graph& g)
    Returns the target vertex of edge *e*.
    (Required by IncidenceGraph.)

degree_size_type out_degree (vertex_descriptor u, const reverse_graph& g)
    Returns the number of edges leaving vertex *u*.
    (Required by IncidenceGraph.)

degree_size_type in_degree (vertex_descriptor u, const reverse_graph& g)
    Returns the number of edges entering vertex *u*. This operation is only available if *bidirectionalS* was specified for the *Directed* template parameter.
    (Required by BidirectionalGraph).

vertices_size_type num_vertices (const reverse_graph& g)
    Returns the number of vertices in the graph *g*.
    (Required by VertexListGraph.)

vertex_descriptor vertex (vertices_size_type n, const reverse_graph& g)
    Returns the *n*th vertex in the graph's vertex list.

std::pair<edge_descriptor, bool>
edge (vertex_descriptor u, vertex_descriptor v, const reverse_graph& g)
    Returns the edge connecting vertex *u* to vertex *v* in graph *g*.
    (Required by AdjacencyMatrix.)

template <class Property>
property_map<reverse_graph, Property>::type
get (Property, reverse_graph& g)

template <class Property>
property_map<reverse_graph, Tag>::const_type
get (Property, const reverse_graph& g)
    Returns the property map object specified by *Property*. The *Property* must match one of the properties specified in the graph's *VertexProperty* template argument.

template <class Property, class X>
typename property_traits<property_map<reverse_graph, Property>::const_type>::value_type
get (Property, const reverse_graph& g, X x)
    This returns the property value for *x*, which is either a vertex or an edge descriptor.

template <class Property, class X, class Value>
void put (Property, const reverse_graph& g, X x, const Value& value)
    This sets the property value for *x* to *value*. *x* is either a vertex or an edge descriptor. *Value* must be convertible to *typename property_traits<property_map<reverse_graph, Property>::type>::value_type*.

```
template <class GraphProperties, class GraphProperty>
typename property_value<GraphProperties, GraphProperty>::type&
get_property(reverse_graph& g, GraphProperty);
```
> This returns the property specified by *GraphProperty* that is attached to the graph object *g*. The *property_value* traits class is defined in *boost/pending/property.hpp*.

```
template <class GraphProperties, class GraphProperty>
const typename property_value<GraphProperties, GraphProperty>::type&
get_property(const reverse_graph& g, GraphProperty);
```
> This returns the property specified by *GraphProperty* that is attached to the graph object *g*. The *property_value* traits class is defined in *boost/pending/property.hpp*.

14.3.3 *filtered_graph*

filtered_graph<*Graph*, *EdgePredicate*, *VertexPredicate*>

The *filtered_graph* class template is an adaptor that creates a filtered view of a graph. The edge and vertex predicate function objects determine which vertices and edges of the original graph show up in the filtered graph. Any vertex for which the vertex predicate returns false and any edge for which the edge predicate returns false will appear to be removed from the graph. The *filtered_graph* class does not create a copy of the original graph, but uses a reference to the original graph. The lifetime of the original graph must extend past any use of the filtered graph. The filtered graph does not change the structure of the original graph, though vertex and edge properties of the original graph can be changed through property maps of the filtered graph.

Example

The following function object is an example of a predicate that filters out edges whose weight is not positive.

```
template <typename EdgeWeightMap>
struct positive_edge_weight {

  positive_edge_weight() { }

  positive_edge_weight(EdgeWeightMap weight) : m_weight(weight) { }

  template <typename Edge>
  bool operator()(const Edge& e) const {
    return 0 < get(m_weight, e);
  }

  EdgeWeightMap m_weight;
};
```

This example uses the *filtered_graph* with the above *positive_edge_weight* predicate to create a filtered view of a small graph. The edges (A, C), (C, E), and (E, C) all have zero weight and therefore do not appear in the filtered graph.

```
typedef adjacency_list<vecS, vecS, directedS,
  no_property, property<edge_weight_t, int> > Graph;
typedef property_map<Graph, edge_weight_t>::type EdgeWeightMap;

enum { A, B, C, D, E, N };
const char* name = "ABCDE";
Graph g(N);
add_edge(A, B, 2, g);
add_edge(A, C, 0, g);
add_edge(C, D, 1, g);
add_edge(C, E, 0, g);
add_edge(D, B, 3, g);
add_edge(E, C, 0, g);

positive_edge_weight<EdgeWeightMap> filter(get(edge_weight, g));
filtered_graph<Graph, positive_edge_weight<EdgeWeightMap> >
  fg(g, filter);

std::cout << "filtered edge set: ";
print_edges(fg, name);

std::cout << "filtered out-edges:" << std::endl;
print_graph(fg, name);
```

The output is

```
filtered edge set: (A,B)  (C,D)  (D,B)
filtered out-edges:
A --> B
B -->
C --> D
D --> B
E -->
```

Where Defined

boost/graph/filtered_graph.hpp

Template Parameters

Graph	The graph type to be adapted.
EdgePredicate	A function object that selects which edges from the original graph will appear in the filtered graph. The function object must model Predicate. The argument type for the function object must be the edge descriptor type of the graph. Also, the predicate must be DefaultConstructible.
VertexPredicate	A function object that selects which vertices from the original graph will appear in the filtered graph. The function object must model Predicate. The argument type for the function object must be the vertex descriptor type of the graph. Also, the predicate must be DefaultConstructible. **Default:** *keep_all*

Model Of

The concepts that *filtered_graph<Graph,EP,VP>* models depends on the *Graph* type. If *Graph* models any one of VertexListGraph, EdgeListGraph, IncidenceGraph, BidirectionalGraph, AdjacencyGraph, and PropertyGraph then so does *filtered_graph<Graph,EP,VP>*.

Associated Types

graph_traits<filtered_graph>::vertex_descriptor
The type for the vertex descriptors associated with the *filtered_graph*.
(Required by Graph.)

graph_traits<filtered_graph>::edge_descriptor
The type for the edge descriptors associated with the *filtered_graph*.
(Required by Graph.)

graph_traits<filtered_graph>::vertex_iterator
The type for the iterators returned by *vertices()*. The vertex iterator is the same type as the vertex iterator of the adapted graph.
(Required by VertexListGraph.)

graph_traits<filtered_graph>::edge_iterator
The type for the iterators returned by *edges()*. This iterator type models the concept MultiPassInputIterator.
(Required by EdgeListGraph.)

graph_traits<filtered_graph>::out_edge_iterator
The type for the iterators returned by *out_edges()*. This iterator type models the concept MultiPassInputIterator.
(Required by IncidenceGraph.)

graph_traits<filtered_graph>::in_edge_iterator
> The type for the iterators returned by *in_edges()*. This iterator type models the concept MultiPassInputIterator.
> (Required by BidirectionalGraph.)

graph_traits<filtered_graph>::adjacency_iterator
> The type for the iterators returned by *adjacent_vertices()*. This iterator type models the same concept as the out-edge iterator.
> (Required by AdjacencyGraph.)

graph_traits<filtered_graph>::directed_category
> Provides information about whether the graph is directed (*directed_tag*) or undirected (*undirected_tag*), which is the same as the adapted graph's *directed_category*.
> (Required by Graph.)

graph_traits<filtered_graph>::edge_parallel_category
> This describes whether the graph class allows the insertion of parallel edges (edges with the same source and target). This is the same as the adapted graph's *edge_parallel_category*.
> (Required by Graph.)

graph_traits<filtered_graph>::vertices_size_type
> The type used for dealing with the number of vertices in the graph.
> (Required by VertexListGraph.)

graph_traits<filtered_graph>::edges_size_type
> The type used for dealing with the number of edges in the graph.
> (Required by EdgeListGraph.)

graph_traits<filtered_graph>::degree_size_type
> The type used for dealing with the number of out-edges of a vertex.
> (Required by IncidenceGraph.)

property_map<filtered_graph, PropertyTag>::type
property_map<filtered_graph, PropertyTag>::const_type
> The map type for vertex or edge properties in the graph. The property map types for the filtered graph are the same as those for the original graph.
> (Required by PropertyGraph.)

Member Functions

filtered_graph(Graph& g, EdgePredicate ep)
> Construct a filtered-edge view of the graph *g* based on the predicate *ep*.

filtered_graph(Graph& g, EdgePredicate ep, VertexPredicate vp)
> Construct a filtered view of the graph *g* based on the edge predicate *ep* and the vertex predicate *vp*.

Nonmember Functions

The functionality supported by *filtered_graph* depends on the underlying *Graph* type. For example, if the *Graph* type does not support *in_edges*(), then neither does *filtered_graph*. Here we list all the possible functions that *filtered_graph* could support, given a *Graph* type that models VertexListGraph, EdgeListGraph, IncidenceGraph, BidirectionalGraph, AdjacencyGraph, PropertyGraph, and BidirectionalGraph.

std::pair<vertex_iterator, vertex_iterator> vertices (const filtered_graph& g)
> Returns an iterator range providing access to the vertex set of graph *g*.
> (Required by VertexListGraph.)

std::pair<edge_iterator, edge_iterator> edges (const filtered_graph& g)
> Returns an iterator range providing access to the edge set of graph *g*.
> (Required by EdgeListGraph.)

std::pair<adjacency_iterator, adjacency_iterator>
adjacent_vertices (vertex_descriptor v, const filtered_graph& g)
> Returns an iterator range providing access to the vertices adjacent to vertex *v* in graph *g*.
> (Required by AdjacencyGraph.)

std::pair<out_edge_iterator, out_edge_iterator>
out_edges (vertex_descriptor v, const filtered_graph& g)
> Returns an iterator range providing access to the out-edges of vertex *v* in graph *g*. If the graph is undirected, this iterator range provides access to all edge incident on vertex *v*.
> (Required by IncidenceGraph.)

vertex_descriptor source (edge_descriptor e, const filtered_graph& g)
> Returns the source vertex of edge *e*.
> (Required by IncidenceGraph.)

vertex_descriptor target (edge_descriptor e, const filtered_graph& g)
> Returns the target vertex of edge *e*.
> (Required by IncidenceGraph.)

degree_size_type out_degree (vertex_descriptor u, const filtered_graph& g)
> Returns the number of edges leaving vertex *u*.
> (Required by IncidenceGraph.)

vertices_size_type num_vertices (const filtered_graph& g)
> Returns the number of vertices in the underlying graph *g*.
> (Required by VertexListGraph.)

edges_size_type num_edges (const filtered_graph& g)
> Returns the number of edges in the graph *g*.
> (Required by EdgeListGraph.)

template <*typename Property*>
property_map<*filtered_graph, Property*>::*type*
get(*Property, filtered_graph& g*)

template <*typename Property*>
property_map<*filtered_graph, Property*>::*const_type*
get(*Property, const filtered_graph& g*)

  Returns the property map object specified by *Property*. The *Property* must match one of
  the properties specified in the graph's *VertexProperty* template argument.
  (Required by PropertyGraph.)

template <*typename Property, typename X*>
typename property_traits<
  typenamae property_map<*filtered_graph, Property*>::*const_type*
>::*value_type*
get(*Property, const filtered_graph& g, X x*)

  This returns the property value for *x*, which is either a vertex or an edge descriptor.
  (Required by PropertyGraph.)

template <*typename Property, typename X, typename Value*>
void put(*Property, const filtered_graph& g, X x, const Value& value*)

  This sets the property value for *x* to *value*. *x* is either a vertex or an edge descriptor. *Value*
  must be convertible to the value type of the specifed property.
  (Required by PropertyGraph.)

14.3.4   SGB *Graph* Pointer

Graph*

  The BGL header *boost/graph/stanford_graph.hpp* adapts a Stanford GraphBase (SGB) [22]
Graph pointer into a BGL-compatible graph. Note that a graph adaptor class is not used;
SGB's *Graph** itself becomes a model of several BGL graph concepts (see the following
"Model Of" section) through the definition of several function overloads.

  Make sure to apply the PROTOTYPES change file to your installation of SGB so that the
SGB headers conform to ANSI C (and hence will compile with a C++ compiler).

  Thanks to Andreas Scherer for help with the implementation and documentation of this
SGB *Graph** adaptor.

Example

See *example/miles_span.cpp*, *example/girth.cpp*, and *example/roget_components.cpp*.

Template Parameters

None.

Model Of

VertexListGraph, IncidenceGraph, AdjacencyGraph, and PropertyGraph. The set of property tags that can be used with the SGB graph is described in "Vertex and Edge Properties" later in this section.

Where Defined

boost/graph/stanford_graph.hpp

Associated Types

graph_traits<Graph>::vertex_descriptor*

The type for the vertex descriptors associated with the SGB *Graph**. We use the type *Vertex** as the vertex descriptor (where *Vertex* is a typedef in *gb_graph.h*.
(Required by Graph.)

graph_traits<Graph>::edge_descriptor*

The type for the edge descriptors associated with the SGB *Graph**. The type used is the *boost::sgb_edge* type. In addition to supporting all the required operations of a BGL edge descriptor, the *boost::sgb_edge* class has this constructor:
sgb_edge::sgb_edge(Arc arc, Vertex* source)*.
(Required by IncidenceGraph.)

graph_traits<Graph>::vertex_iterator*

The type for the iterators returned by *vertices()*. This iterator models RandomAccessIterator.
(Required by VertexListGraph.)

graph_traits<Graph>::out_edge_iterator*

The type for the iterators returned by *out_edges()*. If *EdgeList=vecS* then this iterator models MultiPassInputIterator.
(Required by IncidenceGraph.)

graph_traits<Graph>::adjacency_iterator*

The type for the iterators returned by *adjacent_vertices()*. This iterator models the same concept as the out-edge iterator.
(Required by AdjacencyGraph.)

graph_traits<Graph>::directed_category*

Provides information about whether the graph is directed or undirected. An SGB *Graph** is directed so this type is *directed_tag*.
(Required by Graph.)

graph_traits<*Graph**>::*edge_parallel_category*
>   This describes whether the graph class allows the insertion of parallel edges (edges with the same source and target). The SGB *Graph** does not prevent addition of parallel edges, so this type is *allow_parallel_edge_tag*.
>   (Required by Graph.)

graph_traits<*Graph**>::*traversal_category*
>   An SGB *Graph** provides traversal of the vertex set, out edges, and adjacent vertices. Therefore the traversal category tag is defined as follows:
>   **struct sgb_traversal_tag :**
>   **public virtual vertex_list_graph_tag ,**
>   **public virtual incidence_graph_tag ,**
>   **public virtual adjacency_graph_tag { };**
>   (Required by Graph.)

graph_traits<*Graph**>::*vertices_size_type*
>   The type used for dealing with the number of vertices in the graph.
>   (Required by VertexListGraph.)

graph_traits<*Graph**>::*edges_size_type*
>   The type used for dealing with the number of edges in the graph.
>   (Required by EdgeListGraph.)

graph_traits<*Graph**>::*degree_size_type*
>   The type used for dealing with the number of out-edges of a vertex.
>   (Required by IncidenceGraph.)

property_map<*Graph** , *PropertyTag*>::*type*
property_map<*Graph** , *PropertyTag*>::*const_type*
>   The map type for vertex or edge properties in the graph. The property is specified by the *PropertyTag* template argument, and must be one of the tags described in the "Vertex and Edge Properties" section.
>   (Required by PropertyGraph.)

Member Functions

None.

Nonmember Functions

std::pair<*vertex_iterator* , *vertex_iterator*> *vertices* (*const Graph** *g*)
>   Returns an iterator range providing access to the vertex set of graph *g*.
>   (Required by VertexListGraph.)

std::pair<*edge_iterator* , *edge_iterator*> *edges* (*const Graph** *g*)
>   Returns an iterator range providing access to the edge set of graph *g*.
>   (Required by EdgeListGraph.)

std::pair<adjacency_iterator, adjacency_iterator>
adjacent_vertices (*vertex_descriptor v, const Graph* g*)
  Returns an iterator range providing access to the vertices adjacent to vertex v in graph g.
  (Required by AdjacencyGraph.)

std::pair<out_edge_iterator, out_edge_iterator>
out_edges (*vertex_descriptor v, const Graph* g*)
  Returns an iterator range providing access to the out-edges of vertex v in graph g. If the
  graph is undirected, this iterator range provides access to all edge incident on vertex v.
  (Required by IncidenceGraph.)

vertex_descriptor source (*edge_descriptor e, const Graph* g*)
  Returns the source vertex of edge e.
  (Required by IncidenceGraph.)

vertex_descriptor target (*edge_descriptor e, const Graph* g*)
  Returns the target vertex of edge e.
  (Required by IncidenceGraph.)

degree_size_type out_degree (*vertex_descriptor u, const Graph* g*)
  Returns the number of edges leaving vertex u.
  (Required by IncidenceGraph.)

vertices_size_type num_vertices (*const Graph* g*)
  Returns the number of vertices in the graph g.
  (Required by VertexListGraph.)

edges_size_type num_edges (*const Graph* g*)
  Returns the number of edges in the graph g.
  (Required by EdgeListGraph.)

vertex_descriptor vertex (*vertices_size_type n, const Graph* g*)
  Returns the nth vertex in the graph's vertex list.

template <typename PropertyTag>
property_map<Graph*, PropertyTag>::type
get (*PropertyTag, Graph* g*)

template <typename PropertyTag>
property_map<Graph*, PropertyTag>::const_type
get (*PropertyTag, const Graph* g*)
  Returns the property map object specified by **PropertyTag**.
  (Required by PropertyGraph.)

template <*typename PropertyTag, typename X*>
typename property_traits<
    typename property_map<*Graph*, PropertyTag*>*::const_type*
>*::value_type*
get(*PropertyTag, const Graph* g, X x*)
>   This returns the property value for *x*, which is either a vertex or an edge descriptor.
>   (Required by PropertyGraph.)

template <*typename PropertyTag, typename X, typename Value*>
void put(*PropertyTag, const Graph* g, X x, const Value& value*)
>   This sets the property value for *x* to *value*. *x* is either a vertex or an edge descriptor. *Value*
>   must be convertible to the value type of the property corresponding to the *PropertyTag*.
>   (Required by PropertyGraph.)

Vertex and Edge Properties

The SGB *Vertex* and *Arc* structures provide "utility" fields for storing extra information. We provide BGL wrappers that provide access to these fields through property maps. In addition, vertex index and edge length maps are provided. A property map object can be obtained from a SGB *Graph** using the *get*() function described in the previous section and the property map type can be obtained through the *property_map* traits class.

The following list of property tags can be used to specify which utility field you would like a property map for.

```
// vertex property tags
template <typename T> u_property;
template <typename T> v_property;
template <typename T> w_property;
template <typename T> x_property;
template <typename T> y_property;
template <typename T> z_property;


// edge property tags
template <typename T> a_property;
template <typename T> b_property;
```

The template parameter *T* for these tags is limited to the types in the *util* union declared in the SGB header *gb_graph.h*, which are *Vertex**, *Arc**, *Graph**, *char**, and *long*. The property maps for the utility fields are models of LvaluePropertyMap.

The property map for vertex indices can be obtained using the *vertex_index_t* tag, and this property map is a ReadablePropertyMap. A property map for edge lengths can be obtained using the *edge_length_t* tag, and this property map is a LvaluePropertyMap whose value type is *long*.

14.3.5   LEDA *GRAPH*<*V,E*>

GRAPH<*V,E*>

The LEDA *GRAPH* class template can be used directly as a BGL graph due to some function overloads defined in *boost/graph/leda_graph.hpp*.

The implementation of the BGL interface for the LEDA *GRAPH* class is discussed in §10.3 as an example of how to write BGL adaptors for non-BGL graph classes.

Example

⟨ *leda-graph-eg.cpp* 267 ⟩ ≡

```
#include <boost/graph/leda_graph.hpp>
#include <iostream>
#undef string // LEDA macro!

int main()
{
  using namespace boost;
  typedef GRAPH<std::string, int> graph_t;
  graph_t g;
  g.new_node("Philoctetes");
  g.new_node("Heracles");
  g.new_node("Alcmena");
  g.new_node("Eurystheus");
  g.new_node("Amphitryon");

  typedef property_map<graph_t, vertex_all_t>::type NodeMap;
  NodeMap node_name_map = get(vertex_all, g);

  graph_traits<graph_t>::vertex_iterator vi, vi_end;
  for (tie(vi, vi_end) = vertices(g); vi != vi_end; ++vi)
    std::cout << node_name_map[*vi] << std::endl;

  return EXIT_SUCCESS;
}
```

The output is

> **Philoctetes**
> **Heracles**
> **Alcmena**
> **Eurystheus**
> **Amphitryon**

Template Parameters

V	The type of object attached to each vertex in the LEDA graph.
E	The type of object attached to each edge in the LEDA graph.

Model Of

VertexListGraph, BidirectionalGraph, and AdjacencyGraph. Also, VertexMutableProperty-Graph and EdgeMutablePropertyGraph for the property tags *vertex_all_t* and *edge_all_t* which provide access to the *V* and *E* objects in the LEDA graph. The *GRAPH* type is also a Property-Graph for *vertex_index_t* and *edge_index_t*, which provide access to the ID numbers that LEDA assigns to each node.

Where Defined

boost/graph/leda_graph.hpp

Associated Types

graph_traits<GRAPH>::vertex_descriptor
   The type for the vertex descriptors associated with the *GRAPH*. The type used is the *node* type from LEDA.
   (Required by Graph.)

graph_traits<GRAPH>::edge_descriptor
   The type for the edge descriptors associated with the *GRAPH*. The type used is the *edge* type from LEDA.
   (Required by Graph.)

graph_traits<GRAPH>::vertex_iterator
   The type for the iterators returned by *vertices()*.
   (Required by VertexListGraph.)

graph_traits<GRAPH>::out_edge_iterator
   The type for the iterators returned by *out_edges()*.
   (Required by IncidenceGraph.)

graph_traits<GRAPH>::in_edge_iterator
   The *in_edge_iterator* is the iterator type returned by the *in_edges()* function.
   (Required by BidirectionalGraph.)

graph_traits<GRAPH>::adjacency_iterator
   The type for the iterators returned by *adjacent_vertices()*.
   (Required by AdjacencyGraph.)

graph_traits<*GRAPH*>::directed_category

The LEDA *GRAPH* type is for directed graphs (*directed_tag*).
(Required by Graph.)

graph_traits<*GRAPH*>::edge_parallel_category

The LEDA *GRAPH* type allows parallel edges to be inserted (*allow_parallel_edge_tag*).
(Required by Graph.)

graph_traits<*GRAPH*>::traversal_category

This graph type provides vertex iterators, out-edge and in-edge iterators, and adjacency iterators. The traversal-category tag type is as follows.

struct leda_graph_traversal_category :
    public virtual bidirectional_graph_tag,
    public virtual adjacency_graph_tag,
    public virtual vertex_list_graph_tag { };
(Required by Graph.)

graph_traits<*GRAPH*>::vertices_size_type

The type used for representing the number of vertices in the graph, which is *int*.
(Required by VertexListGraph.)

graph_traits<*GRAPH*>::edges_size_type

The type used for representing the number of edges in the graph, which in this case is *int*.
(Required by EdgeListGraph.)

graph_traits<*GRAPH*>::degree_size_type

The type used for representing the number of out-edges of a vertex. In this case the type is *int*.
(Required by IncidenceGraph.)

property_map<*GRAPH, PropertyTag*>::type
property_map<*GRAPH, PropertyTag*>::const_type

The map type for vertex or edge properties in the graph. The specific property is specified by the *PropertyTag* template argument, and must be either *vertex_index_t*, *edge_index_t*, *vertex_all_t*, or *edge_all_t*. The two "all" tags are for accessing the *V* and *E* objects in the LEDA graph. The *vertex_index_t* and *edge_index_t* tags provides access to the ID numbers that LEDA assigns to each node and edge.
(Required by PropertyGraph.)

Member Functions

No additional member functions (especially since that would require modifying LEDA source code).

Nonmember Functions

std::pair<vertex_iterator, vertex_iterator> vertices(const GRAPH& g)
> Returns an iterator range providing access to the vertex set of graph *g*.
> (Required by VertexListGraph.)

std::pair<adjacency_iterator, adjacency_iterator>
adjacent_vertices(vertex_descriptor v, const GRAPH& g)
> Returns an iterator range providing access to the vertices adjacent to vertex *v* in graph *g*.
> (Required by AdjacencyGraph.)

std::pair<out_edge_iterator, out_edge_iterator>
out_edges(vertex_descriptor v, const GRAPH& g)
> Returns an iterator range providing access to the out-edges of vertex *v* in graph *g*. If the
> graph is undirected, this iterator range provides access to all edge incident on vertex *v*.
> (Required by IncidenceGraph.)

std::pair<in_edge_iterator, in_edge_iterator>
in_edges(vertex_descriptor v, const GRAPH& g)
> Returns an iterator range providing access to the in-edges of vertex *v* in graph *g*. This
> operation is no available if *directedS* was specified for the *Directed* template parameter. It
> is available for *undirectedS* and *bidirectionalS*.
> (Required by BidirectionalGraph.)

vertex_descriptor source(edge_descriptor e, const GRAPH& g)
> Returns the source vertex of edge *e*.
> (Required by IncidenceGraph.)

vertex_descriptor target(edge_descriptor e, const GRAPH& g)
> Returns the target vertex of edge *e*.
> (Required by IncidenceGraph.)

degree_size_type out_degree(vertex_descriptor u, const GRAPH& g)
> Returns the number of edges leaving vertex *u*.
> (Required by IncidenceGraph.)

degree_size_type in_degree(vertex_descriptor u, const GRAPH& g)
> Returns the number of edges entering vertex *u*. This operation is only available if *bidirec-*
> *tionalS* was specified for the *Directed* template parameter.
> (Required by BidirectionalGraph.)

vertices_size_type num_vertices(const GRAPH& g)
> Returns the number of vertices in the graph *g*.
> (Required by VertexListGraph.)

edges_size_type num_edges (*const GRAPH& g*)
  Returns the number of edges in the graph g.
  (Required by EdgeListGraph.)

std::pair<edge_descriptor, bool>
add_edge (*vertex_descriptor u*, *vertex_descriptor v*, *GRAPH& g*)
  Adds edge (u, v) to the graph and returns the edge descriptor for the new edge. For this
  graph type the *bool* flag will always be false.
  (Required by EdgeMutableGraph.)

std::pair<edge_descriptor, bool>
add_edge (*vertex_descriptor u*, *vertex_descriptor v*, *const E& ep*, *GRAPH& g*)
  Adds edge (u, v) to the graph and attaches *ep* as the value of the edge's internal property
  storage.
  (Required by EdgeMutablePropertyGraph.)

void remove_edge (*vertex_descriptor u*, *vertex_descriptor v*, *GRAPH& g*)
  Removes the edge (u, v) from the graph.
  (Required by EdgeMutableGraph.)

void remove_edge (*edge_descriptor e*, *GRAPH& g*)
  Removes the edge *e* from the graph. This differs from the *remove_edge(u, v, g)* function in
  the case of a multigraph. This *remove_edge(e, g)* function removes a single edge, whereas
  the *remove_edge(u, v, g)* function removes all edges (u, v).
  (Required by EdgeMutableGraph.)

vertex_descriptor add_vertex (*GRAPH& g*)
  Adds a vertex to the graph and returns the vertex descriptor for the new vertex.
  (Required by VertexMutableGraph.)

vertex_descriptor add_vertex (*const VertexProperties& p*, *GRAPH& g*)
  Adds a vertex to the graph and returns the vertex descriptor for the new vertex.
  (Required by VertexMutablePropertyGraph.)

void clear_vertex (*vertex_descriptor u*, *GRAPH& g*)
  Removes all edges to and from vertex u. The vertex is still in the vertex set of the graph.
  (Required by EdgeMutableGraph.)

void remove_vertex (*vertex_descriptor u*, *GRAPH& g*)
  Remove vertex u from the vertex set of the graph.
  (Required by VertexMutableGraph.)

template *<typename PropertyTag>*
property_map<GRAPH, PropertyTag>::type
get(*PropertyTag*, *GRAPH& g*)
> Returns a mutable property map object for the vertex property specified by *PropertyTag*.
> (Required by PropertyGraph.)

template *<typename PropertyTag>*
property_map<GRAPH, PropertyTag>::const_type
get(*PropertyTag*, *const GRAPH& g*)
> Returns a constant property map object for the vertex property specified by *PropertyTag*.
> (Required by PropertyGraph.)

template *<typename PropertyTag, typename X>*
typename property_traits<
  typenamae property_map<GRAPH, PropertyTag>::const_type
>::value_type
get(*PropertyTag*, *const GRAPH& g*, *X x*)
> This returns the property value for *x*, which is either a vertex or an edge descriptor.
> (Required by PropertyGraph.)

template *<typename PropertyTag, typename X, typename Value>*
void put(*PropertyTag*, *const GRAPH& g*, *X x*, *const Value& value*)
> This sets the property value for *x* to *value*. *x* is either a vertex or an edge descriptor.
> (Required by PropertyGraph.)

14.3.6   *std::vector<EdgeList>*

std::vector<EdgeList>

The function overloads in *boost/graph/vector_as_graph.hpp* make it possible to treat types such as *std::vector<std::list<int>>* like a graph.

Example

In this example we construct a graph using container classes from the Standard Library and use the BGL *print_graph*() function (which is written in terms of the BGL graph interface) to output the graph.

⟨ *vector-as-graph.cpp* 272 ⟩ ≡

```
#include <vector>
#include <list>
#include <boost/graph/vector_as_graph.hpp>
#include <boost/graph/graph_utility.hpp>

int main()
{
```

```
enum { r, s, t, u, v, w, x, y, N };
char name[] = "rstuvwxy";
typedef std::vector< std::list<int> > Graph;
Graph g(N);
g[r].push_back(v);
g[s].push_back(r); g[s].push_back(r); g[s].push_back(w);
g[t].push_back(x);
g[u].push_back(t);
g[w].push_back(t); g[w].push_back(x);
g[x].push_back(y);
g[y].push_back(u);
boost::print_graph(g, name);
return EXIT_SUCCESS;
}
```

The output is

```
r --> v
s --> r r w
t --> x
u --> t
v -->
w --> t x
x --> y
y --> u
```

Where Defined

boost/graph/vector_as_graph.hpp

Template Parameters

EdgeList   A Container whose *value_type* is convertible to the *size_type* of *std::vector* (so that it can be used as a vertex descriptor).

Model Of

VertexListGraph, IncidenceGraph, AdjacencyGraph,

Associated Types

graph_traits<std::vector>::vertex_descriptor
  The type for the vertex descriptors associated with the graph.
  (Required by Graph.)

graph_traits<std::vector>::edge_descriptor
  The type for the edge descriptors associated with the graph.
  (Required by Graph.)

graph_traits<std::vector>::vertex_iterator
  The type for the iterators returned by *vertices()*.
  (Required by VertexListGraph.)

graph_traits<std::vector>::out_edge_iterator
  The type for the iterators returned by *out_edges()*.
  (Required by IncidenceGraph.)

graph_traits<std::vector>::adjacency_iterator
  The type for the iterators returned by *adjacent_vertices()*.
  (Required by AdjacencyGraph.)

graph_traits<std::vector>::directed_category
  This graph type is for directed graphs, so the category type is *directed_tag*.
  (Required by Graph.)

graph_traits<std::vector>::edge_parallel_category
  This graph type allows parallel edges, so the category type is *allow_parallel_edge_tag*.
  (Required by Graph.)

graph_traits<std::vector>::vertices_size_type
  The type used for representing the number of vertices in the graph.
  (Required by VertexListGraph.)

graph_traits<std::vector>::degree_size_type
  The type used for representing the number of out-edges of a vertex.
  (Required by IncidenceGraph.)

Member Functions

No additional member functions.

Nonmember Functions

std::pair<vertex_iterator, vertex_iterator>
vertices(const std::vector& g)
  Returns an iterator range providing access to the vertex set of graph *g*.
  (Required by VertexListGraph.)

std::pair<adjacency_iterator, adjacency_iterator>
adjacent_vertices(vertex_descriptor v, const std::vector& g)
  Returns an iterator range providing access to the vertices adjacent to vertex *v* in graph *g*.
  (Required by AdjacencyGraph.)

std::pair<out_edge_iterator, out_edge_iterator>
out_edges (vertex_descriptor v, const std::vector& g)
> Returns an iterator range providing access to the out-edges of vertex v in graph g. If the graph is undirected, this iterator range provides access to all edge incident on vertex v.
> (Required by IncidenceGraph.)

vertex_descriptor source (edge_descriptor e, const std::vector& g)
> Returns the source vertex of edge e.
> (Required by IncidenceGraph.)

vertex_descriptor target (edge_descriptor e, const std::vector& g)
> Returns the target vertex of edge e.
> (Required by IncidenceGraph.)

degree_size_type out_degree (vertex_descriptor u, const std::vector& g)
> Returns the number of edges leaving vertex u.
> (Required by IncidenceGraph.)

vertices_size_type num_vertices (const std::vector& g)
> Returns the number of vertices in the graph g.
> (Required by VertexListGraph.)

Chapter 15

Property Map Library

Most graph algorithms require access to various properties associated with the vertices and edges of a graph. For example, problem data such as the length or capacity of an edge may be needed by the algorithms, as well as auxiliary data flags such as color, to indicate whether a vertex has been visited. There are many possibilities for how these properties can be stored in memory, ranging from members of vertex and edge objects, to arrays indexed by some index, to properties that are computed when needed. To insulate generic algorithms from the details of the underlying property representation, the *property map*[1] abstraction is introduced.

Several categories of property accessors provide different access capabilities:

readable The associated property data can only be read. The data are returned by value. Many property maps defining the problem input (such as edge weight) can be defined as readable property maps.

writable The associated property can only be written to. The parent array used to record the paths in a breadth-first search tree is an example of a property map that would be defined writeable.

read/write The associated property can both be written and read. The distance property use in Dijkstra's shortest-paths algorithm would need to provide both read and write capabilities.

lvalue The associated property is actually represented in memory and it is possible to get a reference to it. The property maps in the lvalue category also support the requirements for read/write property maps.

There is a tag struct for each of the categories of property maps.

```
namespace boost {
  struct readable_property_map_tag { };
```

---

[1] In previous papers describing BGL, the property accessor concept was named Decorator. In Dietmar Kühl's master's thesis [24], property accessors are called data accessors.

```
  struct  writable_property_map_tag { };
  struct  read_write_property_map_tag :
    public  readable_property_map_tag,
    public  writable_property_map_tag { };
  struct  lvalue_property_map_tag :
    public  read_write_property_map_tag { };
}
```

Similar to the *iterator_traits* class of the STL, there is a *property_traits* class that can be used
to deduce the types associated with a property map type: the key and value types, and the
property map category. There is a specialization of *property_traits* so that pointers can be used
as property map objects.

```
namespace boost {
  template <typename PropertyMap>
  struct property_traits {
    typedef typename PropertyMap::key_type key_type;
    typedef typename PropertyMap::value_type value_type;
    typedef typename PropertyMap::reference reference;
    typedef typename PropertyMap::category category;
  };
  // specialization for using pointers as property maps
  template <typename T>
  struct property_traits<T*> {
    typedef T value_type;
    typedef T& reference;
    typedef std::ptrdiff_t key_type;
    typedef lvalue_property_map_tag category;
  };
  template <typename T>
  struct property_traits<const T*> {
    typedef T value_type;
    typedef const T& reference;
    typedef std::ptrdiff_t key_type;
    typedef lvalue_property_map_tag category;
  };
}
```

15.1   Property Map Concepts

The property map interface consists of a set of concepts that define a general-purpose mechanism for mapping key objects to corresponding value objects, thereby hiding the details of
how the mapping is implemented from algorithms that use property maps. The property map
requirements are purposefully vague on the type of the key and value objects to allow for
the utmost flexibility. Since the property map operations are global functions, it is possible

to overload the map functions such that nearly arbitrary property map types and key types can be used. The interface for property maps consists of three functions: *get()*, *put()*, and *operator[]*. The following concrete example shows how the three functions could be used to access the addresses associated with various people.

```
template <typename AddressMap>
void foo (AddressMap address)
{
  typedef typename boost::property_traits<AddressMap>::value_type value_type;
  typedef typename boost::property_traits<AddressMap>::key_type key_type;

  value_type old_address, new_address;
  key_type fred = "Fred";
  old_address = get (address, fred);
  new_address = "384 Fitzpatrick Street"
  put (address, fred, new_address);

  key_type joe = "Joe";
  value_type& joes_address = address[joe];
  joes_address = "325 Cushing Avenue";
}
```

For each property map object there is a set of *valid keys* for which the mapping to value objects is defined. Invoking a property map function on an *invalid* key results in undefined behavior. The property map concepts do not specify how this set of valid keys is created or modified. A function that uses a property map must specify the expected set of valid keys in its preconditions.

Notation

The notation used in the following sections is summarized here.

PMap	is the type of a property map.
pmap	is a property map object of type *PMap*.
key	is an object of type *property_traits<PMap>::key_type*.
val	is an object of type *property_traits<PMap>::value_type*.

15.1.1 ReadablePropertyMap

A ReadablePropertyMap provides read-access to the value object associated with a given key via a call to the *get()* function. The *get()* function returns a copy of the value object.

Refinement Of

CopyConstructible

Associated Types

property_traits<PMap>::value_type
> The type of the property.

property_traits<PMap>::reference
> A type that is convertible to the value type.

property_traits<PMap>::key_type
> The type of the key object used to look up the property. The property map may be templated on the key type, in which case this typedef can be *void*.

property_traits<PMap>::category
> The category of the property: a type convertible to *readable_property_map_tag*.

Valid Expressions

> *get(pmap, key)*
> Return Type: *reference*
> Semantics: lookup the property of the object associated with *key*.

15.1.2 WritablePropertyMap

A WritablePropertyMap has the capability of setting the value object associated with the given key object via the *put()* function.

Refinement Of

CopyConstructible

Associated Types

property_traits<PA>::value_type
> The type of the property.

property_traits<PA>::key_type
> The type of the key object used to look up the property. The property map may be templated on the key type, in which case this typedef can be *void*.

property_traits<PA>::category
> The category of the property: a type convertible to *writable_property_map_tag*.

Valid Expressions

> *put(pmap, key, val)*
> Return Type: *void*
> Semantics: assign *val* to the property associated with *key*.

15.1.3   ReadWritePropertyMap

The ReadWritePropertyMap concept refines the ReadablePropertyMap and WritablePropertyMap concepts. It also add s the requirement that *property_traits<PA>::category* be a type
convertible to *read_write_property_map_tag*.

15.1.4   LvaluePropertyMap

An LvaluePropertyMap provides access to a reference to a property object (instead of a copy
of the object as in *get()*). An LvaluePropertyMap can be *mutable* or *immutable*. The mutable
LvaluePropertyMap returns a reference whereas the nonmutable returns a const reference.

Refinement Of

ReadablePropertyMap for immutable and ReadWritePropertyMap for mutable.

Associated Types

property_traits<PMap>::reference
> The reference type, which must be a reference or const reference to the value type of the
> property map.

property_traits<PMap>::category
> The category of the property: a type convertible to *lvalue_property_map_tag*.

Valid Expressions

pmap[key]
Return Type: *reference*
Semantics: obtain a reference to the property identified by *key*.

15.2   Property Map Classes

15.2.1   *property_traits*

property_traits<PropertyMap>

The *property_traits* class provides the mechanism for accessing the *associated types* of a
property map. The unspecialized (default) version of the *property_traits* class assumes that the
property map provides typedefs for all of the associated types.

```
namespace boost {
  template <typename PA>
  struct property_traits {
    typedef typename PA::key_type key_type;
    typedef typename PA::value_type value_type;
    typedef typename PA::reference reference;
    typedef typename PA::category category;
  };
} // namespace boost
```

The *category* typedef should be a typedef for one of the following types, or a type that inherits from one of the following types.

```
namespace boost {
  struct readable_property_map_tag { };
  struct writable_property_map_tag { };
  struct read_write_property_map_tag : readable_property_map_tag,
    writable_property_map_tag { };
  struct lvalue_property_map_tag : read_write_property_map_tag { };
} // namespace boost
```

Often it is handy to use a pointer as a property map object, where the *key_type* is an integer offset from the pointer. The following specialization of *property_traits* and overloads of the map functions are provided to accommodate this.

```
namespace boost {
  template <typename T>
  struct property_traits<T*> {
    typedef std::ptrdiff_t key_type;
    typedef T value_type;
    typedef value_type& reference;
    typedef lvalue_property_map_tag category;
  };

  template <typename T>
  void put(T* pa, std::ptrdiff_t k, const T& val) { pa[k] = val; }

  template <typename T>
  const T& get(const T* pa, std::ptrdiff_t k) { return pa[k]; }

  template <typename T>
  T& at(T* pa, std::ptrdiff_t k) { return pa[k]; }
} // namespace boost
```

Template Parameters

PropertyMap   A property map type.

Where Defined

boost/property_map.hpp

Members

property_traits::key_type
The type of the key object used to look up the property.

property_traits::value_type
The type of the property.

property_traits::reference
The reference to the value type.

property_traits::category
The category tag of the property map.

15.2.2   *iterator_property_map*

iterator_property_map<Iterator, IndexMap, T, R>

This is an adaptor that wraps a type that models RandomAccessIterator to create an LvaluePropertyMap. This adaptor is often useful for creating a property map out of an array, where the key is an integer offset into the array, and the array contains the value objects. When the key type is an integer, then just use *identity_property_map* for the *IndexMap* template parameter. Otherwise, you need to provide a property map that converts from the key type to an integer. For example, a graph may have an internal property for *vertex_index_t* that can be obtained using the *property_map* traits class.

Example

The following example demonstrates creating a property map out of an array.

⟨ *iterator-property-map-eg.cpp* 283 ⟩ ≡

```
#include <iostream>
#include <boost/property_map.hpp>

int main()
{
  using namespace boost;
```

```
  double x[ ] = { 0.2, 4.5, 3.2 };
  iterator_property_map<double*, identity_property_map> pmap(x);
  std::cout << "x[1] = " << get(pmap, 1) << std::endl;
  put(pmap, 0, 1.7);
  std::cout << "x[0] = " << pmap[0] << std::endl;
  return 0;
}
```

The output is

```
x[1] = 4.5
x[0] = 1.7
```

Where Defined

boost/graph/property_map.hpp

Template Parameters

Iterator	The iterator type being adapted. It must be a model of RandomAccessIterator.
IndexMap	A property map that converts the key type to an integer offset. It must be a model of ReadablePropertyMap.
T	The value type of the iterator.
	Default: *typename std::iterator_traits<Iterator>::value_type*
R	The reference type of the iterator.
	Default: *typename std::iterator_traits<Iterator>::reference*

Model Of

LvaluePropertyMap

Associated Types

All the types required by LvaluePropertyMap.

Member Functions

```
iterator_property_map(Iterator iter = Iterator(),
                      IndexMap index_map = IndexMap())
```
Constructor.

```
template <typename Key>
reference operator[ ](Key k) const;
```
Returns *(iter + get(index_map, k))*.

Nonmember Functions

template <typename Iterator, typename IndexMap>
iterator_property_map<Iterator, IndexMap,
  typename std::iterator_traits<Iterator>::value_type,
  typename std::iterator_traits<Iterator>::reference>
make_iterator_property_map (Iterator iter, IndexMap index_map)
    Create an iterator property map.

15.2.3   Property Tags

```
namespace boost {
  enum vertex_index_t { vertex_index = 1};
  enum edge_index_t { edge_index = 2};
  enum edge_name_t { edge_name = 3 };
  enum edge_weight_t { edge_weight = 4 };
  enum vertex_name_t { vertex_name = 5 };
  enum graph_name_t { graph_name = 6 };
  enum vertex_distance_t { vertex_distance = 7};
  enum vertex_color_t { vertex_color = 8 };
  enum vertex_degree_t { vertex_degree = 9 };
  enum vertex_in_degree_t { vertex_in_degree = 10 };
  enum vertex_out_degree_t { vertex_out_degree = 11 };
  enum vertex_discover_time_t { vertex_discover_time = 12 };
  enum vertex_finish_time_t { vertex_finish_time = 13 };
}

namespace boost {
  BOOST_INSTALL_PROPERTY (vertex, index);
  BOOST_INSTALL_PROPERTY (edge, index);
  BOOST_INSTALL_PROPERTY (edge, nane);
  . . .
}
```

15.3   Creating Your Own Property Maps

The main purpose of the property map interface is to introduce flexibility into generic algorithms. It allows properties to be stored in lots of different ways while presenting a common interface to the algorithms. The following section contains an example of using property maps to adapt to a third-party library the Stanford GraphBase (SGB) (see §14.3.4). After that we look at implementing a property map using the *std::map*.

15.3.1   Property Maps for Stanford GraphBase

The BGL adaptor for Stanford GraphBase includes property maps to access the various fields of the *Vertex* and *Arc* structures used in the SGB. In this section we describe one part of the implementation of the SGB adaptor as an example of how to implement property maps.

The SGB uses the following *Vertex* struct to store information about vertices in the graph. The *arcs* pointer is a linked-list for the out-edges of the vertex. The *name* field and the "utility" fields *u* through *z* are properties of the vertex (*util* is a union that allows various different things to be stored in the vertex). This section describes how to create a property map for accessing the *name* field.

```
typedef struct vertex_struct {
    struct arc_struct* arcs;
    char* name;
    util u, v, w, x, y, z;
} Vertex;
```

The main idea in the implementation of this property map is to define the property map functions *operator[]()*, *get()*, and *put()* in terms of access to the struct data member. The job is made easier by the *put_get_helper* class, which implements *put()* and *get()* in terms of *operator[]*. Therefore, only *operator[]* needs to be implemented. In addition, the associated types required of a property map must be defined.

Following is the implementation of *sgb_vertex_name_map*. We use the class *put_get_helper* (defined in *boost/property_map.hpp*) to simplify creating this property map. We implement *operator[]()* and *put_get_helper* implements *put()* and *get()*. The first type argument to the *put_get_helper* class template is the return type for *operator[]*, which in this case is *char**. The second argument is the property map type itself. The *reference* type only needs to be an actual reference if the property map is to be an LvaluePropertyMap. In this case we are creating a *ReadablePropertyMap*. The SGB adaptor uses *Vertex** for the *vertex_descriptor* of the graph, so that is the *key_type* of the property map.

```
class sgb_vertex_name_map
    : public put_get_helper<char*, sgb_vertex_name_map>
{
public:
    typedef boost::readable_property_map_tag category;
    typedef char* value_type;
    typedef char* reference;
    typedef Vertex* key_type;
    reference operator[](Vertex* v) const { return v->name; }
};
```

15.3.2   A Property Map Implemented with *std::map*

In the previous example, the property map object did not need to contain any state, for the value object could be obtained directly through the key. This is not always the case. Often times the key is used to lookup the value object in some auxiliary datastructure. An obvious candidate for such a datastructure is the ***std::map***. A property map that uses ***std::map*** as its implementation needs to store a pointer to this associative container. The following code implements this property map. We have made the container type a template parameter so that the property map can be used with other containers such as a ***hash_map***. The concept that describes this kind of container is named UniquePairAssociativeContainer.

```
template <typename UniquePairAssociativeContainer>
class associative_property_map
  : public put_get_helper<
      typename UniquePairAssociativeContainer::value_type::second_type&,
      associative_property_map<UniquePairAssociativeContainer> >
{
  typedef UniquePairAssociativeContainer C;
public:
  typedef typename C::key_type key_type;
  typedef typename C::value_type::second_type value_type;
  typedef value_type& reference;
  typedef lvalue_property_map_tag category;
  associative_property_map() : m_c(0) { }
  associative_property_map(C& c) : m_c(&c) { }
  reference operator[] (const key_type& k) const {
    return (*m_c)[k];
  }
private:
  C* m_c;
};
```

Chapter 16

Auxiliary Concepts, Classes, and Functions

16.1 Buffer

A Buffer is something in which items can be put and removed. The Buffer concept has very few requirements. It does not require any particular ordering of how the items are stored or in what order they will appear when removed. However, there is typically some sort of ordering policy.

Notation

B	is a type that models Buffer.
T	is the value type of *B*.
t	is an object of type *T*.

Requirements

For a type to model the Buffer concept it must have the following members.

B::value_type
   The type of object stored in the buffer. The value type must be Assignable.

B::size_type
   An unsigned integer type for representing the number of objects in the buffer.

b.push(t)
   Inserts *t* into the buffer. *b.size*( ) will be incremented by one.

b.pop ( )

Removes an object from the Buffer, the same object as would be returned by *b.top()*.
b.size ( ) will be decremented by one.

Precondition: *b.empty* ( ) is false.

b.top ( ) Returns a reference (or const reference) to some object in the buffer.

Precondition: *b.empty* ( ) is false.

b.size ( )

Returns the number of objects in the buffer.

Invariant: $b.size() >= 0$

b.empty ( )

Return type is *bool*, and the result value is equivalent to *b.size() == 0*.

Complexity Guarantees

- *push* ( ), *pop* ( ), and *size* ( ) must be at most linear time complexity in the size of the buffer.

- *top* ( ) and *empty* ( ) must be amortized constant time.

Models

std::stack, *boost::mutable_queue*, *boost::queue*, and *boost::priority_queue*.

16.2   ColorValue

This concept describes the requirements for the type used for color values. Many of the BGL algorithms use color property maps to mark the progress of the algorithm through the graph. The color value type must be EqualityComparable and also the *color_traits* class must be specialized for *T*, such that the following functions are defined. *T* is the type that is a model of ColorValue.

color_traits<T>::white ( )

Return Type: *T*

Semantics: Returns an object that represents the color white.

color_traits<T>::gray ( )

Return Type: *T*

Semantics: Returns an object that represents the color gray.

color_traits<T>::black ( )

Return Type: *T*

Semantics: Returns an object that represents the color black.

16.3   MultiPassInputIterator

This concept is a refinement of InputIterator, adding the requirements that the iterator can be used to make multiple passes through a range, and that if *it1* == *it2* and *it1* is dereferenceable then *++it1* == *++it2*. The MultiPassInputIterator is similar to the ForwardIterator. The only difference is that a ForwardIterator requires the *reference* type to be *value_type&*, whereas Multi-PassInputIterator is like InputIterator in that the *reference* type merely has to be convertible to *value_type*.

16.4   Monoid

A Monoid is a concept that describes a simple kind of algebraic system. It consists of a set of elements S, a binary operation, and an identity element. The C++ representation of a monoid consists of a function object that implements the binary operation, a set of objects that represent the elements of S, and an object that represents the identity element.

Refinement Of

The element type must be a model of Assignable and CopyConstructible. The function object type must be a model of BinaryFunction.

Valid Expressions

The type X is the element type. The objects *a*, *b*, and *c* are objects of type X that represent elements of the set S. The object *i* is an object of type X that satisfies the following properties for the identity element. The object *op* is a function object that implements the monoid operation.

op(a, b)
> Return Type: X
> Semantics: See below.

a == b
> Return Type: *bool*
> Semantics: Returns true if *a* and *b* represent the same element of S.

a != b
> Return Type: *bool*
> Semantics: Returns true if *a* and *b* do not represent the same element of S.

Invariants

- Closure
  The result of *op(a, b)* is also an element of S.

- Associativity
  op(op(a, b), c) == op(a, op(b, c))

- Definition of Identity Element
  op(a, i) == a

16.5   *mutable_queue*

mutable_queue<*IndexedType, Container, Compare, ID*>

This adaptor provides a special kind of priority queue (implemented on a heap) that has an update operation. This allows the ordering of the items to change. After the ordering criterion for item *x* changes, one must call the *Q.update(x)*. In order to efficiently find *x* in the queue, a functor must be provided to map *x* to a unique ID, which the *mutable_queue* then uses to map to the location of the item in the heap. The IDs generated must be between 0 and N, where N is the value passed to the constructor of *mutable_queue*.

Template Parameters

IndexedType	If *ID* is not supplied, then there must be an *index(t)* function defined (where *t* is an object of type *IndexedType*) that returns some integer type.
Container	A model of RandomAccessContainer. The value type of the container must be the same type as *IndexedType*. **Default:** *std::vector*<*IndexedType*>
Compare	A model of BinaryPredicate that takes *IndexedType* as arguments. **Default:** *std::less*<*typename Container::value_type*>
ID	A model of ReadablePropertyMap that takes *IndexedType* as a key type, and whose value type is some integer type. **Default:** *identity_property_map*

Members

value_type
  The same type as *IndexedType*.

size_type
  The type used to represent the size of the queue.

mutable_queue(*size_type n, const Compare& c, const ID& id = ID()*)
  Constructor. Space is reserved for *n* items.

template <*class InputIterator*>
mutable_queue(*InputIterator first, InputIterator last, const Compare& c,*
  const ID& id = ID())
  Constructor. The default container *std::vector* is filled from the range *[first, last)*.

bool empty ( ) const
> Returns whether the queue is empty.

void pop ( )
> Removes the top item from the queue.

value_type& top ( )
> Returns a reference to the top item of the queue.

value_type& front ( )
> Another name for **top ( )**.

void push (const value_type& x)
> Inserts a copy of the object *x* into the queue.

void update (const value_type& x)
> The "value" of an item has changed and the heap ordering should be updated. This method assumes that there is an old item *y* in the heap with **index(y) == index(x)** and that *x* is the new value for the item.

16.6 Disjoint Sets

16.6.1 *disjoint_sets*

disjoint_sets<RankMap, ParentMap, FindCompress>

This class provides disjoint sets operations, sometimes called a union-find data structure. A disjoint-sets data structure maintains a collection $S = S_1, S_2, \ldots, S_k$ of disjoint sets. Each set is identified by a *representative* that is some member of of the set. Sets are represented by rooted trees, which are encoded in the **ParentMap** property map. Two heuristics: *union by rank* and *path compression* are used to speed up the operations.

Template Parameters

RankMap
: must be a model of ReadWritePropertyMap with an integer value type and a key type equal to the set's element type.

ParentMap
: must be a model of ReadWritePropertyMap and the key and value type the same as the set's element type.

FindCompress
: should be one of the find function objects discussed later in this section.
Default: *find_with_full_path_compression*

Example

A typical usage pattern for *disjoint_sets* can be seen in the *kruskal_minimum_spanning_tree* ( )
algorithm. In this example, we call *link* ( ) instead of *union_set* ( ) because *u* and *v* were obtained from *find_set* ( ) and therefore are already the representatives for their sets.

```
// ...
  disjoint_sets<RankMap, ParentMap, FindCompress> dsets (rank, p);

  for (ui   = vertices (G) .first; ui != vertices (G) .second; ++ui)
    dsets .make_set (*ui);
  // ...
  while ( !Q.empty() ) {
    e = Q.front();
    Q.pop();
    u = dsets .find_set (source (e));
    v = dsets .find_set (target (e));
    if ( u != v ) {
      *out++ = e;
      dsets .link (u, v);
    }
  }
```

Members

disjoint_sets (*RankMap r, ParentMap p*)
  Constructor.

disjoint_sets (*const disjoint_sets& x*)
  Copy constructor.

template <typename Element>
void make_set (*Element x*)
  Creates a singleton set containing element *x*.

template <typename Element>
void link (*Element x, Element y*)
  Union the two sets *represented* by element *x* and *y*.

template <typename Element>
void union_set (*Element x, Element y*)
  Union the two sets that *contain* elements *x* and *y*. This is equivalent to *link(find_set(x),-*
  find_set(y)).

template <typename Element>
Element find_set (*Element x*)
  Returns the representative for the set containing element *x*.

template <*typename ElementIterator*>
std::size_t count_sets (*ElementIterator first*, *ElementIterator last*)
  Returns the number of disjoint sets.

template <*typename ElementIterator*>
void compress_sets (*ElementIterator first*, *ElementIterator last*)
  Flattens the parent tree so that the parent of every element is its representative.

Complexity

The time complexity is $O(m\alpha(m, n))$, where α is the inverse Ackermann's function, m is the number of disjoint-set operations (*make_set* (), *find_set* (), and *link* ()) and n is the number of elements. The α function grows very slowly, much more slowly than the log function.

16.6.2 *find_with_path_halving*

find_with_path_halving

This functor finds the representative vertex for the same component as the element x, and at the same time compresses the tree using path-halving.

template <*typename ParentMap*, *typename Element*>
Element operator () (*ParentMap p*, *Element x*)

16.6.3 *find_with_full_path_compression*

find_with_full_path_compression

This functor finds the representative vertex for the same component as the element x, and at the same time compresses the tree using full path compression.

template <*typename ParentMap*, *typename Element*>
Element operator () (*ParentMap p*, *Element x*)

16.7 *tie*

template <*typename T1*, *typename T2*>
tuple<*T1*, *T2*> *tie* (*T1*& *a*, *T2*& *b*);

This is a function from the Boost Tuple Library by Jaakko Järvi that makes it more convenient to work with functions that return pairs (or tuples in general). The effect of the *tie* () function allows the assignment of the two values of the pair to two separate variables.

Where Defined

boost/tuple/tuple.hpp

Example

An example of using the *tie()* function with the *vertices()* function, which returns a pair of type *std::pair<vertex_iterator, vertex_iterator>*. The pair of iterators is assigned to the iterator variables *i* and *end*.

```
graph_traits<graph_t>::vertex_iterator i, end;
for (tie(i,end) = vertices(g); i != end; ++i)
    // ...
```

Here is another example that uses *tie()* for handling operaitons with *std::set*.

```
#include <set>
#include <algorithm>
#include <iostream>
#include <boost/tuple/tuple.hpp>

int main()
{
    typedef std::set<int> SetT;
    SetT::iterator i, end;
    bool inserted;

    int vals[5] = { 5, 2, 4, 9, 1 };
    SetT s(vals, vals + 5);
    int new_vals[2] = { 3, 9 };

    for (int k = 0; k < 2; ++k) {
        // Using tie() with a return value of pair<iterator, bool>
        boost::tie(i,inserted) = s.insert(new_vals[k]);
        if (!inserted) std::cout << *i << " was already in the set." << std::endl;
        else std::cout << *i << " successfully inserted." << std::endl;
    }

    return EXIT_SUCCESS;
}
```

The output is

```
3 successfully inserted.
9 was already in the set.
```

16.8   *graph_property_iter_range*

> *graph_property_iter_range*<*Graph, PropertyTag*>

This class generates a begin/end pair of iterators that provide access to a vertex property across all the vertices in the graph or and edge property across all the edges in the graph.

Example

This example loops through all of the vertices in the graph assigning strings into the name property. It then loops through again printing the names to standard out.

⟨ *graph-property-iter-eg.cpp* 297 ⟩ ≡

```
#include <boost/graph/adjacency_list.hpp>
#include <boost/graph/property_iter_range.hpp>

int main()
{
  using namespace boost;
  typedef adjacency_list<listS, vecS, directedS,
    property<vertex_name_t, std::string> > graph_t;
  graph_t g(3);

  const char* vertex_names[] = { "Kubrick", "Clark", "Hal" };
  int i = 0;
  graph_property_iter_range<graph_t, vertex_name_t>::iterator v, v_end;
  for (tie(v, v_end) = get_property_iter_range(g, vertex_name);
       v != v_end; ++v, ++i)
    *v = vertex_names[i];

  tie(v, v_end) = get_property_iter_range(g, vertex_name);
  std::copy(v, v_end, std::ostream_iterator<std::string>(std::cout, " "));
  std::cout << std::endl;
  return 0;
}
```

The output is

> **Kubrick Clark Hal**

Where Defined

boost/graph/property_iter_range.hpp

Template Parameters

Graph	The graph type must be a model of PropertyGraph.
PropertyTag	The tag specifies which vertex or edge property to be accessed.

Associated Types

graph_property_iter_range::iterator
    A mutable iterator whose value type is the property specified by the property tag.

graph_property_iter_range::const_iterator
    A constant iterator whose value type is the property specified by the property tag.

graph_property_iter_range::type
    The type *std::pair<iterator, iterator>*

graph_property_iter_range::const_type
    The type *std::pair<cosnt_iterator, const_iterator>*

Member Functions

None.

Nonmember Functions

template<typename Graph, typename Tag>
typename graph_property_iter_range<Graph, Tag>::type
get_property_iter_range (Graph& graph, const Tag& tag)
    Returns a pair of mutable iterators that provide access to the property specified by the tag. The iterators range over all the vertices or all the edges of the graph.

template<typename Graph, typename Tag>
typename graph_property_iter_range<Graph, Tag>::const_type
get_property_iter_range (const Graph& graph, const Tag& tag)
    Returns a pair of constant iterators that provide access to the property specified by the tag. The iterators range over all the vertices or all the edges of the graph.

Bibliography

[1] Dimacs implementation file format. http://dimacs.rutgers.edu/Challenges/.

[2] A. Alexandrescu. Better template error messages. *C/C++ Users Journal*, March 1999.

[3] M. H. Austern. *Generic Programming and the STL*. Professional computing series. Addison-Wesley, 1999.

[4] G. Baumgartner and V. F. Russo. Signatures: A language extension for improving type abstraction and subtype polymorphism in C++. *Software–Practice and Experience*, 25(8):863–889, August 1995.

[5] R. Bellman. On a routing problem. *Quarterly of Applied Mathematics*, 16(1):87–90, 1958.

[6] Boost. *Boost C++ Libraries*. http://www.boost.org/.

[7] A. Broder, R. Kumar, F. Maghoul, P. Raghavan, S. Rajagopalan, R. Stata, A. Tomkins, and J. Wiener. Graph structure in the web. In *9th World Wide Web Conference*, 2000.

[8] K. B. Bruce, L. Cardelli, G. Castagna, the Hopkins Objects Group, G. T. Leavens, and B. Pierce. On binary methods. *Theory and Practice of Object Systems*, 1:221–242, 1995.

[9] B. V. Cherkassky and A. V. Goldberg. On implementing push-relabel method for the maximum flow problem. Technical report, Stanford University, 1994.

[10] T. Cormen, C. Leiserson, and R. Rivest. *Introduction to Algorithms*. McGraw-Hill, 1990.

[11] E. Dijkstra. A note on two problems in connexion with graphs. *Numerische Mathematik*, 1:269–271, 1959.

[12] L. R. Ford and D. R. Fulkerson. Maximal flow through a network. *Canadian Journal of Mathematics*, pages 399–404, 1956.

[13] L. R. Ford and D. R. Fulkerson. *Flows in Networks*. Princeton University Press, 1962.

[14] E. Gamma, R. Helm, R. Johnson, and J. Vlissides. *Design Patterns: Elements of Reusable Object-Oriented Software*. Professional Computing. Addison-Welsey, 1995.

[15] M. Garey and D. Johnson. *Computers and Intractibility: A Guide to the Theory of NPCompleteness*. W.H. Freeman, New York, 1979.

[16] A. V. Goldberg. A new max-flow algorithm. Technical Report MIT/LCS/TM-291, MIT, 1985.

[17] A. V. Goldberg and R. E. Tarjan. A new approach to the maximum flow problem. *Journal of the ACM*, 1988.

[18] R. Graham and P. Hell. On the history of the minimum spanning tree problem. *Annals of the History of Computing*, 7(1):43–57, 1985.

[19] C. Hedrick. Routing information protocol. Internet Requests For Comments (RFC) 1058, June 1988.

[20] A. V. Karzanov. Determining the maximal flow in a network by the method of preflows. *Sov. Math. Dokl.*, 1974.

[21] S. E. Keene. *Object-Oriented Programming in Common LISP: A Programmer's Guide to CLOS*. Addison-Wesley, 1989.

[22] D. E. Knuth. *Stanford GraphBase: A Platform for Combinatorial Computing*. ACM Press, 1994.

[23] J. B. Kruskal. On the shortest spanning subtree of a graph and the traveling salesman problem. In *Proceedings of the American Mathematical Sofiety*, volume 7, pages 48–50, 1956.

[24] D. Kühl. Design patterns for the implementation of graph algorithms. Master's thesis, Technische Universität Berlin, July 1996.

[25] J. Lajoie and S. B. Lippman. *C++ Primer*. Addison Wesley, 3rd edition, 1998.

[26] E. L. Lawler. *Combinatorial Opimization: Networks and Matroids*. Holt, Rinehart, and Winston, 1976.

[27] D. Matula. Determining edge connectivity in $o(mn)$. In *Sumposium on Foundations of Computer Science*, pages 249–251, 1987.

[28] J. McQuillan. The new routing algorithm for the arpanet. *IEEE Transactions on Communications*, May 1980.

[29] K. Mehlhorn and S. Näher. *The LEDA Platform of Combinatorial and Geometric Computing*. Cambridge University Press, 1999.

[30] B. Meyer. *Object-oriented Software Construction*. Prentice Hall International Series in Computer Science. Prentice Hall, 1988.

[31] E. Moore. The shortest path through a maze. In *International Symposium on the Theory of Switching*, pages 285–292. Harvard University Press, 1959.

[32] R. Morgan. *Building an Optimizing Compiler*. Butterworth-Heinemann, 1998.

[33] J. Moy. Rfc 1583: Ospf version 2. Network Working Group Request for Comment, March 1994.

[34] D. R. Musser, G. J. Derge, and A. Saini. *STL Tutorial and Reference Guide*. Addison-Wesley, 2nd edition, 2001.

[35] D. R. Musser and A. A. Stepanov. A library of generic algorithms in ada. In *Using Ada (1987 International Ada Conference)*, pages 216–225, New York, NY, Dec. 1987. ACM SIGAda.

[36] N. C. Myers. Traits: a new and useful template technique. *C++ Report*, June 1995.

[37] R. Perlman. Fault-tolerant broadcast of routing information. *Computer Networks*, December 1983.

[38] R. Prim. Shortest connection networks and some generalizations. *Bell System Technical Journal*, 36:1389–1401, 1957.

[39] J. Siek and A. Lumsdaine. Concept checking: Binding parametric polymorphism in C++. In *First Workshop on C++ Template Programming, Erfurt, Germany*, October 10 2000.

[40] A. A. Stepanov and M. Lee. The Standard Template Library. Technical Report X3J16/94-0095, WG21/N0482, ISO Programming Language C++ Project, May 1994.

[41] B. Stroustrup. *Design and Evolution of C++*. Addison-Wesley, 1994.

[42] B. Stroustrup. *The C++ Programming Language*. Addison Wesley, special edition, 2000.

[43] R. Tarjan. Depth-first search and linear graph algorithms. *SIAM Journal on Computing*, 1(2):146–160, 1972.

[44] R. E. Tarjan. *Data Structures and Network Algorithms*. Society for Industrial and Applied Mathematics, 1983.

[45] B. L. van der Waerden. *Algebra*. Frederick Ungar Publishing, 1970.

[46] H. C. Warnsdorff. Des roesselsprungs einfachste und allgemeinste loesung. *Schmalkalden*, 1823.

Index

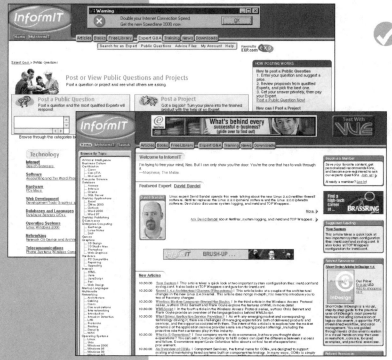